WICCA *for* ONE

Citadel titles by
RAYMOND BUCKLAND

*Wicca for Life: The Way
of the Craft—From Birth to Summerland*

Wicca for One: The Path of Solitary Witchcraft

WICCA for ONE

The Path of Solitary Witchcraft

Raymond Buckland

CITADEL PRESS
Kensington Publishing Corp.
www.kensingtonbooks.com

To my wife, Tara

CITADEL PRESS BOOKS are published by

Kensington Publishing Corp.
119 West 40th Street
New York, NY 10018

All Kensington titles, imprints, and distributed lines are available at special quantity discounts for bulk purchases for sales promotions, premiums, fund-raising, educational, or institutional use. Special book excerpts or customized printings can also be created to fit specific needs. For details, write or phone the office of the Kensington sales manager: Kensington Publishing Corp., 119 West 40th Street, New York, NY 10018, attn: Sales Department; phone 1-800-221-2647.

ISBN-13: 978-0-8065-3866-2
ISBN-10: 0-8065-3866-X

First trade paperback printing: September 2004

19 18 17 16 15

Printed in the United States of America

Library of Congress Control Number: 2004106006

First electronic edition: August 2018

ISBN-13: 978-0-8065-3867-9
ISBN-10: 0-8065-3867-8

CONTENTS

INTRODUCTION

here can be no doubt that television, the movies, and the Internet have all contributed to the everyday person's awareness of Witchcraft as a viable, modern, religious path. This is thanks to the depictions of Witchcraft over the past five or ten years. It used to be that anything shown on the screen—small or large—that touched on the subject, presented it in the now-outdated form of devil worship and black magic. But thanks to the early Wiccan pioneers, and to a Hollywood finally willing to show a little of the authentic side of Witchcraft, we now have movies with characters talking (more or less) knowledgeably about "the Craft."

It seems not so many years ago that I would deliver a lecture on Witchcraft and be greeted with such questions as "Do Witches really fly on broomsticks?" Those days are more or less gone, with today's questions much more likely to be dealing with the relationship between the worshipper and the Old Gods, and with the finer points of Sabbat presentation.

Books have also played their part in this change, of course. In fact it was books that initiated the change. The first book on Witchcraft that was actually written by a Witch did not appear until as recently as 1954 (*Witchcraft Today*, by Gerald B. Gardner), published in England. The first book written by an American practicing Witch appeared in 1970 (*Witchcraft From the Inside*, by Raymond Buckland). Since those days there has been a rapidly increasing library on the subject, covering every possible aspect of the Craft. In the belief that there can never be too much information made available, I add this present volume to the score.

One major confusion that seems to remain for the non-practitioner, is between religion and magic. Magic is a part of many religions, including the major ones. Roman Catholicism's transubstantiation, for example, is pure magic; albeit that magic is just a small part of the whole Catholic religion. Magic is also used by Witches. But as with Roman Catholicism, Witchcraft is first and foremost a religion and any magic done by Witches is but a small part of the whole.

Magic in itself is a practice; anyone may do magic or at least attempt it. You don't have to be a Witch, Jew, Buddhist, Catholic, or anything in particular to do magic. In fact, even atheists practice magic. If, then, your sole interest is in working spells and doing magic, you don't need to become a Witch. I recently read someone's statement that the difference between a Wiccan and a Witch was that a Wiccan practiced the Old Religion and a Witch just did magic. Nonsense! Anyone who "just does magic" is simply a magician. "Witch" and "Wiccan" is basically the same thing, but I will talk more about that later. Anyone can be a magician but, in my view, it takes someone special to be a Witch.

Wicca/Witchcraft is also known as the "Old Religion," since it predates Christianity (the New Religion). It's also sometimes referred to as "the Craft"; a shortened form of "Witchcraft." The oldest type of Witchcraft is that practiced by Solitary Witches. Covens—groups of Witches working together—did not begin to appear until the fifteenth and sixteenth centuries. Admittedly, since that time the idea of Witches always working in covens has taken hold to the point where, even today, many practicing Witches themselves believe that the only "authentic" Witch is one who is part of a coven. But this is incorrect. There have always been Solitary Witches and, I'm sure, there always will be. In England they are sometimes referred to as "Hedge" Witches, because many of them specialized in herbal law, gathering wild herbs from the hedgerows. The word "solitaire" can be applied to a person who lives alone, though mostly as a recluse. This term has been adopted by some as an alternate to "Solitary," for the Witch alone.

In the first part of this book, I'll give you some idea of the background to Solitary Witchcraft and some of the famous Witches who were never associated with covens. I'll go on to show how the whole idea of covens was leapt upon by Dr. Margaret Murray, in the early part of the twentieth century, and took hold from there. I'll then tell of the birth of Wicca, or neo-Witchcraft, with Gerald Gardner's presentation of the working of a modern Witch cult, and examine the various beliefs of Wicca. I'll also look further at the difference between Witchcraft and magic. In the second part of the book, I give the particulars of becoming a Solitary Witch, what is involved and how to study and eventually practice. I'll look at the tools used, the varieties of practice, rituals and celebrations, and the ethics and responsibilities of Witchcraft. Wicca is not a part-time hobby; it is a daily regimen. It is something that you live. It is a belief system and a life path that, if followed diligently, brings tremendous rewards. This is not a book of instant spells to make you greatly desired and incredibly popular (and especially not to make you feared). It is a gateway to a way of life that places you among those special ones . . . the Solitary Witches.

I conclude with a bibliography of those books I feel will really help you. There are hundreds, if not thousands, written on the subject[1] but few that are useful in the practical sense. These are worth acquiring, if necessary seeking out those which have gone out of print. If you haven't already, start a collection of books on this subject. You can't read too much. The more you read, the more you will ascertain those books which make sense for you (we are all individuals, with our own preferences; our own preferred ways of doing things), those which are just not your true path, and those which you consider a waste of time. Read, study, learn, and make your life both enjoyable and worthwhile.

---

[1]See *The Witch Book: The Encyclopedia of Witchcraft, Wicca, and Neo-Paganism* by Raymond Buckland (Visible Ink Press, 2002) for a more comprehensive bibliography.

Part One

THE CASE FOR SOLITARIES

1

From Endor to Endora, and Beyond

How sweet, how passing sweet is solitude!
—William Cowper (1731–1800), *Retirement*

lthough many people think of Witches as part of a group known as a coven, some of the better known ones of fact, fable, and fiction were *solitary* Witches, working without a coven. In fact, Solitary Witchcraft is much older than Coven Witchcraft. Let's have a look at some of these early solo workers.

One of the best known was, in fact, not a Witch at all . . . the so-called "Witch" of Endor. In the King James translation and version of the Bible, James heads the chapter Samuel 1.28: "Saul, having destroyed all the witches, and now in his fear forsaken of God, seeketh to a witch . . ." Yet nowhere in the actual biblical text is the word "Witch" used. The woman is simply described as having a "familiar spirit." Although there is no description of her, of her age, or her house, later writers continue to refer to her as a Witch and depict her as an old hag living in a hovel. Indeed, Montague Summers, a supposed authority on Witchcraft, said of her, "In a paroxysm of rage and fear the haggard crone turned to him (Saul) and shrieked out." Where he got the idea that she was a "haggard crone" we do not know. In the Bible she is described simply as "a woman that hath a familiar spirit at Endor." Endor is a small hamlet on the northern slope of a hill, four miles south of Mount Tabor. Saul, despite the fact that he had tried to purge the land of her sort, went to consult her on the eve of the battle of Bilboa, because he was afraid of the massed armies of the Philistines. She immediately recognized him, despite his disguise, but Saul assured her he would cause her no harm. The woman of Endor was, in fact, no more than a spiritualist medium and psychic—not a Witch at all. She described to Saul what she saw clairvoyantly and she was able to connect him with the spirit of Samuel. Reginald Scott, as early as 1584, doubted the existence of Witches and suggested that Saul actually saw nothing but "an illusion or cozenage."

> We shall define a Classic Witch as follows: a person (usually an older female) who is adept in the uses of herbs, roots, barks, etc., for the purposes of both healing and hurting (including the making of poisons, aphrodisiacs, hallucinogens, etc.) and who is familiar with the basic principles of both passive and active magic, and can use them for good or ill—as she chooses.
>
> —Isaac Bonewits, *Witchcraft: A Concise Guide*

But there were other well-known figures described as Witches for whom the label would seem appropriate. First of these was Circe. The fair-haired Circe was the daughter of Oceanid and the sun god Helios. She became famous for her magical arts. Her brother was Æëtes, wizard king of Colchis and father of Medea. For poisoning her husband, Circe was banished to the island of Aeæa. She lived on the west side of the island, and it has been said that she was a moon goddess. It seems more likely, however, that she was a goddess of love. She was, in many ways, comparable to the Babylonian Ishtar. Homer, in the *Odyssey*, described Circe as a "goddess with lovely hair . . . singing in a lovely voice . . . [in] a white shining robe, delicate and lovely, with a fine girdle of gold about her waist."

If any men ever landed on her island, it was Circe's custom to change them into swine. This she accomplished by getting them to drink a potion from her magic cup. When Odysseus landed there she tried the same treatment on him and his companions, managing to change all but Odysseus himself. The god Hermes had given Odysseus a magical herb called moly, and this protected him. Odysseus forced Circe to restore his men to their normal shape and then spent the next year living with her. Circe later gave birth to Odysseus's son Telegonus. When Odysseus finally left the island it was thanks to the warnings that Circe gave him that he was finally able to reach his home. Circe may be related to the ancient Mediterranean goddess known as the "Lady of the Beasts," whose likeness is depicted engraved on Minoan gems. She was finally slain by Telemachus, Odysseus's son by Penelope.

Another famous woman who could accurately be described as a Witch was Medea. She was the Witch of Colchis, in Greek myth, and was a priestess of Hecate, goddess of the moon. She was also a niece to Circe in Greek mythology. Medea was the daughter of Æëtes, king of Colchis and was famed for her magical arts. Like Kerridwen (discussed later), she possessed a magic cauldron and there are stories of kings and others being boiled in it and then being reborn. These included King Minos, King Æson, and Pelops, son of the king of Phrygia. Medea fell in love with Jason and, with magic, helped him acquire the Golden Fleece from her father. Jason said of her that "[her] loveliness must surely mean that she excels in gentle courtesy." However, when Jason betrayed her, Medea brought about the death of their two children and also the death of Jason's second wife. Medea married King Ægeus and by him had a son, Medus. She later married Achilles, in the Elysian Fields, and was honored as a goddess at Corinth, though the chief seat of her cult was Thessaly, the home of magic. She was made immortal by Hera and became known as "the Wise One."

The goddess Artemis was daughter of Zeus and Leto, and twin sister of Apollo. Artemis was one of the twelve great Greek gods and goddesses of Olympus. As a goddess, she was mainly associated with wild life and with human birth. She was originally one of the great Mother Goddesses, with emphasis on her aspect of virgin huntress and patroness of chastity. As twin sister to Apollo, she is regarded as a divinity of the light, albeit the light of the moon, and, as such, has been an influential archetype for Witches. Her symbol is the female bear and she is associated with the constellation Ursa Major. Legend has it that she was born (on the sixth day of the month of Thargelion) a day before her brother. As she grew up in her favorite Arcadia, she would hunt accompanied by sixty young Oceanids and twenty nymphs. Armed with bows and arrows, given to her by Zeus, she gained the epithet Apollousa, "the destructress," and was a deity of sudden death. She was especially venerated in Arcadia but worshiped throughout Greece, Crete, and Asia Minor.

Artemis's Roman equivalent is Diana, described as "the eternal feminist." She is the source of magical power for Witches, who gather to adore her at the full moon. The *Canon Episcopi*, of the tenth century, condemned those who "believe and profess themselves, in the hours of the night to ride upon certain beasts with Diana, the goddess of the pagans." She is the slim, beautiful virgin, usually depicted with her hair drawn back and wearing a short tunic—a Dorian *chiton*. She is frequently accompanied by either a young hind or a dog. As goddess of fertility, she is sometimes depicted with many breasts. Artemis made chastity a strict law, though she did fall in love with Orion. Unhappily, Apollo later tricked her into shooting Orion in the head. She had a dark and vindictive character and many were punished by death or torment when they crossed her or forgot to pay her reverence. Yet she could be gentle and loving. She

> *The Great Goddess . . . is the incarnation of the Feminine Self that unfolds in the history of mankind as in the history of every individual woman; its reality determines individual as well as collective life.*
>
> —Erich Neumann, *The Great Mother*

was also a music goddess and lover of singing and dancing. Most Wiccans honor Artemis/Diana as part of the triple goddess aspect of the moon, and as a nurturer and protector. She has inspired the Dianic, strongly feminist, tradition of Wicca.

Another Witch was Kerridwen, the ancient Welsh fertility and mother goddess who, like Medea, possessed a magic cauldron. She was also referred to as a goddess of the underworld and as "the goddess of various seeds." Many Welsh-tradition Wiccans give their goddess the name of Kerridwen (or Cerridwen). Myth says that she lived with her two children on an island in the middle of Lake Tegid. Her daughter was Creirwy, the most beautiful of girls. Her son was Afagdu, the ugliest of boys. To compensate for her son's ugliness, Kerridwen brewed a magic potion in her cauldron, which would make him the possessor of all knowledge. This potion was made from six herbs and had to boil for a year and a day.

While she went off collecting herbs, Kerridwen had a mortal boy, Gwion, sit and stir the mixture. As Gwion stirred the cauldron, the hot liquid bubbled and three drops splashed out onto his finger, burning him. He put his scalded finger in his mouth and, by tasting the drops of the potion, gained knowledge. He could suddenly hear everything in the world. Frightened that Kerridwen would be angry, Gwion ran off. When Kerridwen found him gone, she guessed what had happened and pursued him. He shape-shifted, turning into a hare, but Kerridwen changed into a greyhound and continued the pursuit. When Gwion turned into a fish, she became an otter; when he became a bird, she became a hawk. Finally, exhausted, he spied a pile of wheat grain, jumped into the middle, and turned himself into a single grain. As a hen, Kerridwen scratched him out and ate him. As a result of eating Gwion, the goddess became pregnant and eventually gave birth to a boy, whom she abandoned to the waves in a tiny coracle. He was rescued by a prince and grew up to be Taliesin, the greatest poet; a Welsh bard. It is in *The Book of Taliesin* that the story of Kerridwen is found. Lewis Spence feels that the Cauldron of Kerridwen must have been the same as the Cauldron of Inspiration alluded to in the myths of Annwnn.

Other perhaps lesser-known female Witches were Canidia and Erichthoë, both of whom were described as beautiful women. Canidia was the Witch from Naples, Italy, who had a conversation with the Roman poet Horace, in the *Epodes of Horace*. Lucan's Witch Erichthoë, according to the Roman historian in his *Pharsalia*, was a Thessalian who sent Virgil to Hades and advised Sextus Pompey during the Civil Wars.

Lilith features in Jewish folklore, deriving from a Babylonian-Assyrian spirit named Lilit, or Lilu. In the rabbinical literature, Lilith was Adam's first wife but, being his equal, she refused to lie underneath him during intercourse. When he tried to force her, she fled. Some Witches regard Lilith as a patroness and as a moon goddess, whose beauty is more than human. Charles Godfrey Leland identifies Lilith with Herodias, or Aradia.

Morgan le Fay was King Arthur's sister in Arthurian legend. Her name comes from the French Morgain la Fée, where *fée*, or *fay*, means "of the fairies." Her character has been assimilated from the Welsh Modron, daughter of Avallach, and from a water nymph of Breton folklore. There are also ties to the ancient river goddess Matrona, and the goddess known to the Irish as Morríghan. Such writers as Geoffrey of Monmouth, Chrétien de Troyes, Giraldus Cambrensis, and Guillem Torrella of Majorca have sullied the waters to the extent that there is no unequivocal pedigree for the lady. She appears as a noblewoman, a temptress, an enchantress, as Arthur's sister, Guingamor's mistress, and as a "good fairy." She also appears in two aspects: as a young girl and an old woman. According to some legends, she was sister to Merlin. Whatever her true identity, Morgan le Fay was usually presented as adept in the healing arts. On the one hand she was working against Arthur yet on the other hand she magically healed his wounds after the battle of Camlan. She was certainly a most powerful Solitary Witch.

Another person generally thought to have been a Witch—or accused of Witchcraft—was Joan of Arc, or Jeanne d'Arc (1412–1431). She didn't cast spells or work magic, nor did she work with a coven, so in many senses of the word she was not a Witch. But she was described in the trials as "a liar and witch" and also described by the Bishop of Beauvais as having committed such crimes as "sorceries, idolatries, calling-up evil spirits and many other instances touching and opposed to our faith." She did display some signs that might have been interpreted as Witchcraft, such as communicating with spirits. When only thirteen she was in her father's garden when she heard a voice that she believed came from God. During the next five years she heard voices two or three times a week. She also saw visions of the people communicating. Due to her upbringing, she interpreted the voices as those of God and some of the saints. From these visions and voices, she determined that her mission was to place the dauphin (the King's eldest son) on the throne of France. This she managed to do but was later betrayed by the Duke of Burgundy and handed over to the Bishop of Beauvais. When she went to trial she was charged as being a diviner, prophetess, sorceress, Witch, and conjurer of evil sprits, but she was finally burned at the stake for heresy and for the "sin" of wearing men's clothes. This took place on May 30, 1431, in the Old Market square at Rouen.

A more genuine Witch who was similarly accused and brought to trial in 1324 was Dame Alice Kyteler, focus of the most famous Witch trial in Ireland. Dame Alice was a woman of substance. There is some evidence that there was a group of Witches operating in the county of Kilkenny at the time but Dame Alice seems to have been of an independent nature. The bishop, Richard de Ledrede, who was an unpopular man, became convinced that Dame Alice was a sorceress involved in Witchcraft and, in 1324, charged her with heretical sorcery. He indicted her on the following counts: that she denied the faith of Christ; sacrificed animals at a crossroads (always considered a meeting place for Witches); used sorcery to communicate with demons; attended nightly meetings to "blasphemously imitate the power of the church"; caused disease and death and aroused love and hate; used potions, powders, candles, and ointments; had an incubus demon lover named Robin Artison; and that she caused her previous husbands (she was married four times) to bequeath all their money to her son William. The bishop wrote to the chancellor and asked for the arrest of Dame Alice, but it so happened that the chancellor was related to Alice's first husband. The seneschal of Kilkenny, Sir Arnold Le Poer, was related to her fourth husband. The bishop proceeded to excommunicate Dame Alice but she, in turn, used her influence to have him arrested. He served seventeen days in jail. Dame Alice then moved to England where she spent the rest of her life. Meanwhile, the bishop was himself later accused of heresy by the Archbishop of Dublin and was exiled for almost twenty years.

Although the term wizard is more generally applied to a male Witch (the true term is "Witch," whether male or female), there have been a number of well-known solitary male practitioners throughout history, myth, and fiction. Merlin is probably the best known. The name Merlin is a Latinized form of the Welsh name Myrddin. He was a magical figure who appears in literature ranging from medieval manuscripts to modern novels. References to him may also be found in a wide variety of place names and specific sites throughout Great Britain. He was a wizard, or Witch, frequently linked with King Arthur, though Rosemary Guiley suggests he may have originated as a version of the Celtic god Mabon, the British Apollo. According to Geoffrey of Monmouth's life of Merlin, the great wizard together with the bard Taliesin took the wounded King Arthur to the Fortunate Isles. One of the best known portrayals of Merlin is found in Sir Thomas Mallory's *Le Morte d'Arthur*, which was first published in

1485. In this story, Merlin helps raise the young Arthur and, on Arthur's accession to the throne on the death of his father, Uther Pendragon, becomes the young king's magical advisor. Although more recent portrayals of Merlin show him as an old man—usually bearded—earlier representations depict him as a young, beardless man. It seems possible that features from the Scottish Lailoken, a wild man of the woods with powers of prophesy, became incorporated into the essentially Welsh Merlin.

In many respects, the Greek god Apollo, twin brother to Artemis, might have been considered a male Witch. The son of Zeus and Leto, Apollo assumed various functions including god of divination and prophecy and, in that capacity, resembled the Assyro-Babylonian sun god Shamash. Apollo was also patron of healing. He was connected with the sun, being frequently referred to as Phœbus, "the shining one." As a solar deity, Apollo made the fruits of the earth ripen and also protected the crops by destroying mice that infested the fields. Raven Grimassi says that Apollo was also known as Lycius, a wolf god, and as Smintheus, the mouse god, saying that "the mouse appears in tales of Italian Witchlore where it is related to Diana, the stars, and to the souls of Witches."

Joan of Arc's bodyguard Gilles de Laval, Baron de Rais (1404–1440), was descended on his father's side from Tiphaine du Guesclin, whom many considered to be a fairy. He fought bravely against the English and, at Charles's coronation, was appointed Marshall of France at the age of twenty-five. In 1432, he retired to his estates where he enjoyed his tremendous wealth and, among other things, amassed a library of rare manuscripts. He dabbled in alchemy and, it was said, Witchcraft. From his alchemical work, and being misguided by a Florentine priest named Francesco Prelati, Gilles de Rais rapidly went through his fortune and had to start selling off his land and buildings. Prelati guided his employer by claiming to be able to conjure a demon he called Baron. This demon made a variety of demands, including blood sacrifices, which were obtained by luring children into the castle. Eventually Gilles de Rais was accused of a variety of crimes and forty-seven charges were brought against him, including being a "heretic, apostate, conjurer of demons," among others. After his servants had been tortured into confessions, de Rais was found guilty; on October 26, 1440, he was strangled and his body placed on a pyre. It was not burned, however, as relatives were allowed to remove it for proper burial.

For several centuries Witches were persecuted by the Christian church. Most of those initially accused were solitary people, acting alone. It wasn't until the sixteenth century that the idea of Witches forming into covens was accepted. The first such coven, so-called, was mentioned in the trial of Bessie Dunlop, in Ayrshire, Scotland, in 1567. Prior to that, those charged with Witchcraft were charged as individual, or solitary, Witches. They ranged from very young to very old.

"Cunning Man" Murrell (1780–1860) was a notable solitary Witch. A Cunning Man was not uncommon in England from the fifteenth through the nineteenth centuries, and even into the twentieth century. They were sought out for anything from the removal of a wart or tracing lost property to the curing of a major disease. Cunning Men invariably worked alone, were quite often proficient astrologers, and had an immense knowledge of herbs and their uses. Many claimed to be the seventh child of a seventh child, as did some Witches. Such a person was believed to have inherent psychic and magical powers. The word "cunning" came from the Old English *kenning*, meaning "wise." James Murrell of Hadleigh, Essex, England, was perhaps the best known Cunning Man. As a young man, he was apprenticed to a surveyor and later worked for a chemist's stillman, but ended up as a shoemaker. It is said that he fathered twenty children. Murrell lived in a small cottage opposite the church in Hadleigh. Bunches of drying herbs hung from the beamed ceilings and old, colored bottles, filled with mysterious liquids, lined shelves and mantelpieces. The house became the center for what Eric Maple describes as "the Murrell cult." From simple beginnings, his reputation as a Cunning Man grew to the point where even the wealthy would travel from as far away as London to get his advice and make use of his services. His herbal knowledge was vast and he was also a great healer, sometimes by the laying on of his hands and sometimes by the use of magic, amulets, and/or talismans. Murrell had a huge wooden chest in which he stored his many books and instruments. It was referred to as a "wizard's chest." Murrell rarely charged more than a shilling for his services, even if asked to work complicated magic. For minor miracles he charged only sixpence, though this was still a considerable sum for the laborer of the time. The client was always asked if he or she required "high" or "low" assistance. The former was spiritual while the latter was material. For "high," Murrell would need to conjure good angels to fight the forces of evil.

Astrology was a major part of Murrell's business. He consulted the tomes he kept in his wooden chest and cast horoscopes. His predictions were so accurate that many people who consulted with him, of all classes, returned again and again. After his death, Queen Victoria's horoscope was found among his possessions. Skrying was also part of Murrell's stock in trade. He had a gazing mirror hanging on the wall, which he used most often, but he would also utilize a pail of water or other reflective surface. He would travel to where he was needed although, in later years, he came to insist that the client come to him. There is a story of Murrell using a Witch bottle to counter an evil spell put on a farm girl. The girl had been cursed by an old woman and was having fits. Murrell placed a variety of items in a small metal bottle, along with some of the girl's urine. The bottle was placed over a fire and heated. This resulted in the perpetrator—an old woman—beating on the door and crying out for him to stop what he was doing. Then the bottle exploded and the sounds of the old woman died away. The young girl immediately recovered. Although Murrell hoped that one of his children would carry on his work, none of them did. In fact, when Murrell died, his son Buck proceeded to burn most of the contents of the wizard's chest. The novelist Arthur Morrison came across the cottage in 1880 and was just in time to see what remained of the items, mostly books on astrology and herbalism.

In literature, one of the more famous Witches is the Russian Baba Yaga (or Baba Jaga), who is analogous to Frau Berchta (or Brechta) of Germany. Baba Yaga was a female Witch who lived in a hut in a forest beyond a river of fire. The hut stood on chickens' legs and was forever spinning around. It was surrounded by a picket fence topped with human skulls. Baba Yaga liked to steal young children, cook them in her oven, and then eat them. She often traveled with Death, who provided her with human souls on which she also feasted. She rode through the air in an iron cauldron, conjuring up tempests with her magic wand. She swept away her tracks with a besom. Baba Yaga was a guardian of the fountains of the water of life. Sometimes she is presented in triple form, with two sisters, all of whom are called Baba Yaga, but most of the time she acts alone. The usual attitude in which she is found is lying on her back in the hut, a foot in each of two corners, her head to the door, and her nose either touching the ceiling or even growing up out of the chimney.

The evil queen of *Snow White* is another well-known Solitary, albeit of the most negative variety. There are also the Witches of *Hansel and Gretel* and of *Sleeping Beauty*, both of whom work as Solitaries. Witches—one good and one bad—appear in L. Frank Baum's *The Wizard of Oz* as the Good Witch of the East and the Wicked Witch of the West.

Perhaps two of the best-loved Witches are those of the television series *Bewitched*, which ran in the 1960s. It was based on the Thorne Smith novel *The Passionate Witch* (which in turn inspired the 1942 Paramount movie *I Married a Witch*). The lead in the Screen Gems' comedy television show was the Witch Samantha, played by Elizabeth Montgomery. Her mother was Endora, played by Agnes Moorehead. Samantha, married to a mortal, tried hard to live without using her powers but invariably weakened and resorted to them. Her mother, who intensely disliked Samantha's husband Darrin, did not hesitate to use her powers, usually against Darrin. Another of the television family of Witches who is basically solitary is Sabrina, in the series *Sabrina, the Teenage Witch.*

> *Witchcraft is more than just a religion or a set of philosophies. It is a way of life, a way of existing within the Universe. It comes from ancient sources, but can change with the times; it is very serious in nature, but can laugh at itself.*
>
> —Jennifer Hunter, *21st Century Wicca*

There is, then, quite a catalog of prominent solitary Witches from earliest times up to the present, proving that there is as much "validity" in the Solitary Witch as there is in the Coven Witch. It therefore follows that anyone wishing to become a Witch can do so alone, without having to join with a group. ✤

2

Whence Came Covens?

*[Wicca is] for those who have become
enchanted by the moon shining through the
trees; who have begun to investigate the
sublime world that lies out beyond the fabric of
daily life, and who stand in smoke-shrouded
circles, raising aloft their hands to greet the
Goddess and the God as the candles flicker
on the altar . . . for those who, through
choice or circumstance, meet with the
Silver Lady and the Horned God alone.*
—Scott Cunningham, *Living Wicca*

r. Margaret Alice Murray (1863–1963), according to
Michael Jordan, was "a pioneer in the study of a subject
which had, hitherto, been virtually devoid of academic
research." That subject was Witchcraft. Margaret
Murray was born in Calcutta, India, on July 13, 1863. At the age of
thirty-one she entered University College, London. Her main interest was in archaeology but at that time it was difficult for a woman

to receive an advanced degree in the subject, so instead she obtained a degree in linguistics. This in turn led her to the study of Egyptian hieroglyphics and to specializing in Egyptology. She joined Sir Flinders Petrie in his excavations at Abydos, in Egypt. Then, in 1899, she became a Fellow and then a junior lecturer in Egyptology. She remained at University College, as an Assistant Professor, until her retirement in 1935.

The works of Sir James Frazer led Murray to take an interest in Witchcraft, which she eventually came to view as possibly being a pre-Christian pagan religion. She studied the records of the Witch trials during the persecutions and, in 1921, published her findings in the book *The Witch Cult in Western Europe*. There she proposed that Witchcraft was not merely a product of the Christian Church of the Middle Ages but had, in fact, been a religion in its own right. Its adherents, she said, formed into groups known as "covens." Although Sir James Frazer, in *The Golden Bough* (1890), had discussed the possible prehistoric origins of Witchcraft rituals (he made no mention of covens), and Charles Godfrey Leland in his book *Aradia, the Gospel of the Witches* (1899), had examined the workings of Italian Witches, no one had previously done the detailed examination that Murray did, nor drawn quite the same conclusions. She referred to the cult as a "Dianic" one (as did Leland), centering on

The historical view is that what is now known as Witchcraft was the Old Religion, embracing presumably theology, occult powers, and ceremonial rituals . . . and which was driven underground by the onslaught of the emergent Church and associated power politics.

—Justine Glass, *Witchcraft: The Sixth Sense—and Us*

the worship of the goddess Diana. According to Murray, evidence from the trials showed an organization of groups led by a male leader, who was regarded by the Christian chroniclers as the Devil. She saw connections to Witchcraft in all strata of society. Such conclusions, by a scholar of some note, caused a minor sensation. Many were quick to dismiss her findings out of hand. Others were just as quick to join forces with her. In 1931 she published a complementary volume, *The God of the Witches*, that looked more closely at the male deity, a horned god, and attempted to trace back the origins of the pagan cult to Palæolithic times.

Murray remains a controversial figure, yet much of what she uncovered, from the records of the early Witchcraft trials, was valid. It's impossible to read her first two books on the subject without acknowledging that there is a core of truth to her theory of Witchcraft being an organized, pre-Christian, pagan religion. Her argument for covens was weak but the evidence from the trials was genuine. Many of her detractors are nowhere near as qualified as she was herself. In the mid-1950s, she was the president of the prestigious Folk-Lore Society, and she received a number of academic honors.

In the trial of Bessie Dunlop, in Ayrshire, Scotland, in 1567, there is the first mention of a coven, with Bessie speaking of there being five men and eight women in her group. However, she didn't actually use the word "coven." That was not used until the trial of Isobel Gowdie, in Auldearne, in 1662. At that trial the specific number of thirteen for the group was given. Murray claimed that "the number in a coven never varied, there were always thirteen," but it seems she made the figures fit her theories. In 1932 Cecil L'Estrange Ewen "checked over the corresponding figures for the alleged covens for England and found the lady's (Murray's) groups of thirteen had in each case been obtained by an unwarranted omission, addition, or inconcinnous disposition." However, later writers such as Montague Summers picked up on Murray's words and referred to covens of thirteen.

> *This degeneracy of the legal system, the taking of evidence of children, the tricks to obtain confessions, and the bland acceptance of evidence of flying, shape-shifting and familiars, was to continue until the fanaticism of Protestantism purged itself in bloodshed and regicide. Because most of the educated classes believed in witches the judges and magistrates did not dispense justice, but rather administered procedures which had as little connection with normal criminal procedures as those of the Inquisition when witchcraft cases were involved.*
>
> —Ronald Holmes, *Witchcraft in History*

Today many modern Wicca groups feel that the only "valid" way for a Witch to work is in a coven. Yet, as was shown in chapter 1, there is absolutely no reason why coven working should be considered any more valid than solitary working. That covens are here to stay is definite and the majority of today's Witches seem to prefer them. But the tradition of the Witch alone is far older and, although in many ways it is a more difficult path to tread, it is equally as satisfying. Solitary Witchcraft is the oldest form of Witchcraft. Solitaries are Witches in their own right; they are not simply working alone until such time as they can locate and join a coven. Despite today's emphasis on covens, there is a place, if not a need, for solitary Witches. ✀

3

——◆——

Religion or Practice?
Coven or Solitary?

*One day draweth on another, and I am well pleased
in my being here, for methinks solitariness collecteth
the mind as shutting the eyes doth the sight.*
—Sir Francis Bacon (1561–1626)

argaret Murray's theories were no more than theories, until as recently as the mid-1950s. In 1954, the book *Witchcraft Today*, by Gerald Brousseau Gardner (1884–1964), was published. This was the very first book about Witchcraft that was actually written by a practicing Witch. Until then—from the very beginning of printing in the mid-fifteenth century—everything written on the subject had been written by the persecutors of Witchcraft, or by those whose only sources of reference were such biased writings. The publication of Gardner's book was to change all that and its appearance was only made possible by the repeal of the old British Witchcraft Act in 1951. With this repeal, any Witches still surviving could finally come out into the open once more, free of the fear of persecution. But those few Witches who *had* survived had learned their lesson; they were content to continue in secret, away from prying eyes. All, that is, except Dr. Gardner.

Throughout his life, Gerald Gardner was fascinated by, and spent time investigating, religio-magic. He lived the majority of his life in the Far East and there had become acquainted with the Dyaks, the headhunters of Borneo, and with many local native tribes learning of their practices and beliefs. On his retirement and return to his home-land of England, in the 1930s, to his great surprise and delight Gard-ner encountered a surviving coven of Witches, in the area of the New Forest. They made themselves known to him because of his background and religio-magical expertise, plus the fact that an ances-tress of his had been burned at the stake as a Witch, in Scotland in 1640. He was invited to join the group and was subsequently initi-ated. Finding that Witchcraft was actually the survival of an ancient pre-Christian religion, and not at all the dark, evil practice he had always been led to believe it to be, Gardner was delighted. He wanted to run out and tell the world how wrong it was. Of course, he was not allowed to. It was explained that the group had only man-aged to remain alive by keeping quiet about its existence. But some years later, on the death of the group's leader and with the last law against Witchcraft finally repealed, Gardner published a book (*Witch-craft Today*, Rider, London 1954), which was the first book actually written by a Witch and giving the Witches' side of the story. This was to be the start of the whole re-emergence of Witchcraft as a reli-gion and the eventual establishment of Wicca as an accepted every-day practice around the world. Today it is the fastest growing religious movement in America.

If Gerald Gardner had not sown the seeds that sparked the revival of interest in Witchcraft, it is almost certain that the Old Religion would have eventually died out. In the United States it was myself, a protégé of Gardner, who introduced Wicca and started the first modern American coven. When Gardner's book went out of print, I wrote *Witchcraft From the Inside* (Llewellyn: St. Paul, 1970) to fill the gap and continue the line of information from the source.

The reaction to Gardner's revelations was mixed, as might be expected. However, in what he had to say, a large number of people saw the tempting glimmer of a way of life they had not previously dared hope for. Apparently there were a great many people who were dissatisfied with organized religion of the Christian persuasion, and they had—consciously or unconsciously—been seeking such an honest, earth-oriented religion as Witchcraft was now shown to be. Additionally, when Gardner presented his work and expressed his belief that the coven to which he belonged was probably the last still alive, he was surprised and delighted to then hear from other scattered groups across Europe, each in turn believing that *they* were the last. It seemed that Witchcraft had not been completely stamped out after all but had, in fact, managed to stay alive, if holding on only by a thread.

People started writing to Gardner, expressing their desire to become a part of the Old Religion. Witchcraft, or *Wica*, as Gardner preferred to call it (more usually spelled *Wicca* these days), was a religion of initiation and, in Gardner's experience, organized into covens. There was a hierarchy, with the leaders representing the god and goddess of the Old Religion. As Gardner experienced it, there was a degree system of advancement. All this meant that it took time to absorb newcomers. Painfully slowly (for those waiting to enter the Craft), existing covens expanded and new ones came into being. Gardner received many queries from the United States but knew of no existing covens there to which he could send people. He therefore prevailed upon me to act as his clearinghouse in the U.S. and to start the American line of Wicca. In 1963, I went to Scotland to stay for a while with Gardner's High Priestess, was eventually initiated and, with my wife, raised to the appropriate degree to do this.

It took many years for Witchcraft to establish itself in America, mainly because of the structure of Gardnerian and other imitative forms of Wicca. It is interesting to speculate, with hindsight, on how much faster the Old Religion might have spread had Solitary rather than Coven Witchcraft been the initially accepted form. The bottle-neck for the spread and the development was unquestionably the need for initiation by others and, for many systems, the degree pro-gram of advancement. With self-initiation, or "self-dedication," all who so strongly desired to be a part of the movement, could have been—and with far greater alacrity. In fairness, it must be pointed out that it wasn't just a question of initiation, of being "made" a Witch. There was the whole Witchcraft education to be considered and, at that time, this was definitely better taught in coven style.

> *What is Witchcraft but the human control of natural forces through a supernatural power? . . . With fasting and incantation, with conjuring, men snare that power and use it—without actually knowing what it is that they use. So Witchcraft is the science of that power.*
>
> —Theda Kenyon, *Witches Still Live*

In those formative years (and this is often still the case today) there were many who believed that Witchcraft was nothing but working magic: casting spells and, perhaps, healing and divining the future. As mentioned earlier, if that were the case we would be talk-ing about magic and magicians rather than Witchcraft and Witches. What must always be borne in mind is the fact that Witchcraft is a religion—the "Old Religion." As a religion, its primary focus is wor-ship of the deities. This applies just as much to the Solitary Witch as the Coven one. Hedge Witches and others who, for whatever reason, do not belong to a coven, still believe in the old gods. They still pray to them, asking them for what they need and thanking them for what they receive. Specific rituals of celebration are usually practiced at set times throughout the year. It must be acknowledged that there may be varying degrees of proportion of religion to magic. Some did in the past, and some do today, put far more emphasis on the magical side than on the religious aspects, but the religious side is still there; the God and Goddess are always acknowledged. Back in the Middle Ages the farmer and his wife might have been more concerned with scraping together a living—surviving—than with performing rituals to deity and immersing themselves in liturgy. But they still asked the gods for a good harvest, if only in the form of a mumbled prayer whilst plowing, and they thanked the gods when they harvested the crops. The growing of the crops, the birthing of the animals, and the hunting for food were always associated with the god of hunting and the goddess of fertility.

> *The cycle of light and dark, of planting and harvesting, of leaves budding, opening and falling, is an ever-turning wheel that has no beginning and no end. It rolls through the seasons, changing the landscape and influencing the things we do and the way we feel. Each time of the year is special, with its own particular feelings, smells, and atmospheres— and, if we allow it, its effect on our lives.*
>
> —Gail Duff, *Seasons of the Witch*

If you have the desire to be a practicing Witch, then you need to examine yourself and find exactly what it is you want. If you have absolutely no interest in religion, or perhaps have no belief in deity in any form, yet want to work magic, then you do not need Witchcraft. There are many forms of magic that you can focus upon and that will serve your purpose. But if Witchcraft is definitely what you

> . . . *That inward eye*
> *Which is the bliss of solitude.*
>
> —William Wordsworth (1770–1850),
> *I Wandered Lonely as a Cloud*

wish to be a part of, then the only remaining question is: Coven or Solitary?

Covens are usually part of a specific tradition of Witchcraft. Just as in Christianity there are various denominations, the same is true in Witchcraft. Many of these are only found in coven form; for example, you will never find a Solitary Gardnerian Witch, because Gardnerian is a tradition that has a very rigid coven system. But there are others, such as Saxon, where the Witches may join together in a coven or work equally well as Solitaries. If your preference is for Coven Witchcraft, then you will have to find a coven and persuade them to accept you and initiate you into it. If your preference is for Solitary Witchcraft, then you can start right away and "initiate" yourself (see chapter 9). There are advantages and drawbacks to both systems, as you'll see. ✺

4

Beliefs

THE LORD

Behold! I am he who is at the beginning and the end of time.
I am in the heat of the Sun and the coolness of the breeze.
The spark of life is within me as is the darkness of death;
For I am the cause of existence
And the Gatekeeper at the end of time.

Lord-dweller in the sea,
You hear the thunder of my hooves upon the shore
And see the fleck of foam as I pass by.
My strength is such that I might lift the world to touch
   the stars,
Yet gentle, ever, am I, as the lover.

I am he whom all must face at the appointed hour,
Yet am I not to be feared, for I am brother, lover, son.
Death is but the beginning of life
And I am he who turns the key.

—Raymond Buckland, *Buckland's Complete Book of Witchcraft*

ome of the basic beliefs of Wicca include the Witch ideas of deity, of God and Goddess; a belief in honoring the earth; in reincarnation; in retribution in this life; in the ability to work "magic"; and a belief in spirits of various types. Most, if not all, of these depend upon no more than common sense. There is no dogma here; nothing that depends solely on "faith" propounded by a stern priesthood, with admonitions that it is a sin *not* to believe!

God and Goddess

Many have been brought up in a Christian world, with a concept of one (male) deity. If you stop to consider life in our world, you see that in everything there is actually a duality: male and female are necessary for life. This is so with humans, animals, birds, fish, and even with plants and trees. Why, then, would it not be so with the gods? It makes far more sense to believe in a God *and* a Goddess (if it were to be a solitary figure, then why wouldn't it be a female, anyway?). Although this idea of male and female, with the deities, is very ancient it is absolutely relevant to today's society, where the female is finally being recognized as equal to the male.

With early humankind, going back to the cave dwellers, there was a very real feeling for the gods. In order to survive it was necessary to be successful in hunting for food and, later, successful in growing crops. Fertility of both wild and domestic animals was paramount. With a belief, at that time, in many deities, the prominent ones became the god of hunting and the goddess of fertility. As time passed, and humans learned not only to grow food but also to store it for the winter, success in hunting became of less importance. The God still remained, however, for how could the animals and the crops germinate without that male element? The concept of god and goddess remains even today, for that same reason, even though our food may come to us by way of the supermarket and fast-food restaurants.

The belief in deity is the core of religion, and there have been many attempted definitions of it. Sir James G. Frazer (*The Golden Bough*) defined religion as "a propitiation or conciliation of powers superior to man, which are believed to direct and control the course of nature and of human life." Certainly religion is a belief in powers that may be beyond the comprehension of humankind, and those powers may need to be petitioned or shown gratitude for apparent boons. But in order to do so, how are these "powers" perceived? Many say they are a vast, inconceivable energy force that is so mighty it would be impossible even to describe it. Yet, if this is so, how can you relate to it? You can't pray to something you can't even conceive of. In religious rites, although you may understand it to be such a tremendous energy force, you do need to relate to it in order to ask for what you want and to give thanks for what you receive. To do this you must personalize it—usually anthropomorphizing it also—so that you can see it in your mind and even make images of it, in order to relate to it. In Wicca, since we relate this "All-That-Is" to life as we know it on earth, we see it in the form of a male and a female: a god and a goddess. To these we even give names, the better to relate. And here is another of the joys of Witchcraft: you don't need an intermediary, such as a priest, to "allow" you to commune with deity. *Everyone is his or her own priest/priestess*, fully able to connect with deity in a personal, intimate fashion.

Names are no more than labels. For this reason you will find a wide variety of names used for the deities of Wicca. There is no one set of labels. The God and the Goddess are known by a wide variety of names; some classical, some local, some even made up. As one writer has put it, "[The Goddess] has many names in many lands and pantheons. If you examine their mystery you will find not names but titles, attributes, 'job descriptions,' even, spelled out in many tongues."[2]

Religion is, or should be, a very personal thing with the individual able to feel completely comfortable in its form. There should be no

[2]Marian Green, *A Witch Alone* (London: Aquarian Press, 1991).

reason for compromise. Someone whose background is, for example, Scandinavian might not feel comfortable trying to relate to deities with ancient Greek names. Such a person would be far more at ease communing with the gods using names such as Thor, Odin, and Freyja. Similarly, someone of Celtic background would be better able to relate to the names Belenos, Lugh, Dagda, Scáthach, and Epona. So take time to decide on those names that have real meaning to you personally. This is another benefit of being a Solitary Witch; you do not have to compromise even on the names of the gods. Throughout this book I am going to use the name Herne for the God and Epona for the Goddess. Having been born and raised in England, these are names I can feel comfortable with. But *you choose your own names*. Feel free, should you use the rituals given in this book, to substitute your own choices where Herne and Epona are shown.

The Wiccan Goddess is usually viewed in three aspects: Maiden, Mother, and Crone, and sometimes referred to as the Triple Goddess. She is associated with the moon. As the Maiden, she is linked to the new moon; as the Mother to the full moon; and as the Crone to the waning moon. As the Maiden she is also linked to youth and freshness, renewal, beginnings, promise, and potential. As the Mother she is especially close to mothers and tied in to childbirth. In her Crone aspect she is a goddess of wisdom, prophesy, magic, and also retribution and destruction. Above all, in whatever aspect, she is a goddess of love. Other attributes which might be given her are healing, beauty, compassion, and concern.

In the same way the Wiccan God may be seen in three aspects; as a young man, a middle-aged man, and as an old man. He is associated with the sun, with hunting, with nature and the forest, and with death and whatever follows death. In modern day Wicca there often seems to be more of an emphasis on the Goddess than on the God. In fact, there are some groups (mainly feminist) who actually direct their worship exclusively at the Goddess. To my mind this is as unbalanced as is the Christian concept of an all-male deity. There is certainly room for more emphasis to be placed on one over the other, to suit the individual, but both are necessary and both should be acknowledged. Both deities are associated with the earth and with fertility, and also with rebirth, compassion, and retribution.

In worship and in magical rites, there are usually images of the deities placed on the altar. Initially it may be a good idea to use symbols rather than actual figures. An antler or a pinecone for the God and a seashell for the Goddess are possibilities, or colored candles can be used. I suggest this because it will probably take some time for you to form a picture in your mind of exactly how you see the God and the Goddess. Even when you have their figures firmly in your mind, it may take a very long time to find statues or paintings that are the same. Of course, if you are an artist you can create something appropriate, which is a nice idea. If you can sculpt, fine. If not, then a drawn/painted figure can be mounted on a piece of wood or decoupaged to a stand.

A: Decoupage on Wood   B: Paint on Rock

Deity Figures for the Altar

I'll talk more about the altar and what is on it in chapter 7, *Temple*.

Although I have stressed a god and a goddess, which would make Wicca duotheistic, many actually view the Craft as polytheistic; believing in *many* deities. Some see these only as various "aspects" of the main God and Goddess but others view them as separate deities, albeit perhaps of lesser importance. It is not difficult to conceive of a whole hierarchy with specific deities in charge of, for example, health, the arts, divination, the animals, the waters, death, and so on. But this is one of the joys of Wicca—there are no hard and fast rules, no laws carved into stone. You work with what is right for *you*, as an individual.

Along with this belief in gods it should be pointed out that there is a *non-belief* in any divine figure of ultimate evil, such as the Christian Satan. Satan, and his minions, was an invention of the Christian church—actually an adaptation of a Persian concept put forward by Zoroaster (c. 800 B.C.E.) in the writings known as the *Avesta*. Wiccans, then, do not believe in Satan . . . and most certainly do not worship him!

The Goddess and God are always with us and their story is played out within the Wheel of the Year.
Over the course of thousands of years their different aspects have been turned into a myriad other deities, all of which are parts of the one.

—Gail Duff, *Seasons of the Witch*

Honoring the Earth

This is something that should probably be looked at while we still have the God and Goddess in mind, since it is part of the Gaia thesis that the earth's biosphere is a living being. Happily, recent years have seen an awareness of the need to work with the earth, to recycle and conserve. Everyone should recycle items such as paper, newspaper, cardboard, plastic, bottles—anything that can be recycled. If your community doesn't recycle, make the effort of taking the items to a recycling center yourself. Witches do not pollute, so don't throw trash out of the car window (or anywhere else). If you see someone else's trash blowing about the landscape, pick it up and deposit it in an appropriate place. A lot of Witch groups, and some Solitaries, have adopted sections of highway to keep clean. This is an excellent idea. It not only keeps that section clean, but it also demonstrates to others how much we care about our environment, about Mother Earth. Consider joining or donating to worthwhile movements such as the Ocean Conservancy and/or the World Wildlife Fund.

In *Wicca For Life* (Citadel, 2001) I gave some facts and suggested some projects that might be undertaken by Wiccans. They can certainly be considered by Solitary Wiccans. These were taken from the booklet *50 Simple Things You Can Do to Save the Earth* (Berkeley: The Earth Works Group, Earth Works Press, 1989) and bear repeating here:

* It takes one fifteen-year-old tree to make enough paper for just seven hundred grocery bags, so save that tree by taking your own cloth bags to the store with you. Plastic grocery bags are *not* biodegradable (even though some claim to be) so don't use them.

* Permanent press clothes and non-iron bed linens are treated with formaldehyde resin. Avoid them and use natural fabrics whenever possible.

* Use water-based markers and pens, since permanent ones contain harmful solvents such as ethanol, toluene, and xylene.

* Use paper plates and cups, not styrofoam ones. Styrofoam is actually polystyrene foam made from a carcinogen. It is completely nonbiodegradable.

❀ Add brewer's yeast and garlic to your pet's food. Fleas hate it and this way you can avoid your pet absorbing the nerve-damaging chemicals in commercial flea collars.

There are many things such as the above that you can do to help the environment. Work at them and get your friends and relatives to do the same.

Most Wiccans also do all they can to help save the animals. One worthwhile and enjoyable thing you can do is to build a backyard wildlife refuge. It can be as simple or as complex as you like. The extra benefit is for you: you get to see a lot of wildlife up close and enjoy the antics of birds and animals, which you might never normally see. Hummingbirds are attracted by brightly colored plants, especially red-colored ones such as morning glories. Bird feeders can be set up with sunflower seeds, corn, and thistle seeds. Heated birdbaths are appreciated in the winter. Food scraps of all sorts are enjoyed by crows. Bluejays like peanuts (crack them, if possible, to help them get into them). Check with your local office of the Audubon Society and with the National Federation of Wildlife, to see what you can best do for the animals native to your area. Where I live, we get a tremendous variety of birds, plus rabbits, chipmunks, wild turkeys, deer, foxes, skunks, opossums, and others. We have a small farm, and we have created hedgerows and planted trees to help

In the cycle of water, we have rain that falls to the earth, is heated by the sun, and evaporates back into the sky, forming clouds again and eventually raining back down to the earth. These cycles are visible manifestations of the Law of Cyclicity. Both reincarnation and karma work in accordance with this Law.

—Monte Plaisance, *Reclaim the Power of the Witch*

the wildlife. But even in a city environment you can work at it. If nothing else, bird feeders on balconies and heated birdbaths are good.

Reincarnation

One of the main tenets of Witchcraft is a belief in reincarnation. Witches acknowledge that they live a number of lives on this earth. Some have fleeting memories of past lives, though not everyone does. I like to explain reincarnation by drawing a parallel with a person going through the grades in a school. At each grade level there is a certain curriculum, with things that are taught and have to be learned. Together with these are experiences that are gained, in turn teaching life lessons. At the end of the proscribed period there is a graduation, followed by a short break. Then the person comes back to the next grade, with its attendant curriculum of new lessons and experiences. This continues on for a number of levels until the final graduation, when all has been accomplished. This, then, is how our lives progress. We are born into a particular body, learn lessons, and

It is not particularly surprising to find that reincarnation is among the oldest beliefs held by mankind. As a matter of fact, Stone Age practitioners of "the old religion" . . . already believed in reincarnation. It is such a basic part of their religion, that witchcraft is unthinkable without the firm conviction that man does return time and again, and that the life cycle continues forever or at least until such time as the individual has fully discharged his obligations toward self, or perhaps toward deity.

—Hans Holzer, *Born Again: The Truth About Reincarnation*

have certain experiences in that body, eventually reaching an end and graduating/dying. At that point our spirit goes back to the gods, reviews what we have learned, and plans what needs to be studied in the next incarnation. We are then reborn into a new body and continue the learning process.

Exactly how many lives we go through, and what happens at the end, we don't know. I think the number of lives would depend on the individual and how quickly he or she learns and assimilates. You often hear talk of "old souls" and "new souls." These are people who have lived either a number of previous lives or are in the early stages. As to what happens at the end, we will have to wait and see. There is the theory that we "become at one with the gods," whatever that may mean. There is another theory that after a number of lives on this earth we go on to a round of lives on some other planet or in some other life-form. But that still begs the question, what happens at the end?

Along with reincarnation, there are also various thoughts on karma, on rewards and punishments for how we live our lives. The following section discusses this.

Whosoever formulates, even subconsciously, a wish to study the higher knowledge, will be given the opportunity to do so. Life by life, he will be given the training necessary to fit him for its study, until finally, if, through all the hard discipline to which he has been subjected, it has still maintained its place in his esteem as the one thing worthwhile, this subconscious wish will work through into consciousness.

—Dion Fortune, *The Training and Work of an Initiate*

Retribution

A popular interpretation of karma is that in the next lifetime you will be rewarded or punished for what you do in this lifetime; for example, if you kill someone in this life, then in the next life you will be killed. But this does not follow the general Wicca belief, which is of retribution taking place *during this present lifetime*. Only by such belief, it is felt, is there any influence to do good and avoid the bad.

Some other religions state that there is a judgment, followed by rewards and/or punishments, that will come in the afterlife, or the next life. However, this seems to lead to people hoping to "get away with" actions, since there are no immediate consequences. But in Wicca there is the belief not only that what you do will return, but that it will return threefold, *in this lifetime*. (This is a very real deterrent against harming others or doing any type of ill deed.) In other words, if you do harm to someone, that harm will reflect back onto you, and at three times the intensity. However, do good and that too will come back at three times the original. It's not necessarily literally three times; for example, if you knock out someone's tooth it doesn't follow that you'll have three of your own teeth knocked out. Rather, you will suffer something that might be considered three times as bad as having a tooth knocked out. The main principle, here, is that the return belief reinforces the Wicca principle that you should do good and not harm anyone (and that includes yourself). Not all Wiccans subscribe to the threefold principle (though the majority seem to) but all subscribe to the payback in this lifetime. This might be the place to mention—and emphasize—that Witches do not do drugs, or anything that would harm themselves.

Since we eventually experience all things, over a number of lifetimes, then certainly you might experience (for example) killing someone and also being killed yourself. But the two are not linked and do not follow from one lifetime immediately into the next. In other words, the one is not dependent upon the other; it is two separate experiences that must be gone through.

This idea of the working of retribution contributes to what is the only "law" of Wicca. That law, known as the Wiccan Rede, is "An it harm none, do what thou wilt." (The meaning of the old word "an" is "if.") It is saying that you can do whatever you like, just so long as you do not harm anyone. That includes yourself, of course.

Magic

In Witchcraft there is a belief in what is termed "magic." What exactly *is* magic? The occultist Aleister Crowley defined it is "the art and science of causing change to occur in conformity with will." In other words, making something happen that you want to happen. Any act of magic—any claim of making something happen—could be passed off by a skeptic as "coincidence." But if you make things happen enough times, just as you want them to and at exactly the time you want them to, then "coincidence" becomes a very inadequate explanation.

From what was said in the "Retribution" section, it should be obvious that the only magic that is done in Wicca is positive magic. No magic is ever done that would harm anyone in any way. Negative, or black magic, is only done by magicians who do not share the Wiccan beliefs.

The term "black magic" has absolutely nothing to do with race, nor does it in any way imply negativity toward any race. It dates from pre-Christian times when it was felt that the forces of good were somehow tied to the daytime and to light, while the forces of evil were tied to night and darkness. From this grew reference to light and dark magic (meaning positive and negative), more generally called white and black magic. Having been used for over two thousand years, these terms are not likely to go away. Today's Wiccans, however, prefer to refer to positive and negative magic.

There are a large number of ways to actually work magic and I will be dealing with many of them in Part Two.

> *In times past, those who followed the work of the village witch or Cunning Man started gaining their knowledge from their cradles, learning by watching, questioning and taking part in those tasks wherein the psychic skills are developed and brought into controlled use . . . You can learn how from a book, where, even when, but you cannot turn that information into real understanding without doing it. Most practical knowledge is remembered because of what we did, rather than what we saw or heard.*
>
> —Marian Green, *A Witch Alone*

Spirits

Do you believe in fairies? Or elves? Gnomes, sprites, hobgoblins, leprechauns, buccas, brags, selkies, or similar? Most, though not all, Witches believe in a spirit realm. Many claim to have seen or encountered spirits of one sort or another. The nature spirits are often referred to by the general term *devas*. It is generally accepted that very young children, who have not been browbeaten into accepting that such things are "not possible," often see and speak with spirits or devas.

In England one of the earliest recorded cases of an encounter with spirits who might be called fairies occurred in the middle of the twelfth century, in the county of West Suffolk, at a place known as Wolfpits, about five miles from Bury St. Edmunds. A small boy and his sister were found wandering there by some villagers. The pair was described as of normal size and appearance, except for a greenish hue to their skin. They did not speak English but a language unknown to anyone there. They were taken to the house of Sir Richard de Calne, at Wilkes, and given food and drink. Although they seemed hungry, they wouldn't eat. Eventually they were per-suaded to eat some beans. The boy forever remained depressed and eventually died but the girl survived, her greenish coloring gradu-ally fading. As she learned to speak English she explained that she and her brother were from a country she described as being beneath the earth. They had been drawn out by the sound of bells, but then found they couldn't get back. Being beneath the earth, the land had no sunshine but was lit with a light much like twilight.

There are many elements of this story that have been repeated time and again, over hundreds of years. Different people, variously known as fairies or similar, are said to dwell "underground." Some are described to be of a greenish color. It is interesting that originally such spirits were invariably of human size. In fact, even Shakespeare described them that way in his earlier works. In *The Merry Wives of Windsor* he has Anne Page, a grown woman, dress as a fairy and expect to be taken as one. Later, however, he was to become one of the main promoters who shrank fairies to become diminutive creatures.

The point here is that there seems to be some evidence for the existence of "spirits," for want of a better term, from some other world or, perhaps, parallel universe. Certainly many gardeners say they have seen nature spirits among the flowers and vegetables. In the 1960s, Peter Caddy founded a community known as Findhorn on the barren, windswept coast of Inverness, Scotland, and watched it blossom into a rich, fertile paradise worked by fairies and elves.[3] When Peter Caddy and his wife Eileen started to work the area it was a truly inhospitable place, with sandy soil and little, if any, sparse desertlike life. But in a few short years the Caddys, and some few others who joined them, were producing huge vegetables (forty-two-pound cabbages and sixty-pound broccoli plants), beautiful flowers, twenty-one types of fruit, forty-two herbs, and a total of sixty-five different vegetables. The focus of their work, they said, was through love, and it was always acknowledged that what was done came about with the help of the spirits of the land: fairies and elves.

[3]See *The Magic of Findhorn* by Paul Hawken (London: Souvenir Press, 1975).

There is plenty of evidence for such spirits. There is evidence that others, besides Peter Caddy, have successfully called on them for help when needed. As a Witch, you are not expected to automatically believe in them . . . but the more people you meet with similar interests to your own, the better the chance that you will eventually come into contact with others who believe in them. Don't be a skeptic, simply keep an open mind.

Part Two

SOLITARY PRACTICE

ALTHOUGH IN MANY WAYS it is easier to be personally taught by another, when it comes to Solitary Witchcraft it *is* possible to learn from a book. With the gradual spread of information on what Witchcraft really is (as opposed to how people were led to believe it to be, through centuries of misrepresentation), thousands of people have recognized that this alternate religion is the one they had been searching for—consciously or unconsciously—for much of their lives. Here, then, are the details that can teach you all you need to know to become a practicing Witch.

Anyone who is sincere in their desire to become a Witch, will have no hesitation in studying to become the best possible Witch they can become. Don't let the word "study" frighten you. It's not like going back to school, with an enforced curriculum and periodic grading and tests. This is study for your own enjoyment and fulfillment. You set the time scale, or schedule; you decide when you are ready to move on to other things; you decide when it is time to "graduate." You will find that there is such pleasure in this study that it will be ongoing. I have been a Witch for over forty years, yet I still read and research when and where I can; I still look for further information. Learning of the Craft becomes such a pleasure that you don't ever want it to stop.

5

Tools

*It is an old belief that the best substances for
making tools are those that have once had life
in them, as opposed to artificial substances.
Thus, wood or ivory is better for a wand than
metal, which is more appropriate for swords or
knives. Virgin parchment is better than
manufactured paper for talismans, etc. And
things which have been made by hand are
good, because there is life in them.*
—*Gardnerian Book of Shadows*

s a Witch you will need certain tools. You won't necessarily need *all* the ones listed here. You can choose,
deciding what you want to use and what you don't.
(Choice will be discussed along the way.) In fact, you can
actually practice as a Witch without *any* tools! But the use of something tangible helps immeasurably, at least in the early stages, so I
strongly suggest using them. To stand and manipulate a wand or
athamé as an integral part of your rituals really brings power to what

you do and say, so I recommend it. You can always discard any tools sometime in the future, if you find you don't really need them.

With all of the tools used in Witchcraft, the very best—by which I mean the most "powerful," the most capable of holding and dispensing energy—are the tools you make yourself. Don't immediately think, "But I could never make a knife!" It's not too difficult really,[4] and you don't necessarily have to make the *whole* knife. To end up with a magically powerful tool you just need to have *put some of your own energy into it*. The more energy you can channel into the tool, the better, so the greater percentage of the tool that you make, the better. But it's a case of any is better than none. For this reason you can simply buy an appropriate commercially produced knife to use as your ritual tool. If you carve signs, symbols, sigils, or just your initials, into the handle, you will have put something of yourself into the knife. Your own personal energies will have gone into it, making it a very different knife from any other. All the tools you make, will be consecrated before you actually use them in ritual, making them even more special and making them very much "sacred" tools. The consecration will be detailed at the end of this section.

Athamé

The most common Wicca tool is a ritual knife called an athamé, pronounced a'*tham*'ay. I have heard various other pronunciations used, some of which are peculiar to particular traditions and some just out of ignorance. This pronunciation is the one I recommend but it is up to you. Of course, you can call the knife something completely different if you wish. In the Saxon tradition, for example, it is the *seax*, an old Saxon word for knife. You could call it a bodkin, needle, spike, rowel, bristle, tusk, tine, lancet, or any one of a number of old terms. You can even make up your own name for it. Keep in mind that this is a tool rather than a weapon (a definite distinction). For the sake of this book, however, I will stick to athamé as its name.

[4]See *Buckland's Complete Book of Witchcraft* by Raymond Buckland (St. Paul: Llewellyn, 2002).

> *The symbolism of the athamé connects it to the Moon, the silver blade representing the full moon and the black handle representing the new moon. It is also a representation of the male phallus and thus the masculine aspect of nature. Some traditions attribute the athamé to the element air . . .*
>
> —Monte Plaisance, *Reclaim the Power of the Witch*

Athamé

The type of knife you use is again a matter of choice. Traditionally, it should be a knife with a straight, double-edged blade. The double-edged blade is recommended because of the way it is used in ritual work, which will be explained more fully. Since, as I've said, it's a tool and not a weapon, the blade does not need to be sharp. It's not used for any actual, physical cutting. The blade is usually metal (steel, iron, brass, copper) but it could be stone (flint is an interesting choice), bone, wood, or whatever. The handle should be of a natural material, such as wood or bone, rather than plastic or anything synthetic. Many Witches say the handle should be black or some other dark color. This is a good idea since a dark color helps absorb your energies. The size of the knife is up to you. Some like to have a large, impressive one with a long blade, while others prefer something small and delicate.

As to what to carve on the handle, this again is your choice. Various Wicca traditions are very specific about what is on the athamé, so if you are a coven member you must follow the rules of that tradition. Gardnerian Wiccans, for example, use various symbols taken from ceremonial magic. But as a Solitary, the decision is yours. One possibility would be to use your Witch name (see chapter 13, "Magic/Witch Name" section), your initials, or pertinent astrological signs. You might put your name (magical or mundane) on one side of the handle and the signs for your sun sign, moon sign, and rising sign on the other side. As I've said, what is important is simply that you do some work on the tool to imbue it with your energy.

Wand

Many Witches—Solitaries especially—see the wand as an alternative to the athamé. In covens, the arrangement is usually that all the Witches have their own personal athamés and, in addition, there is one wand available for use in ritual by the coven leaders. But the wand and athamé actually are interchangeable in terms of properties and use, so both are not necessary. And of the two (and for Solitaries especially), I feel the wand is the more appropriate Witch tool. If we cast our minds back to early fairy stories, we see Witches and fairy godmothers waving wands rather than knives. For these reasons, the rituals in this book will be detailed with the Witch using a wand. If you are more attracted to the athamé, then simply substitute that whenever the word is used.

The size, shape, and substance of the wand are not strict. First of all, the wood may be any type. Some favor rowan, willow, ash, or hazel, but oak, pine, walnut, ebony, or virtually any other wood, will work just as well. Many simply buy a length of wood dowel from the hardware store. However, as with all things connected to the Craft, I feel a little effort should go into the acquiring and making of the tools. Since even those people who live in the middle of a city can gain access to a park, or even a tree-lined street, then ideally a wand should be cut from a tree by the Witch who will be using it. I favor cutting a branch from a felled or dead tree but realize that's not always possible. If it must be cut from a living tree, then permission should be asked of the tree and an explanation given as to what the branch will be used for. Let's not forget that we are all part of nature and that plants, flowers, and trees all have feelings.[5] If the tree is in a public park, make sure it is legal to cut off a branch. In old books of magic, the length of the wand is given variously as twenty-one inches or as equivalent to the distance from your elbow to the tip of your middle finger. These dimensions are according to various ceremonial magic *grimoires*. But as with all things for the Solitary Witch, it's whatever suits you. Again, though, put some of your energies into the wand, whether carving, staining, painting, decorating, or engraving it.

There is also a tool known as the Priapic wand, which is used in some rituals. (Some Solitaries use it all the time, as their regular wand.) It is named after the Greek fertility deity Priapus, son of Dionysus and Aphrodite. The "true" form of this is a wand with its end carved to look like a phallus. Obviously it represents the male organ of generation. Rather than a lifelike phallus, some prefer to carve the end in the form of a pinecone, or even attach an actual pinecone to it, as a symbolic phallus. This is certainly acceptable, having been used for thousands of years.

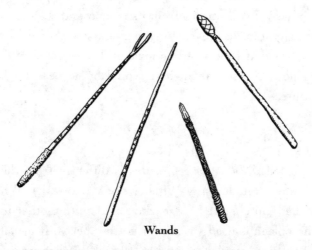

Wands

[5]See *The Secret Power of Plants* by Peter Tompkins and Christopher Bird (New York: Harper & Row, 1973) and *The Secret Life of Plants* by Brett L. Bolton (New York: Berkley, 1957).

Sword

Many covens like to use a sword to draw the ritual circle and for initiations and other specific rituals. As a Solitary, you will probably have no call to use a sword unless you particularly hanker for one. If you do, then the same applies to it as I have said of the athamé.

White-Handled Knife

A white-handled knife is another common coven tool that may or may not find a home with a Solitary Witch. You may prefer a burin (see following description). Basically, while the athamé is the ritual knife, the white-handled knife is the utilitarian one, the one that is used for actual cutting. It can be used for carving the signs on the other tools, for marking candles and other items with necessary sigils for rituals, and for any other cutting and shaping that becomes necessary. It does not usually have anything carved on its handle and does not have to have a double-edged blade.

Although the athamé is regarded by most as a ritual tool not used for actual cutting, there are those Witches who think otherwise. To them, the more the athamé is used—for whatever purpose—the more *mana*, or power, it will absorb from its owner, and they see nothing wrong with its total use, even for things outside the ritual circle. I have to confess that I see a certain logic in this argument. Of course, if the athamé is so used, then there would be no need for a white-handled knife.

Boleen

Sometimes spelled *bolline* or *boline*, this is different from the white-handled knife (though many Witches don't realize it). Where the white-handled knife is used for marking and cutting other tools and similar, the boleen is used strictly for cutting herbs. It usually has a short, curved blade similar to a sickle. Not all Witches are herbalists, so not all Witches have a boleen.

Burin

Its use is similar to that of the white-handled knife. It is used for marking such things as candles. It is a pointed tool, much like an awl. In fact, many Witches will simply adapt an awl. It is especially useful when doing candle-burning magic (see chapter 14, "Candle Magic" section). One way to make a burin is to take a piece of wood for the handle and drive a nail into it. Then cut off the head of the nail, and sharpen the end on a grinding wheel. You can carve or decorate the handle as you wish.

Staff

A larger version of the wand is the staff. We've all seen wizards with staffs (Gandalf in J. R. R. Tolkien's *Lord of the Rings*, for example). The staff was a useful dual-purpose instrument in the old days, when it could not only be a magical tool but could also be a handy walking stick (not to mention a useful cudgel for protection). Today, most of us don't do too much walking so it may not be so appealing. But to some it can replace not only the wand but also the sword, being useful for marking and consecrating a magic circle. It is another tool that deserves to be well decorated and marked with magical signs and sigils.

Crafting ceremonial objects, such as ritual staffs, from wood is a tradition handed down to contemporary pagans from ancient wise men and women. In constructing such an item, you are making a ritual tool with a thousand-year history and reclaiming its sacred role in religious and magical practices.

—Eleanor & Philip Harris,
The Crafting & Use of Ritual Tools

Cord/Cingulum

This is a special cord that is used for working cord magic (and can also have other more mundane uses). It is usually red and nine feet long. The Witch will generally keep the cord by doubling it over and then wrapping it and tying it around his or her waist. Sometimes referred to as a cingulum, it can serve as a belt for a robe or something from which to hang the athame's sheath, if you use an athamé. The main thing to remember is that by being worn in the magic circle all the time it does absorb much of your energy, making it that much more suitable for cord magic work.

Nine feet is a good length for a number of reasons, not least because it is a magical number.[6] Also, at that length it can be very handy for marking on the ground a magical circle of anything up to the traditional nine-foot diameter. If you stick something in the ground and then loop your cord around it, you can then hold a stick or knife at the extended two ends and walk around the center point, marking the circle. If you have looped it at the halfway point of the cord's length, the circle will be exactly nine feet in diameter. By shortening the length you can get a smaller circle.

The cord is usually made of a soft material such as silk. In the tradition of making all your tools yourself, you can take three long lengths of cord and plait or braid them together to form your magical cord. A word of caution if you are planning to dye the finished product (red, green, or whatever color you prefer): if it does have to be dyed, then do the dyeing first before cutting it to length. I have known many Witches who have made beautiful cords, exactly nine feet long, then have dyed them only to find they shrink! When you're ready to cut to length, then bind the ends with thread so they won't unravel. Your finished cord should be consecrated before use, just as with the other tools.

---

[6]Three has always been regarded as magical, mainly because of the three aspects of the Goddess: Maiden, Mother, Crone. Nine, then, is especially magical since it is three times three.

Besom

A besom is a broomstick. This has a place in the history of Witch-craft, being looked upon by many as the "traditional" instrument of the Witch. But since we don't actually fly on a broomstick, it doesn't have the appeal that perhaps it should. Some Witches use a besom to sweep their magic circles, ritually cleansing the circles of all nega-tivity. Others use the besom like a staff and will mark the circle with it. It can certainly have a place in specific isolated rituals (for exam-ple, being jumped over at a wedding rite). For most Witches, how-ever, it is an interesting adjunct but by no means mandatory.

Bell

A bell is another of those tools or instruments that is used by some but not by all. However, the sounding of a bell can add tremendously to the charged atmosphere of a magical ritual. Its vibrations work like the olfactory vibrations of burning incense, increasing the energy being built for magical work. If you decide to include a bell in your working tools, choose carefully. The tone and purity of the sound count a lot. You may like something deep and gonglike or something high and ethereal. Of course, there's no reason you shouldn't have both and utilize two bells.

Goblet

A cup, or goblet, is essential. In virtually all rites there is a drinking of wine (or fruit juice) to toast the gods. Some Witches refer to the goblet as a "chalice" but this smacks of the Eucharistic cup of Chris-tianity, so I tend to avoid it. The shape of the goblet is not important. It can be plain, with a handle or two, or even can be a drinking horn rather than a cup. It can be of metal, crystal, pottery, or any other material. Libations are always poured during the ritual, so a libation dish might be another required instrument. Again, this can be of any shape and any material.

Censer

A censer, or *thurible*, is another essential, since incense is burned at both religious and magical rituals. This can be a store-bought incense burner for powdered incense, stick incense, or cone incense, or it can be something you make; for example, you can simply fill a saucer with sand (to absorb the heat) and burn the incense on top of that. If you are really into ritual, I would recommend using the powdered incense burned on charcoal briquets and having one of those incense burners that you swing on a chain—the swinging of it adds tremendously to any performance of ritual.

There are other tools or instruments that can be used for specific purposes but that are not generally looked upon as major, essential, working tools. An example would be the skrying mirror, used for divination (see chapter 15), or the mortar and pestle used in herbal preparations.

Dress

What you wear as a Witch is important, both in terms of your clothes and any jewelry. I'm not talking about your everyday wear, and don't confuse ritual wear with everyday wear. Unfortunately, there are those few who, for whatever reason, feel they must wear black robes, heavy makeup, and masses of occult jewelry everywhere they go to show they are Witches! These are most often people who have no idea about true Witchcraft and who don't know that ritual robes should be kept for ritual. In contrast, there are those who are Witches and who wear their everyday clothing, such as T-shirt and jeans, even when practicing their art, seeing no need to "dress up" at any time.

Yet for ritual purposes, it's not "dressing up"! There are two aspects to Witchcraft: one is the religious side and the other is the magical side. Neither should be treated lightly. They both deserve respect. Perhaps it's more obvious that there should be respect shown (both to the gods and to yourself) when doing religious rituals. But magic practice should be treated with equal respect. First of all, magic is/should be practiced only when there is a very real need for it. (More on this in chapters 13 and 14, on magic.) It is not, then, something that is done on a whim and so should also be carefully prepared for. And that preparation should include dress.

If you don't care for special robes, then it's all right to wear T-shirt and jeans (my late good friend and fellow Witch, Scott Cunningham, never wore anything but T-shirts and jeans). However, they should not be the same T-shirt and jeans you've been wearing all day, for working in the office, garage, garden, or wherever. They should be a T-shirt and pair of jeans kept especially for ritual use. The consecrated circle, or other space, is sacred space; it is regarded as being "between the worlds"—between this world and the next— and as such is sacred to the gods and to the Witch. Show some respect for this space by not "contaminating" it with clothing that might well carry negativity from the mundane world.

Before stepping into sacred space, Witches usually take a spiritually cleansing bath and then either dress in ritual clothing or step naked into the sacred space. Ritual purification is common among many religious groups. The bath should be of comfortably warm water—neither hot nor cold—to which a handful of sea salt has been added. (These days sea salt is available at many supermarkets. If you can't find it there, try a health food store. If all else fails use regular salt, but try to find sea salt if you can.) This bathing can be made a ritual in itself. You can light one or two votive candles and turn off electric lights. Burn some incense too, if you like. The purpose of the bath is purification, so you can add herbs or oils to it if you wish. The oils that carry the property of purification include acacia, cinnamon, clove, frankincense, jasmine, lavender, myrrh, olive, and sandalwood. The herbs of purification include alkanet, anise, bay, benzoin, bloodroot, broom, cedar, chamomile, fennel, hyssop, iris, lavender, lemon, lemon verbena, parsley, peppermint, rosemary, sagebrush, thyme, turmeric, valerian, vervain, and yucca. You can drop some oil into the water— one or two (not more than three) of the ones mentioned—or you can put not more than three herbs in a piece of muslin and hang the bag in the bath water. This is a spiritual cleansing, so you don't have to soap up and rinse off. Just relax for a few moments in the salted water, with or without oil or herbs, then get out and dry off.

The majority of Witches wear special ritual robes. These usually are floor or ankle length with long bell sleeves. They can be with or without a hood and with or without a cord at the waist. There are patterns readily available or you can purchase such robes from a number of sources these days. You will hear, and should heed, cautions about trailing long sleeves and hems around lighted candles. This should be common sense and is no reason to reject the traditional robes. The color of the robe is up to you. All colors plus black and white have been and are used by Witches around the world. There's no reason why you shouldn't have more than one robe and perhaps have a different colored one for different seasons. The material of the robe, as with all things connected with the Craft, should be natural: cotton, wool, or silk. Avoid polyesters and other synthetics.

Robes are not the only choice. I have known many Witches who have been captivated by the past, or who are fans of fantasy, and have adopted various medieval forms of dress. Many Witches (especially in Europe) work naked—what is known as "skyclad"; clad only by the sky—seeing this as the purest and simplest of methods. Certainly any number of paintings and illustrations of Witches from the past show them naked. Of course, the climate in your area may govern how suitable that would be.

> *Robes have another interesting effect. They act as a very strong auto-suggestion, which has the power of keying the mind to the operation in hand. Merely to vest oneself in the robes of one's grade automatically quickens the emotional link . . . During the many magical operations undertaken through the years, the robes become "charged" with a certain etheric energy or "magnetism."*
>
> —W. E. Butler, *The Magician: His Training and Work*

Jewelry

Along with dress you might want to consider jewelry. Again, there may be a distinction between what you would wear in the mundane world and what you might wear only when doing rituals. There are no hard and fast rules. You may wear, for example, a pentagram ring or pendant necklace at all times. But you might feel empowered in ritual by wearing a crown of some sort, which you would never wear outside the circle. With covens there are certain conventions; for example, in many degree-oriented traditions the High Priestess, as leader, will wear a particular bracelet as a badge of office. If she is the leader of a number of covens, she might also wear a crown. Other Witches in the group would not wear either bracelet or crown. However, all are encouraged to wear a necklace, which symbolizes the circle of rebirth. As a Solitary, you can please yourself. If your pleasure is to wear a crown, then wear one; if you want a bracelet, have one! Over the years, the number of Wicca supply houses and jewelers has increased and they offer a wide variety of beautiful rings, bracelets, pendants, crowns, and other implements and adorn-ments. Check out Web sites and the many available catalogs to see what is being offered. Not only do you need to feel comfortable in your religio-magical environment, you also need to feel good about yourself, to feel "empowered." As a Solitary, you can do whatever best suits you and no one—*no one*—can tell you you're wrong, invalid, unauthentic, or anything else!

I've spoken about the various tools but any and all of them are just "tools" until they are consecrated. That act makes them sacred, mag-ical items. In the *Temple* chapter, creating your sacred space will be discussed. This is the place where you will do your rituals. This also is where you will do your consecrations, whether of these initial tools or of any future tools, talismans, amulets, or anything else requiring the sacred cleansing treatment. And that is what a consecration is. It is a cleansing of all negativity and any and all vibrations previously attached to the object, allowing you to start using it with nothing but the positive energies and designs in it that you want there. A Christian baptism is such a consecration (and is done with salted water, as is the Craft consecration). It is a rebirth—a new beginning. This is also something that you will be doing at the start of any and all rituals. You will be cleansing yourself of the vibrations of the mundane world and making yourself pure for whatever religious and/or magical purposes you have in mind.

Book of Shadows

Every Witch owns a book in which he or she keeps all the rituals, prayers, chants, spells, and notes on everything pertaining to the Craft. This is traditionally known as the "Book of Shadows." The name dates from the time when what had previously been an oral tradition was finally being recorded, but when it was necessary for Witches to meet "in the shadows," as it were, because of the persecutions. The tradition is that the book is written in the Witch's own handwriting and is bound in a black cover. Today, the cover does not have to be black, but it is strongly recommended that you keep to writing the whole thing yourself—no computer printouts or the like! As with all things Wicca, there is a reason for this. Here the reason is "power." I have already discussed doing work on each and every one of your tools, to put your energy and power into them. It's the same thing with the book. If you write it yourself, you are concentrating on each and every letter that is written on the pages and, in doing so, you are imbuing your Book of Shadows with tremendous energy, which is actually drawn upon when you do the rituals or work the particular magic. You don't have to write it in stylish Spencerian script or in one of the so-called secret or magical alphabets. You certainly can use an elegant and graceful writing if you are so inclined, though I caution you to use something easily readable when writing out rituals that need to be read in candlelight! Be proud of your book and make it a thing of beauty, if you can. There also may be a place for using one of the old alphabets.

Some Witches buy commercially produced, blank books and use those. Others make the book from scratch, gathering together the sheets of paper (parchmentlike paper can look really effective) and placing them between handmade covers of tooled leather or wood-burned plywood. It can be a fun project and one which, in years to come, makes the book very precious to you.

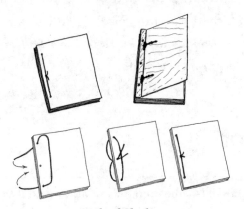

Book of Shadows

If you have an interest in astrology, then you can keep all your astrological notes and reference materials in your Book of Shadows. Similarly, if your main interest is in herbs, then part of your Book of Shadows becomes your herbological notebook. Incorporate your occult interests with your religious rituals and your magical spells. Your Book of Shadows becomes a depository of arcane wisdom.

Some Witches lay the Book on the altar for the rituals but it can take up a lot of room and, when it's lying flat, it's not easy to read from. (It can be very awkward bending over to read while at the same time trying to raise an athamé or wand in salute to the gods.) I'd recommend getting, or making, some sort of a stand, much like a music stand. This can be placed alongside the altar, at the best height for reading. Hopefully you will get to the point where you know all of your rituals by heart, but it still helps to have the Book there, in case you need to refer to it. It's better to be able to concentrate on putting real feeling into what you are saying than to struggle to remember the exact wording. More on that later.

> [My Book of Shadows] came from my teacher . . .
> and, no matter how many other books I have read
> over the years, I always return to it. Like the folk
> singer, I need to hear or read the original song and
> develop from that, rather than developing a modern
> version. This way, I stay close to the tradition and
> maintain its themes and ideas but am still able to
> incorporate my own writing.
>
> —Gail Duff, *Seasons of the Witch*

Anointing Oil

I include this as one of the tools, though it is only used occasionally.
It is used at your self-dedication, or initiation, and if you are doing a
Wiccaning. There may be other occasions where you would like to
use it. In fact, some Witches anoint themselves at the start of every
ritual, which is a nice idea. Here is an old recipe for making the oil:

> Take a small bottle and fill it with mint. There are many
> different types of mint, but Catmint, Nepeta cataria, is
> preferable. Pour in enough olive oil to cover the mint and
> fill the bottle. Again there are many types of olive oil.
> Choose a good quality, extra-virgin olive oil. Cap the bottle
> and let it stand in a cool, dry place for twenty-four hours,
> turning the jar upside down every six hours. At the end of
> the twenty-four-hour period, carefully strain the liquid
> through a piece of cheesecloth into a bowl. Refill the bottle
> with fresh mint and pour in the oil from the bowl. Again
> cap it, store it, and turn it every six hours. Repeat this
> process over at least a three-day period, using the same oil
> but refreshing the mint each time. At the end of that time,
> again strain it and this time bottle the liquid. This is your
> anointing oil. ⚴

6

Consecration of Tools

For all the rhetorician's rules
Teach nothing but to name his tools.
—Samuel Butler (1600–1680), *Hudibras*, Part I, Canto I

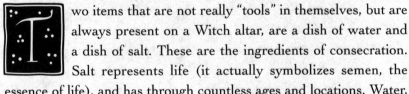 wo items that are not really "tools" in themselves, but are always present on a Witch altar, are a dish of water and a dish of salt. These are the ingredients of consecration. Salt represents life (it actually symbolizes semen, the essence of life), and has through countless ages and locations. Water, of course, is essential to life. Along with these two items, you will need to have incense burning in order to consecrate anything.

To consecrate an item, in the circle first place some of the salt into the water and mix it. As you do this, ask the gods to purify the salt and water, making them the objects of their (the gods') blessings and instruments to purify and cleanse any and all other objects on which they may be used. You can do this in your own words, out loud or in your head. Sprinkle the object (athamé, wand, talisman, or whatever) with the salted water, making sure to cover all sides and angles. If you'd prefer, you can dip your finger into the salted water and then rub it all over the object. As you do this, see the negativity going out of it and being replaced by white, positive energy. Hold the object in the smoke of the incense, turning it so that all facets get censed, and see the positivity being sealed in. Now, either hold the object between the palms of your hands or hold it flat to your body over the heart. Concentrate your thoughts on the purpose of the item: If it is a working tool then see it as a powerful, effective tool to aid in your work; if it's a talisman, for protection for example, then see it as a powerful protector. Ask the gods to bless it and help it work for and with you.

When you've initially consecrated your first working tools, wrap them in a piece of white linen or silk and carefully put them away until you are ready to start working with them. Do not let anyone else handle them. These are *your* ritual tools; they are sacred and special. ⚮

7

Temple

*The purpose of Temples today should be to
provide us with an artificial environment that
will stimulate and strengthen spiritual abilities
and create favorable conditions for
communication with inner intelligences.*
—William G. Gray, *Temple Magic*

ince Wicca is a religion, its rites are held in what is
described as "sacred space." This is actually no more than
the particular area where you decide to do your rites and
rituals. It can be as elaborate or as simple as you want it
to be. I term it the "temple," even though such a grandiose term
might only be appropriate within your own mind. In early days,
when the farmer walked the fields planting his seeds and asking the
gods to bring good crops, this temple was no more than the plowed
furrow of the field. Over time, it has become a sacred circle of tooled
stones, a clearing in a forest, a dark cottage standing alone, a corner
of a small kitchen, a modern office cubicle. As I've said, it is simply
the sacred space where you will work.

Your temple doesn't even have to be the same place every time. You may be out in the countryside, walking along a deserted beach at the seashore, or even sitting on the floor of your bedroom when you feel the need to commune with the gods; it doesn't matter. All are appropriate for the Solitary Witch.

In Coven Witchcraft there has to be a consecrated circle of certain dimensions that encloses the members of the group. The altar is positioned in the center and the ritual action goes on around that. Let's look at the many different ways that a Solitary may work, enjoying the freedom of working alone. I'll start with what might be considered the ideal, most elaborate setup and then go on to alternatives that can be called upon to fit your situation.

The space where you have your rituals is indeed sacred; it is a special place where you commune with the Lord and the Lady, the God and the Goddess of Wicca. This is the space that is "between the worlds." You should feel completely safe there. It is somewhere you can go not only to worship the gods or to do magic, but just to feel safe, comforted, and secure. I feel very strongly that such space is very special and so is deserving of some effort. There will certainly be times when it is necessary to work in far from ideal circumstances, perhaps at short notice, but if possible, I advise you to plan ahead and do the very best you can. Ideally, then, you will work in a circle. The size of it is up to you. I would imagine that a circle roughly six feet in diameter would be sufficient but that will depend on the size of the centrally placed altar, if you have one. It might also depend on whether or not you plan to do much dancing around the circle (see chapter 8, *Ritual*).

Most Witches work either at night or at least in the evening hours. You don't have to, of course, but it's generally acknowledged that the airwaves, or "vibes," are more attuned to things then. (Have you ever noticed, when traveling by car in the late evening, how it's possible to tune in the radio to faraway stations that you can never get during the day?) You will therefore need illumination; traditionally this is candlelight.

Candles are placed around the circle. Most Wiccans place one each at the four "quarters": east, south, west, and north. These directions are associated with the four elements: east—air, south—fire, west—water, north—earth. If that's not enough illumination then don't hesitate to add more between those (and these extras can be lit before any ritual actually starts, while the quarter candles are lit as part of the ritual itself). The quarter candles themselves can be white or colored. You may like to use the colors associated with the directions and elements: yellow to the east, red to the south, blue to the west, and green to the north. You may prefer to use all of one color, with the color dependent upon the season. There may be one or two candles on the altar as well.

If there are reasons you cannot use candles, or have no inclination to use them, then there is no reason why electric light cannot be used. If you use electricity, the lights should be a low wattage or be dimmed down through a rheostat. Just as there's nothing to stop you doing your rites in bright daylight, so there's nothing to stop you from having bright, blaring lights. For the vast majority of Witches, however, low lights, quiet, and a sense of reverence not only add to the look of the setting but actually contribute to the energy available, so the majority use candles.

Altar

It is useful to have an altar in the circle. This is not a catchall for anything and everything you want to have with you but a sacred piece of furniture. It will hold a candle (or two), the incense burner, your athamé and/or wand, goblet and libation dish, salt and water, and a small bell. Your representations of the God and the Goddess also will be on the altar. If you use candles to represent the deities then you don't really need any other candle(s) there. But if you have statues or antlers/seashell, or similar, to represent the gods, then I'd recommend a main altar candle in the center of the altar. Place it at

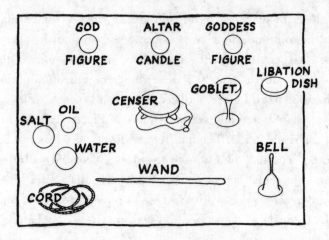

Suggested Altar Layout

the rear, so you are not likely to knock it over as you reach for other items during the rituals.

Any incense, matches, spare candles, wine, and so on, should be kept either underneath or alongside the altar, depending upon its design. And its design is fluid: you could use a cardboard box, if necessary, or a coffee table. A wooden trunk or chest of drawers will do. If you can do your rites outdoors, then a flat rock or an old tree stump are ideal. I've said that the altar is a sacred piece of furniture, and so it is—even if it's also a cardboard box! While it's in use within the sacred space, it is a sacred piece of furniture. What it is and how it is used otherwise can be quite different.

The shape is also immaterial. I favor a round altar myself, but it can be square, rectangular, or irregular. Its height should be one that will be comfortable for you. If you are standing before an altar that is too low and working with the objects on it, it can really strain your back after a while! Many Witches do their rites kneeling, or even sitting down, while others prefer to stand, so adjust the height of your altar accordingly. The orientation of the altar also is up to you. Many Witches favor the altar facing north (in other words, as you stand before it using the items on it, you would be facing north), while others favor east. It doesn't matter which but you should have a good reason for what you choose, as you should for all your choices in Witchcraft. Don't just do something simply because that's the way you think it should be done or because "that's the way they did it in that movie." With the altar placement, you might prefer to face the east because that's the direction in which the sun rises, or you might prefer north because that's equated with the element of earth and you feel very earth-oriented (perhaps your astrological sign is an earth one). If you don't have a good reason now, keep it in mind and don't be afraid to change things around later on.

The altar doesn't have to be of bare wood. Many Witches like to decorate it with an altar cloth or cloths (changing the colors for the different seasons). This can make a big difference to the look and feel of the altar. Some will even decorate the altar cloth with embroidery, paint, and so on. Also, you can add to the look by decorating the altar with flowers, branches, and fruit that are appropriate for the different seasons.

Ideally you should have a circle of about six feet or so in diameter, with an altar in its center and candles around to indicate its area. But suppose you don't have that luxury? To go to the other extreme, suppose you only have a small space alongside your bed? Here again is the joy of the Solitary. You could simply sit on the edge of your bed and "construct" a circle about you, in your mind. You can put your tools on top of a chest of drawers or, if there's not even a chest of drawers, then again imagine the altar there. You will have to do almost everything in your imagination, but *it can be done*. It is far from

> *Much has been written of the details of various positions of ritual furniture but it is really more desirable for each student to experiment for himself and find out how things work best for him.*
>
> Gareth Knight, *The Practice of Ritual Magic*

ideal, but it is possible. It does take tremendous discipline, but if you really want to be a Witch despite the most trying circumstances, you can do it. But let me leave that scenario for now. I'd like to treat the more complete working of Witchcraft first, and later suggest modification dependent upon restrictions.

The circle that we have been discussing is actually the line on the ground showing where a great, invisible globe of energy passes through the surface of the earth. When you start to construct your magic circle, you are actually starting to build a large globe, or egg, of energy that will encompass you and your altar and tools. It is a protective shell and forms a space between the mundane world and the world of spirit. It is within this shell that is "between the worlds." Although it is actually more spherical in shape, it is generally referred to as the "Cone of Power."

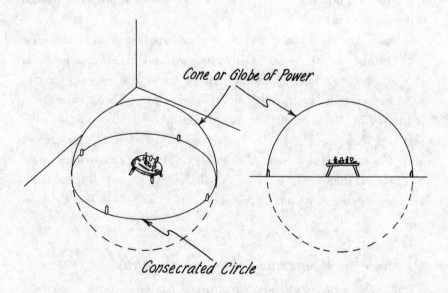

The Magic Circle and Cone of Power

To start the process, you need to physically mark a circle on the ground. This can be done by laying down a length of cord, drawing the line with chalk, making a circular trail of sand or salt, and so on.

In the days of the Witch persecutions, Witches would simply set down a variety of pots and pans on the ground, in a rough circle, to indicate where the line was. This way, if they were surprised by the authorities, they could simply kick the pots and pans out of the way, thus getting rid of any evidence of a magic circle.

If you're lucky enough to be having your ritual outdoors, then you can use something to mark the circle. This was where a coven sword came in handy; the priest or priestess would walk around with it stuck in the ground and thus mark the circle. As a Solitary, you can use a wand, staff, broomstick, or whatever. But indoors, as I've indicated, cord, chalk, or similar is good. (A length of cord is probably best.) Having marked the size and shape of the circle, place the altar in its center, place the tools on it, and position the candles around the circle's line. All this is simply preparation, not part of the ritual itself.

Try to do your rituals at a time when all is quiet and, especially, when you are not likely to be interrupted (this is why most Witches do their rituals late at night). Lock the door and disconnect the telephone. ⚜

8

Ritual

*It may seem hard to believe that the utterance
of a few words or the gathering together of a
few items may produce magical effects.
Nevertheless, unbelievable as it may seem,
that is exactly what happens when a
knowledgeable magician casts a powerful spell.*

—Migene González-Wippler,
The Complete Book of Spells, Ceremonies & Magic

 rite, or ritual, is a combination of speech and actions for a set purpose. Scott Cunningham defined it as "A specific form of movement, manipulation of objects or series of inner processes designed to produce desired effects." (*Wicca*) He went on to say that in religion it is geared toward union with the divine and that in magic it produces a specific state of consciousness that allows the magician to move energy toward needed goals. Isaac Bonewits said that "the crucial point is to do things in the proper order, in the proper way, usually as prescribed by custom or tradition." (*Real Magic*) Arnold van Gennep divides ritual into three parts: separation, transition, and incorporation. (*The Rites of Passage*)

Why are all these definitions important? So that you will get a good sense of the part that ritual plays in Wicca. It is not just a particular, and perhaps peculiar, way of doing things, it is a very specific act.

Classic ritual contains what is termed *legomena* and *dromena*; that is, "things said" and "things done," and usually follows a traditional structure. I have mentioned that within the sacred, or magic, circle you are between the worlds. This is the separation of which van Gennep speaks. The actions of the ritual itself bring about the transition, for you will be a different person after the ritual from the one you were before it. The results of the ritual are then incorporated into your life, especially into your Wicca life. Most effective rituals encompass such elements as special dress, the altar and its working tools, chants, prayers, mystery dramas, song, and dance. These adhere to a prescribed formula determined by the purpose of the ritual, though not all elements are present in every ritual.

The very act of a ritual can give you a tremendous feeling of power. For this reason rites should not be mumbled and hurried through. It is a much more magical, empowering ritual to speak loudly and boldly, to move about the circle, and to use elaborate gestures. (I always recommend that my students take acting classes, if possible, to obtain a good "stage presence.")

Ritual can be much easier and far more satisfying for the Solitary than for the Coven Witch. First of all, when in a coven most of the ritual is actually done by the coven leaders, with other members playing at the most only minor roles. When other members *are* called upon, it is easy for them to feel self-conscious or even intimidated. For the Solitary, you have no call to feel embarrassment, to be at all nervous or self-conscious, for you have no "audience" (other than the gods, who love and respect you). You can shout, if you feel like it, can sing off-key, and can dance like a lunatic! This might be a good time to point out that the gods do have a sense of humor. Where you might never dare to laugh out loud in a Christian church, or to even consider telling a joke (least of all an "off-color" one!) in such straightlaced surroundings, in Wicca it is recognized that humor is a very important part of life and that the gods enjoy the sound of laughter. This is not to say that you can clown your way through the rites of Wicca. No. They are sacred rites and deserve respect. But it does mean that if you mess up—saying the wrong words, or accidentally dropping the anointing oil, for instance—you can have a good laugh about it before continuing.

I'll get into the details of magic rituals later, when talking about magic itself. For now, let's concentrate on the religious rituals. These are constructed almost like a sandwich. They have a specific opening and closing (like the two slices of bread) with various "fillers" between those two, dependent upon the purpose of the ritual. For the Sabbats, the fillers are seasonal celebrations. For the Esbats, they are oriented toward healing, divination, or other more mundane purposes. Let's examine the two "slices of bread" first: the opening and the closing of the ritual.

Opening the Circle (sometimes called "Erecting the Temple")

The circle has been marked in or on the ground (see chapter 7, *Temple*), with candles all about it and the altar in its center. The incense, the main altar candle (and deity candles if you have them), and any extra circle candles—though not the four quarter candles— are alight at the start. Your working tools are on the altar. Wine (or fruit juice, or similar, if you don't wish to have anything alcoholic) is handy beside the altar, as is incense for topping-up the censer when necessary. [*I'd suggest also having a taper on the altar, by the main altar candle. As you'll see, this will be used for lighting the circle candles. A taper is much more in keeping with the "feel" of the ritual than, say, a lighter or even matches.*] You have taken your ritual bath and are either naked or wearing your robe or other ritual garb.

Ring the bell three times. Take up your wand (or athamé), hold it high, and announce that you are about to start the ritual. You can say something like the following, but feel free to use your own words:

"All hail, Lord and Lady; Herne and Epona! [substitute your own deity names if you wish] **I alert you to the building of this temple."**

Move out, around the altar, and go to the east point of the circle. [*Most Witches start their rites in the east (which is the direction in which the day itself starts) though some few start in the north. Think about it and do whatever feels right to you. There is no wrong point at which to start.*] Take a moment there to gather yourself and to focus your energies on what you are about to do, which is to lay the foundation of the ritual circle. Extend your hand and point the wand at the circle marked on the ground. As you breathe in, see and feel powerful, positive energies flowing into you from the deities. Feel them filling your body with their power and then moving down your arm and into the wand. From there, direct those energies, like a light force, from the end of the wand into the line of the circle. Slowly walk forward, continuing to direct this powerful energy through your body, down your arm, through the wand, and down into the circle. [*You are moving clockwise, known as* deosil *(pronounced "jess-il"), with your right shoulder to the altar.*] Walk all the way around until you arrive back where you started. Then you can relax and withdraw the extended wand, turning away from the circle and moving back to stand at the altar. Lay down your wand then ring the bell once.

Take up the dish of salt. Take three good pinches of the salt and drop them into the water. Replacing the dish of salt, stir the water clockwise with your forefinger, and ask the gods to bless the resultant mixture. You can say something like the following but again, as with all of these rituals, feel free to use your own words:

"Through the blessings of Herne and Epona, may the life energies of the salt join with the life force of the water to form a sacred union that will cleanse, guard, and protect in any way I shall use it."

Take up the sacred water and again go to the east. From there, again walk slowly around the circle and back to the starting point, this time sprinkling salted water along the length of the circle. As you walk and sprinkle, concentrate on cleansing the circle, and all within it, of all negativity. Return to the altar and replace the water. Ring the bell once.

Take up the censer [*Here is where a swinging censer can be most apt*] and go to the starting point in the east. Walk the circle again, swinging the censer along its line and again concentrating on removing all negativity. [*If you don't have a swinging censer, then just move what incense burner you have along the line of the circle.*] Go back to the altar and return the censer to its place. Light the taper from the altar candle. With it in one hand and your wand in the other, move out and around to the east and light the east candle. Standing and facing east, raise the wand and say:

"I ask that the Guardians of the Watchtowers of the East may guard this Sacred Circle and protect it from any negative force that may try to enter."

Describe a pentagram in the air and then proceed along to the south. In the south, light that candle, stand, and raise your wand. Repeat the call, calling upon the "Watchtowers of the South," and describe the pentagram. Then on to the west and then the north. At each point, light the candle and make the call. And at each direction, after you've called, describe a pentagram in the air with your wand.

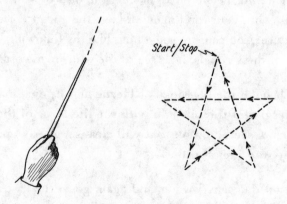

Describing a Pentagram

Returning to the altar, ring the bell three times. You have now erected the magic circle. You are now between the worlds, with no negativity able to intrude. Now, standing before the altar, again raise your wand and say:

"Lord and Lady; Herne and Epona! I invite you to join me in this sacred space. Please unite with me and witness these rites I perform in your honor. Be with me to guide me and guard me in all things I do. So Mote It Be!"

Lower your wand and place it on the altar. Pour some wine into the goblet then raise it in salute, saying:

"Lord and Lady; Herne and Epona."

Pour a little of the wine into the libation dish, from the goblet, saying **"To the gods!"** then drink.

[*After you have finished your ritual, when the circle has been closed, take the libation dish outside and pour the offering to the gods onto the ground, again saying* **"To the gods."** *If you are not able to get out of doors (perhaps you live in a high-rise apartment building), then you can pour the libation on a potted plant or into a window box. As a very last resort, pour it down the sink but even then say* **"To the gods."**]

The circle has now been cast and you may proceed with the "filler" of the occasion, which might be working magic, doing healing, giving thanks, asking a boon, or celebrating a Sabbat. I'll look at all of these later. You will eventually finish the occasion with Closing the Circle, which I will deal with now.

Here I might mention that in the above ritual, when calling upon the four watchtowers, some Witches will say something like: "Spirits of the East, attend!" or will even call upon specific elementals (for example, Sylphs, Salamanders, Undines, and Gnomes) and demand that they guard the circle. There are two points here that I feel are worthy of consideration. The first is that nothing and no one should be *told* to attend or should be *demanded* to do anything. There should only be an *invitation* extended. And second, most certainly any elementals, or any spirits of any kind, should *not* be conjured or their presence demanded. You could well end up with something you can't get rid of!

Closing the Circle

At the end of the ritual, when you have done all you wish to do, you can't just stop and walk away. You have to officially close the circle, being sure to thank the gods for attending and witnessing what you've been doing. Some Witches speak of "releasing" the deities at the end of the ritual. This suggests that they have been bound there, which is nonsense. Thanking them for their attendance is sufficient.

Standing before the altar and facing the east (or whichever direction you've decided is the main one), ring the bell three times then raise your wand and say:

> **"Hail, Herne and Epona; mighty ones! This Circle is now brought to an end. I thank you for attending and for witnessing these rites. As we came together in peace and love, so let us leave in peace and love. Merry did we meet. Merry may we part. And merry may we meet again. So Mote It Be!"**

Kiss your wand, or the blade of your athamé, then extinguish the candles on the altar. [*Some Witches will not blow out a candle; believing that it must be snuffed out. There is really no valid (magical or spiritual) reason why you should not blow it out if you feel like it. Personally, I use an antique candlesnuffer, but do what you want.*] Cross to the east point and extend your arm outward, thrusting the wand through the (invisible) wall of the circle. The circle is now opened and you can extinguish the other candles and generally move around and clean up. It is not necessary to "deconsecrate" the circle, to undo it, to dance around widdershins (counterclockwise), or anything like that. The announcement has been made, the gods have been thanked and dismissed, and the "bubble" has been burst, so the ritual circle is no more . . . until next time.

Moving In and Out of a Consecrated Circle

There may be times, while the circle is cast, that you need to momentarily move out of it and then return. Perhaps you left some object you need outside; perhaps you just need to go to the bathroom. Don't break the circle unless you really have to, but if you do have to, here's how you do it.

Stand at the inside edge of the circle and extend your wand (or athamé) across the line of the drawn circle. In effect it is cutting through the consecrations. Put it through low down, near the ground, then bring it up, over, and down again, as though you were literally cutting a doorway in the side of the globe or cone. You can then step out, through this doorway. Unless you are just grabbing something and coming immediately back inside, you need to close this doorway behind you. Turn and, again with your wand or athamé, "draw" a line to reconnect the line of the circle you cut through. In fact, there are three circles in one there: remember, you consecrated the circle by first walking around with the wand, then with the salted water, and finally with the censer. So move your wand back and forth to reconnect the three lines, in effect. Now you may move away and the circle is sealed behind you. When you return, you must do the same thing, first opening it from the outside, then passing through, then turning and closing it again with the three lines. Now that you are back inside, you should "seal" it, as a sort of extra patch over where it had been opened. You do this by simply facing the line of the circle and, with your wand, describing a pentagram, as was done at each of the four quarter candles when the circle was first cast. Now the circle is reconsecrated and all is as it should be.

Although it is all right to leave the circle like this if you have to, try not to break it any more than absolutely necessary.

Dance

Dance has been a part of ritual for millennia. From earliest times, dancing has been an integral part of religious worship and of magical practice. In many ways, the dance was considered a prayer, a spell, or an invocation. Throughout the world, humankind has always celebrated life and celebrated communion with deity in dance. Its origins can probably be traced to early humans mimicking the stalking and slaying of game, as part of a hunting magic ritual. Dance was even a part of Christian worship up until the seventeenth century, especially in Spain. In 1282, at Inverkeithing in Scotland, the village priest was admonished (but not punished) for leading his parishioners in a dance about a phallic symbol, as part of the Easter celebrations. According to Pennethorne Hughes (*Witchcraft*), dancing still occurs in the Church of Abyssinia. It should be no surprise, therefore, that dancing should have been an integral part of a religion so full of life as is Witchcraft. Leaping dances astride pitchforks, poles, and broomsticks were a part of fertility rites to promote the growth of crops, and were also a big part of Witches' Sabbat celebrations.

Many surviving examples of old Pagan dances can be found today, with May Day celebrations for example, and also in Morris dancing. The "dibbling" of sticks into the ground, as part of some of the Morris dances, ties in with the planting of seeds, while the clashing of sticks and waving of handkerchiefs were intended to disperse negative spirits. In many of the Morris dances, the dancers leap high in the air in much the same way that the Pagans and Witches of old leapt high as part of imitative magic, when showing the crops how high to grow.

Dancing is one of the ways for Witches to raise the power required to work magic, as I'll discuss in the chapters on magic. By moving rhythmically, clapping or slapping the body, perhaps also chanting, a state of *ekstasis* is brought on, leading to directing the raised power to bring about the end sought. In Voodoo there is a similar ekstasis achieved through dancing, which is done to the rhythmic beating of the drums; the ensuing ecstasy leading to the entry of the *loa*, the Voodoo deities.

A Solitary Witch can employ dancing whenever he or she feels like it. It doesn't have to be any formalized style of dance; it can be simple or intricate, just as the Witch feels moved. It can be standing in one spot or it can be progressing around the circle. It can be as simple as just running, skipping, or hopping around the circle. As with the rest of ritual, there is no need for embarrassment or for feeling self-conscious, since the Solitary has no one to please but him or herself. I encourage all Solitaries to incorporate dance into their rituals as much as possible. It makes the rituals enjoyable and makes them come alive.

Music

Witches seem to love music, especially homemade music. At Wiccan festivals around the country you can see and hear individuals and groups, with drums, pipes (such as flutes, penny whistles, and recorders), dulcimers, and guitars, happily making their own music to and of the gods. Hand drums of many different types are very popular. Those who have no instruments but feel sufficiently moved, will bang sticks together, hit anything that produces a sound, and even clap hands or beat thighs to produce a rhythmic sound.

These are the sounds of music—using the word in its broadest sense—that every Solitary Witch can produce in his or her circle: stamping on the ground; slapping hands on thighs; and beating a tambourine. Let the spirit move you and incorporate such excitement into your rituals. For both your dancing and your singing, you can use recorded music if you wish. It seems that the majority of Witches prefer live music, however crudely produced, but there is certainly nothing wrong with using a tape recorder, stereo, CD player, or similar, if that is your desire. There are wonderful recordings of appropriate and inspiring music, such as Carl Orff's *Carmina Burana* (an orchestral and choral rendition of pagan-inspired poems of the goliards of the twelfth and thirteenth centuries). Or your tastes may go to more modern music. Favorites with many Witches are the recordings by Enya and Loreena McKennitt. It doesn't matter what it is as long as it fits with your personal feelings of communion with deity.

Song

As with dance, so with song. You don't have to just speak everything in the rites; you can sing some or even all of the ritual. You can add songs wherever you feel inclined. Make up your own tunes or use ones you know. It will add a whole new dimension to the rituals. And as a Solitary, it doesn't matter whether or not you can carry a tune! If you use recorded music, then you can sing to that.

There are a number of Wicca-oriented songs that have been written and are generally available (some of them available on tape or CD). In my book *Wicca For Life* (Citadel, 2001) I include two possible songs—with words, music, and guitar chords—for each one of the eight Sabbats. I similarly include a variety of songs in my *Buckland's Complete Book of Witchcraft* (Llewellyn, 2002). Many other books on the Craft include songs as well. ✄

9

First Step

*Initiation is equivalent to a basic change in
existential conditions; the novice emerges from
his ordeal endowed with a totally different
being from that which he possessed before his
initiation; he has become another.*

—Mircea Eliade, *Rites and Symbols of Initiation*

he first step is *becoming* a Witch. If you were joining an
established coven of Witches then this would be your initiation. Just as there are many different denominations
of Christianity, for example, so are there many different
forms, or "traditions," of Wicca. In modern times, the first such was
that established by Gerald Gardner; it became known as Gardnerian
Wicca. Today there are a tremendous number of different traditions,
including Celtic, Welsh, Færie, Saxon, Alexandrian, Druidic, Scottish, and so on (not to mention innumerable groups that describe
themselves as "eclectic"). All worship the same deities (though use
different names to relate to them) and celebrate the same festivals,
but the makeup of the rituals is different. Also different is the form
of initiation. Some traditions have degree systems with graduated

---

forms of advancement; others do not. Anyone initiated into Gardnerian, for example, would not be accepted as a Welsh Witch, and
vice versa. Unfortunately, there is a lot of rivalry between some of
the traditions, with claims to being the most ancient, most "legiti-
mate," most "authentic," and so on. Such claims are all spurious—
and pointless. If you wanted to become a member of any one
particular tradition, then you would have to track down a coven of
that type and persuade them to accept you into their group. The joy
of a Solitary Witch is that he or she does not have to be beholden to
anyone or any group. You can initiate yourself and practice right
away. However, you will not then be automatically accepted into any
coven or tradition, not without going through their specific initiation
and acknowledging their set of rules. Yet there should be no reason
you'd want to be accepted into any coven, since you would be a fully
fledged, totally authentic Witch by your own self-initiation. And here
is where some of the extremely petty squabbling can come into
modern-day Wicca. Many Coven Witches will claim that there can
be no such thing as a Solitary Witch. Ignore such ramblings! As I
have already pointed out, the Solitary Witch is actually much older,
and therefore much more "authentic," than the Coven Witch. Apart
from that, since you are doing your own "thing," it really doesn't
matter in the least what anyone else thinks about it!

Initiation is, in effect, a rebirth. It is starting life anew, one of the
reasons for taking a new name. In fact, I'd suggest you settle on a
Witch name for yourself before you do this self-dedication. Read
what I say about choosing a name and do this before proceeding (see
chapter 13, "Magic/Witch Name" section). The ritual should be done
in private, with no onlookers. I strongly recommend that you do it
skyclad, or naked, going along with the idea of being reborn.

The Beginning: Initiation, or Self-Dedication

Open the circle in the usual way. Have a small dish of anointing oil
on the altar. Ring the bell nine times in all, in three sets of three

(with a brief pause between each set). Take up the anointing oil and dip your index finger into it. Draw a cross inside a circle on your forehead, in the position of the Third Eye (between the eyebrows). Then draw a pentagram, with the point upward, over your heart. Touch the oil to your genitals, right breast, left breast, genitals, in this way describing a triangle. Replace the oil on the altar and pick up your wand. (If you do not yet have a wand, you may use your index finger in its place.) Hold it high in salute. Say:

> "God and Goddess; Lord and Lady. I am here a simple seeker of knowledge, a lover of life. I here dedicate myself to you and to your service. You are the ones I have chosen to serve. I do this of my own free will, with no pressure from any other. Guard me and guide me in all that I do, for all that I do is in love of you and of all life. Help me live my life with harm to none. Help me acknowledge the depth and beauty of all life, animal, vegetable, and mineral. The animals, birds, fish, reptiles, and all living things are my brothers and sisters. The trees of the forest, the plants, flowers, herbs, and all growing things are my brothers and sisters. The rocks, soil, sand, the rivers, lakes, seas, all waters of the earth, and all that is of the earth, are my brothers and sisters. Make me one with this family. Let me guard them and work for them as they all work for me.
>
> "Lord and Lady, from this day forth I accept and will ever abide by the Wiccan Rede: 'An it harm none, do what thou wilt.' I pledge myself to you, the gods. I will always protect you as you do me. I will defend you against those who speak ill of you. You are my life and I am yours. So Mote It Be."

Lower your wand and ring the bell three times. Take up the goblet of wine and raise it. Say:

> "To the gods!"

Pour a little into the libation dish (your offering to the gods) saying:

> "As this wine drains from the cup, so let the blood drain from my body should I ever do anything to harm the gods, or those in kinship with their love. So Mote It Be!"

Drink to the gods. (You do not have to drain the cup! You can always pour more into the libation dish.) Replace the goblet and raise both hands high in salute. Say:

> "As a sign of my being born again into the life of Wiccacraft, I here take upon myself a new name, by which I shall always be known within the Sacred Circle, which is the place between the worlds. Henceforth I shall be known as (Your Witch name) So Mote It Be!"

Lower your arms and ring the bell three times.
Now hold the wand over the altar and say:

> "Now I consecrate this, the true tool of a Solitary Witch. It has all the powers of an athamé. I here consecrate it, so that it may be properly used within this Circle and in the service of the gods."

Sprinkle some of the water on the wand then hold it in the smoke of the incense.

> "I cleanse and consecrate this, my magical wand, that it may serve me as I serve the Lord and the Lady. May it be my strength and my love and may it never be used in anger nor to harm anyone or anything. So Mote It Be!"

Draw a pentagram in the air with it, then kiss the wand and lower it. You may now sit and meditate on what the Craft means to you. At this time, you may receive some indication from the gods that you are indeed in touch with them—some sight, sound, or inner feeling. Whether you do or not, relax and enjoy the knowledge of having finally come home to the Craft, of having finally become one of the members of the Old Religion.

If you feel like singing or dancing, or celebrating in any other appropriate way, now is a good time to do it. Now should follow the ritual of Cakes and Wine, but I will give the details of that below. The final step is always the Closing of the Circle.

Note that nowhere in the self-dedication does the initiate repudiate his or her previous religion. There are no words against any other faith. Should you, at any future date, decide that Wicca is not the right religion for you after all, you are free to leave and either return to your previous faith or continue seeking elsewhere. Note, also, that there's no longer an oath of secrecy taken. In times of persecution, it's obvious that an oath of secrecy served a useful purpose. It also served a purpose in the very early days of paganism, long before the arrival of Christianity. This oath of secrecy is still a part of some modern-day Wicca initiations (Gardnerian Wicca, for example. Although it may no longer be necessary, it remains as part of that tradition's heritage). I don't include such an oath in the material in this book. If you feel strongly that you would like one, by all means add your own.

As in all the rituals I offer, it's actually far better that you use your own words and speak "from the heart." You can study the rituals as I've presented them, and get a good sense of them, then use the words that come to you at the time. This way you are not attached to a piece of paper or book. But do be sure you have a good understanding of what you are saying and doing, and when, so that you can perform the ritual without having to concentrate on the words and hence lose the "feel" of the rite itself. ✖

10

---◆---

Esbats

The talk they had with the Shining Ones
was about the glory of the place;
who told them that the beauty
and glory of it was inexpressible.
—John Bunyan, *The Pilgrim's Progress*

sbat is the name given to the regular working of a Witch, as opposed to the big seasonal celebrations known as *Sabbats*. The word Esbat comes from the French *s'esbat-tre*, meaning "to amuse oneself." However, the Esbat is a serious occasion for it involves worship of the God and the Goddess, though that worship is joyous. You should have an Esbat at least once a month, at the full moon. You can certainly have one more often than that—on a regular weekly or bi-weekly basis, or as the need/desire arises—but it shouldn't be less than once a month.

Format

The format of the Esbat is to start, as with all Wicca rituals, with the Opening of the Circle. This establishes your sacred space for the

Esbat. At this, as you've seen, the gods are invited to attend and witness the rites. Once the circle has been cast and the gods invited in, then it is customary to give a prayer of thanks for the blessings you have and to ask for what aid you feel you need. This can be done silently or out loud. If it is a full or new moon, then that rite is now performed (see "Full Moon" section). It is followed by the Cakes and Wine ceremony (see description that follows), which is a thanking of the gods for the necessities of life. If you then want to do any magic, divination, or healing, this is the time to do it. (During the Cakes and Wine, which is a relaxing time, you can run through, in your mind, exactly what you plan to do.) When you have done the magic, then relax for a moment before closing the circle. I'll here give a suggested Esbat ritual, and mark the separate parts where necessary. Feel free to change this to suit yourself.

Esbat Rite

The circle has been cast and you are back at the altar. You may continue standing, may kneel, or even sit if you prefer. With wand raised, say:

> **"Lord and Lady; God and Goddess; Herne and Epona. I am here to share my love and my thoughts, thanks, and desires with you. I am here to reaffirm my feelings for the gods and for the Craft. Be with me always, in everything I do, both in and out of this Sacred Circle."**

Lower the wand and spend a few minutes silently (or out loud, in your own words) thanking the gods for all that they have done for you. This is a very real "count your blessings" time and don't hesitate to give thanks, knowing that there are many people who are far worse off than you are. At the very least, thank the gods for bringing you to the Craft and for making you one of the family of Witchcraft. When you have spent some time giving thanks, ring the bell three times and say:

"'An it harm none, do what thou wilt.' Thus runs the Witch's Rede. May I always remember that whatever I would do, and whatever I would ask of the gods, let it be done with harm to no one, not even myself."

Now is the time to ask for favors that you feel you need. Always keep in mind that the gods help those who help themselves. This being the case, don't ask the gods for some miracle and expect to have it happen right away! Ask for what you want and then continue to work toward that goal yourself. You will probably find that the goal is achieved very much more easily than you might have hoped. But, as with magic, there will be no flash and bang as you wave your magic wand. Ring the bell three times. If this is a full moon, or a new moon, then do that rite here (see "Full Moon" section). If it is not a special moon, then go straight into the Cakes and Wine rite that follows.

Cakes and Wine

Also known as "Cakes and Ale," this is the thanksgiving part of every Wicca ritual. Make sure that there is wine (or ale or juice) in the goblet. On the altar, or on the ground beside it, there should be a small plate with a cake or cakes on it (cookies will do just as well). Many Witches make their own, often in the shapes of moons, stars, cats, and so on, sometimes utilizing Hallowe'en cookie cutters. I give a special Wicca cake recipe in the sidebar, if you want to try making your own. Raise your wand in salute and say:

"May I ever be aware of all that I owe to the gods. Now is the time for me to give thanks for all they provide that sustains me."

Take up the plate of cakes and lay it in the center of the altar, beside the goblet. Slowly dip the tip of your wand into the goblet, touching the surface of the wine. As you do so, say:

"In just such a fashion as this does male join with female, for the happiness of both. Let the fruits of union promote life. Let all be fruitful and let wealth be spread amongst all. As the wand is the male, so the cup is the female. Conjoined they bring blessedness."

Touch the wine-dipped tip of the wand to the cake(s) and say:

"Here is the food of the gods, which sustains all life. May it be blessed. May all people be able to partake of it freely. Let there be enough for all, and let those who have plenty share with those who have little. So Mote It Be."

Lay aside the wand. Take up the goblet, pour a libation to the gods [*Remember to say "To the gods"*], then drink from the goblet. Put it down and take up a cake. Break off a small piece and drop it [*"To the gods"*] in the libation dish, in the wine. Then eat some of the cake. Say:

"May I hold the gods in my mind and see their acts in all things. May I always share and give thanks. May I never forget that without the gods I would have nothing. So Be It."

You can now relax and enjoy wine and cake. If you are planning on doing some magic, divination, or any other circle-based activity, then now is a good time to go over your plans. Review any key words or chants (chapter 13, *Magic (General)*). Make sure you have all the ingredients you need. When you have done your work, or if there is no work to be done, then you may relax with some music, songs, or dancing until you are ready to close the circle. That closing will be done as has been described previously.

Full Moon

Do your utmost to perform this ritual either on the night of the full moon, or at the least on one of the three nights leading up to it. This rite is also known as "Drawing Down the Moon," since you are

The cakes we use we make ourselves from scratch. They are oat cakes and we start by grinding oat groats to make into flour. This we do in a stone-wheel hand grinder, though it can be done in a small electric coffee grinder. For about half a dozen people we would use 4 ounces of flour. To this add ½ teaspoon of baking powder, ⅓ teaspoon of salt, 1 egg, and about a teaspoon of butter or oil. Mix and add water until it is a smooth texture, not too watery. If you want sweetened cakes then also add sweetener to taste, and you can also add small pieces of fruit such as diced apple, if you wish. Preheat a cast iron pan—you can use cast iron muffin tins if you like—lightly greased. Preheat the oven to 410°F. Pour the batter into the pan and place in the oven for 30 minutes. Good served hot or cold.

—Ray and Tara Buckland

invoking the Goddess and asking her to descend into you. Incidentally, it doesn't matter whether you are female or male, you can still draw down the Goddess into you.

As stated earlier, the Opening of the Circle is done, then thanks are given and prayers offered to ask for what is needed. Then, if it's the appropriate time of the month, the Full Moon rite is done.

The bell is rung seven times. Stand at the altar with your feet together and your arms crossed on your chest. Say:

> **"Goddess of the Moon; my Lady Epona! You have been known by many different names in many different lands**

and times, yet do you remain constant. You give your light at the darkest of times, smiling down upon us and watching over us. I ask you now, as Queen of all Witchcrafts, to come down and join with me, blending your voice with mine, as I say:

[*Stand with your legs roughly shoulder-width apart, and raise your arms upward and outward, to welcome the Goddess energy. You should learn the following to say at this time. But don't be surprised if the Goddess herself manifests here and takes over your voice. You may suddenly find yourself saying words you hadn't even thought about. Don't be alarmed. This is the Goddess herself making her presence felt. Try to remember what it is that she says through you. If she does not come into you (it won't always happen and for some people it never happens), simply say these written words and feel yourself blending with the Lady and speaking for her.*]

"I am she who watches over all, whether they be awake or asleep. I am the Mother of all Life. It gives me great pleasure that you should pay me homage at the full of the moon. Let my worship always be within your heart. Behold! All acts of love and pleasure are my rituals, therefore let there be beauty and strength, power and compassion, honor and humility, mirth and reverence within you. If you seek me, know that your seeking and yearning avail you not unless you know the mystery—that if you cannot find what you seek within you, you will never find it without. For behold! I have been with you from the beginning and I am that which is attained at the end of desire.

"Know that, together with my Lord, I weave the web of life for everyone. I am at the beginning and at the end of life and of time. I am Maiden; Mother; Crone. Wherever you may be, if you need me then call upon me and I will be there. I live deep within you; I am Life and I am Love. Be true to me and I will always be true to you. Harm none and love all life. So Mote It Be."

Lower your arms and spend a few moments digesting what has been said. When you are ready, ring the bell three times and proceed with the Cakes and Wine rite (see previous section).

Dark Moon or New Moon

As with the Full Moon rite, do your utmost to perform this ritual either on the very night of the new moon, or at the least on one of the three nights leading up to it. As stated above, the Opening of the Circle is done, then thanks are given and prayers offered to ask for what is needed. Then, if it's the appropriate time of the month, the Dark Moon rite is done.

The bell is rung seven times. Stand at the altar with your feet together, your arms crossed on your chest, and your head bowed. Say:

> **"At the darkest time of night there is a turning point. From darkness to light; from death to life; a journey completed; a new journey begun."**

Slowly raise your head, stand with feet shoulder-width apart, and slowly raise your arms up and outward. Say:

> **"Behold! The Lady of Darkness; mother; grandmother. Hail to the Crone! Old yet young. Mother darksome and divine."**

Pause and be prepared for the Goddess to speak through you, as at the Full Moon rite. But if she does not, then say:

> **"As the wheel turns, we see birth, death, and rebirth. Know, from this, that every end is a beginning. Maiden; Mother; Crone . . . I am all these and more. Whenever you have need of anything, call upon me and I will be there. I abide within you, even at the darkest of times. When there seems no single spark to warm you or to**

light the darkness, when all seems blackest of all, then
know that I am here, watching and waiting to grow with
you in love and in strength. I am she who is at the
beginning and at the end of time. Harm none and love
all life. So Mote It Be."

Lower your arms and spend a few moments digesting what has
been said. When you are ready, ring the bell three times and proceed with the Cakes and Wine rite. ❧

11

Rites of Passage

*The characteristics of this event [initiation]
are marked by an expansion of the
mind to include an awareness of
higher levels of consciousness.*
—Chic Cicero and Sandra Tabatha Cicero,
Self-Initiation into the Golden Dawn Tradition

s a Solitary Witch, you will generally be doing your rituals alone. But being a Witch means that you are a priest or priestess of the Old Religion. As a priest or priestess, you could be called upon to perform a rite of Wiccaning, Handfasting, Handparting, or Crossing Over (these are the equivalents of baptism, marriage, divorce, and death). On such occasions, the only change to your regular circle-forming is to enlarge the size of the sacred space to encompass everyone concerned. Treat the occasion as though you were inviting guests into your home, which is really what you are doing. Aim to make them comfortable but do things your way!

Let's look first at Wiccaning, which is the equivalent of baptism. It is naming a child and dedicating it to the gods.

Wiccaning

As soon as possible after a birth, Witches will dedicate the child to the gods. At this ritual, the parents of the child announce to the Lord and the Lady that they will raise their child to honor the old gods. It is *not* making the child a Witch. Whether or not the child becomes a Witch is up to that child him or herself, at a later date, when able to make such a decision. At that later time, the child will either go through a coven initiation or, as a Solitary, will do a self-dedication (see chapter 9, "The Beginning" section). For now, though, there is the Wiccaning. This would be done at any Esbat rite. It may be done as a rite in itself, in which case the circle is cast and the Wiccaning is performed followed by Cakes and Wine and Closing of the Circle. If the Wiccaning is done as part of an Esbat, it is performed just prior to the Cakes and Ale.

Open the circle in the usual way. Have a small dish of anointing oil on the altar. The parents stand just inside the circle, to the east, holding the child. [*If it is a single parent, that parent will speak both parts. I designate your part, as Solitary Priest/ess, by "SP."*] When you have finished casting the circle, take the dish of salted water and go to the parents. Dip your fingers into the water and mark a pentagram on the forehead of each of them (not the child), kiss them, and say **"Blessed Be."** This will serve as a cleansing in lieu of the bath that you have taken. Return to the altar. The bell is rung three times. Turn to face the parents and child and raise your wand in salute.

SP: **"All hail, and welcome to parents and child!"** (*Lower your wand and ask:*) **"What is the name of this child?"**

The parents give the name by which the child will be known when in the Sacred Circle, until such time as it chooses its own name.

SP: **"I welcome you [Name of child] and greet you with much love."** (*to the parents*) **"Do you wish your child to join in worship of the Lord and the Lady?"**

PARENTS: "We do, for without knowledge of the gods of old, no life is complete."

SP: "Well said! May you be doubly welcome. Now, present your child to the Four Quarters."

Parents turn outward, at the east, and raise the baby in their arms to the gods.

PARENTS: "Here do we present [Name of child] as a child of the Old Religion, to be accepted by the Lord and the Lady. So Mote It Be."

They move around to the south and repeat the presentation, then to the west and north. They return to the east and turn back in to face the altar.

SP: "Now bring the child before the altar."

Parents move around to stand alongside the Solitary Priest/ess, facing the altar. SP rings the bell seven times then dips fingers in the anointing oil and draws a cross within a circle on the baby's forehead and a pentagram on the chest, over the heart.

SP: "Lord and Lady, we ask that you bless this child. Watch over her (or him), guarding and guiding her throughout life. When the time is right, bring her to this Sacred Circle once again, to dedicate herself anew to the gods on her own behalf."

FATHER: "May the Lady and the Lord smile down upon [Name of child] always."

MOTHER: "May they guard her and guide her along the path of life."

FATHER: "May they help her see that which is right and discard that which is wrong."

MOTHER: "And may they bring her at last, of her own desire, to this our Old Religion family."

ALL: "So Mote It Be!"

SP: "I charge you both, in the names of the Lord and of the Lady, to take this child by the hand and to lead her along the winding road of life. Teach her the ways of the Craft, but tell her also of other religions and their beliefs, that when the time comes she may make a reasoned decision. Tell her the tales of the Craft of old, of the Burning Times and the times in hiding. Tell her of our many lives, both here and hereafter. Teach her to love all life. To live in harmony with all nature and all things. Teach her of the Lord and the Lady, of love and happiness. Teach her the Wiccan Rede."

PARENTS: "All this we swear to do, for the child and for the family of the Craft."

SP: "I bid welcome to [Name of child]."

ALL: "Welcome!"

Then shall follow the ceremony of Cakes and Wine.

Handfasting

Handfasting is the Wiccan marriage ceremony. Witches may or may not wish to go through a legal marriage ceremony. If they do, it will be before a Justice of the Peace, or appropriate local official, or it may be at a Unitarian-Universalist church with a ceremony of the couple's own devising. But what really matters to them is the ritual of Handfasting performed in the Sacred Circle. If the Solitary Priest/ess performing the ritual holds the requisite ministerial credentials, then that ceremony is sufficient for all things. But if not, then there should be a legal ceremony at some time in addition to the one in the Circle, if the couple sees fit.

The dress of the couple depends upon their tradition. Some wear white robes, some go skyclad, some will wear traditional cowan dress, such as a white wedding gown for the bride and a white tuxedo for the groom. Wicca Handfasting rituals vary considerably, depending upon the tradition of the Wiccans involved. Here is a typical one which could be used by an officiating Solitary.

This ritual should be performed in the waxing cycle of the moon. The circle and the altar are suitably decorated with flowers. Additional to the regular tools on the altar is a dish of anointing oil and a three-foot length of red silk ribbon and, if the couple wishes to exchange rings, the marriage rings. The wine goblet is full.

The Opening of the Circle is performed in the usual way, with bride standing in the east and groom standing in the west. After casting the circle, the Solitary Priest/ess goes first to the bride, and then to the groom, and anoints each of them with oil, drawing the cross within the circle on the forehead and pentagram over the heart, saying:

SP: **"Here I do consecrate you in the names of the Lord and the Lady. Be here in peace and love, with honor to all life."**

SP returns to the altar and rings the bell three times. Bride and groom move forward to stand at the altar, facing the SP.

SP: **"Welcome, and doubly welcome, to you who come to this sacred place to be joined in the time-honored Handfasting rite."** (*to bride*) **"What is your desire?"**

BRIDE: **"To be made one with my soul mate [Name of groom], in the eyes of the gods and of my brothers and sisters of the Craft."**

SP (*to groom*): **"What is your desire?"**

GROOM: **"To be made one with my soul mate [Name of bride], in the eyes of the gods and of my brothers and sisters of the Craft."**

SP: **"Do you both wish this in the names of the Lord and the Lady, God and Goddess of the Craft?"**

BRIDE AND GROOM: "We do."

SP (*to bride*): "What do you bring with you to this marriage?"

BRIDE: "I bring love and respect. I love [Name of groom] as I love myself, honoring and respecting him in all things. I will always support him in everything he does and join with him in love and praise of the gods in whom we believe. I will defend his life before my own. May the gods give me the strength to keep these my vows."

SP (*to groom*): "What do you bring with you to this marriage?"

GROOM: "I bring love and respect. I love [Name of bride] as I love myself, honoring and respecting her in all things. I will always support her in everything she does and join with her in love and praise of the gods in whom we believe. I will defend her life before my own. May the gods give me the strength to keep these my vows."

SP: "Lord and Lady, here stand two of your folk. Witness now that which they have to declare."

SP rings the bell seven times. Bride and groom face each other. They grip right hand to right hand and left hand to left hand. SP binds the hands together with the red ribbon then holds the censer under their hands, censing them. SP then waves the wand both over and under the tied hands.

BRIDE AND GROOM: "We come into this Sacred Circle of our own free will, to join together as one in the eyes of the Ancient Ones. We are no longer two individuals but are now two halves of one whole. Each of us is incomplete without the other. Be with us in all things, dear Lord and Lady, and help us cleave together throughout this life and beyond. All this we ask in your names. So Mote It Be!"

ALL: "So Mote It Be!"

SP unties the hands, gives the bride the groom's ring and the groom the bride's ring. Bride and groom put the rings on each other's fingers. They then hold hands.

SP: **"As the grass of the fields and the trees of the woods bend together under the pressures of the storm, so too must you both bend when the wind blows strong. But know that as quickly as the storm comes, so equally quickly may it leave. Yet will you both stand, strong in each other's strength. As you give love, so will you receive love. As you give strength, so will you receive strength. Together you are one; apart you are nothing. Know that no two people can be exactly alike. No more can any two people fit together, perfect in every way, no matter how hard they may try. There will be times when it will seem hard to give and to love. But see then your reflection as in a woodland pool: when the image you see looks sad and angered, then is the time for you to smile and to love (for it is not fire that puts out fire). In return will the image in the pool smile and love. So do you change anger for love and tears for joy. It is no weakness to admit a wrong; more is it a strength and a sign of learning. Ever love, help, and respect each other and then know truly that you are one in the eyes of the gods. So Mote It Be!"**

ALL: **"So Mote It Be!"**

Bride and groom kiss each other, then SP. Then follows the Cakes and Wine rite followed by celebrations and the Closing of the Circle.

There are many variations on the Handfasting rite. If the ritual can be performed out in the open, with plenty of space, then it is not unusual to have a small fire burning at the east entrance and for the couple to leap over the fire at some point. This was an ancient fertility action enacted at fire festivals in many areas across Europe and elsewhere. Similarly, a besom, or broomstick, might be laid down for the couple to jump over, for promoting fertility.

Handparting

However much love exists at the start of a relationship, there can be no guarantee that it will last forever. In today's society it seems to be not uncommon for married couples to split and go their separate ways. Although not encouraging marriage vows to be taken lightly, Witchcraft allows for this, believing that no one should be forced to stay bound together if that magic tie of love has gone. It is thought to be far better to make the break and go separate ways, perhaps in that way being able to find love and happiness again with someone else. To this end, the Wicca rite of Handparting is performed to give an official seal to the separation. The couple should meet together with the Solitary Priest or Priestess to decide upon a fair division of property, plus provision for the support of any children of the marriage. Everything should be put into writing and be signed by both partners. Neither should be coerced into signing what he or she does not believe to be fair.

The Circle is cast in the usual way, as at the start of an Esbat or any other ritual. Husband and wife stand with the Solitary Priest/ess at the altar. The written agreement is present on the altar. A length of red ribbon also lies on the altar. The bell is rung three times.

SP: **"What matter is it that brings you both before the gods, in this our Sacred Circle?"**

HUSBAND: **"I desire to be Handparted from [Name of wife]."**

WIFE: **"I desire to be Handparted from [Name of husband]."**

SP: **"Do you both desire this of your own free will?"**

HUSBAND AND WIFE: **"We do."**

SP: **"Has a settlement been reached between you, regarding the division of your property [*if appropriate:*] and the care for your children?"**

HUSBAND AND WIFE: **"It has."**

SP takes up the document, examines it, shows it to the husband and wife, then returns it to the altar.

SP: **"You are both certain that this is the step you wish to take?"**

HUSBAND AND WIFE: **"We are."**

SP: **"Then let us proceed. But be mindful, both of you, that you stand here in this Sacred Circle in the presence of the Mighty Ones."**

SP rings the bell three times. Husband and wife join right hand to right hand and left hand to left hand. SP loosely loops the red ribbon around their hands. The couple repeat the following line by line after the Solitary Priest/ess:

SP: **"Together repeat after me: 'I, [Name], do hereby most freely dissolve my partnership with [Name of spouse]. I do so in all honesty and sincerity, before the Lord and the Lady as my witnesses. No longer are we as one. Now we are two individuals free to go our separate ways. We release all ties, rights, and obligations to one another, yet we will ever retain respect for one another as we respect and love all our fellow Wiccans. So be it!'"**

SP pulls the ribbon away and the couple release their hands.

SP: **"Handpart!"**

The couple remove their wedding rings, if they have them, and give them to the Priest/ess, who sprinkles and censes them.

SP: **"I here cleanse these rings, in the names of the Lord and the Lady."**

The rings are returned to the individuals to do with as they may.

SP: **"Now you are Handparted. Let everyone know that you are so. Go your separate ways in peace and love. Let there be no bitterness between you. Go in the ways of the Craft, as brother and sister. So Mote It Be."**

ALL: **"So Mote It Be!"**

The bell is rung seven times. The couple kiss one another then kiss the SP.

The Cakes and Wine rite follows, as does the Closing of the Circle.

Crossing Over

Witches have many different names for the death ritual: "Crossing Over," "Crossing the Bridge," "Remembrance," "Into the Shadows," "Summerland Journey," and more. With our belief in reincarnation, and knowing that all lives have been planned from before birth, Witches are probably better prepared for death than most people. However, it can still be devastating to experience the death of a loved one, someone who was especially close to you. It's not so much that we are sorry for the person who dies; after all, they are experiencing a type of "graduation." No, we are sorry for ourselves, that we have been deprived of that person's energy, love, and companionship.

This rite may be performed by the Solitary Witch at any of the other rituals or as a rite in itself, preceded by Opening the Circle and followed by Cakes and Wine. If done with another ritual, it should be done just before Cakes and Wine.

There should be an extra white candle standing unlit in the center of the altar. Flowers may be arranged around it.

Ring the bell thirteen times, then say:

> **"I toll the bell of remembrance, rung today for [Name of deceased], who has moved on across the bridge to the Summerland. That [Name of deceased] is not here today, in body, is my loss and truly saddens me. Yet although I sorrow I also rejoice, for she/he has left this plane to move on toward the next lifetime. She/he has completed the life work that had been planned and now moves forward, through the light, to that which lies ahead."**

Light the central candle on the altar. Touching the wand to it, say:

"Here I send my love and my energies to help you pass across the bridge, into the light and into the arms of the Lord and the Lady. May your spirit burn as brightly as does this candle flame. You have touched many hearts in your time here and I, and others, will miss you. Blessed be!"

If there is anything you wish to say to the deceased, or about the deceased, now is the time to do so. If it is only **"I love you,"** or **"I'll miss you,"** or whatever, it may be said to yourself or out loud (out loud would probably be better). Reminisce about the deceased, preferably remembering the good times, the laughter, and the jokes. Send love to the one who has gone and then, if you've been sitting or kneeling, rise. If you feel so inclined, dance deosil around the circle. You may chant the name of the one gone, or may simply chant **"I love you."**

Ring the bell seven times, then take your wand and point it at a spot behind the altar, imagining the deceased standing there smiling at you. In fact, he or she may appear. Concentrate on sending love and joy, projecting your feelings along the line of your wand. When you feel satisfied, say:

"I wish you all the love and happiness I may. I will always remember you with love. You are always welcome at my Circles. Do not forget me. We will meet again. So Mote It Be."

Then follow with the Cakes and Wine, followed by Closing the Circle. ✳

[*Note: This ritual may also be done for an animal, on the death of a pet.*]

12

Sabbats

he main celebrations of the Witch year are known as the Sabbats. Gail Duff (*Seasons of the Witch*, 2003) suggests that the word Sabbat comes from the Greek *sabatu*, meaning "to rest." There are eight of these celebrations. The four major ones—also known as the "cross-quarter days"—are Samhain (pronounced *Sow-in*), Imbolc (*Im-'olk*), Beltane, and Lughnasadh (*Loo-n'suh*). They fall on November Eve, February Eve, May Eve, and August Eve respectively. The four minor celebrations fall on the Summer Solstice (also known as *Litha*), the Winter Solstice (*Yule*), the Spring Equinox (*Ostara*), and the Autumn Equinox (*Mabon*). The date for the Summer Solstice is approximately June 21 (it will change slightly each year, dependent upon the calendar). The Winter Solstice is approximately December 21, the Spring Equinox approximately March 21, and the Autumnal Equinox approximately September 21. The solstices mark the longest day/shortest night (Summer) and the shortest day/longest night (Winter), while the equinoxes mark the time when the day and night are of equal length. The eight festivals are roughly six weeks apart. It used to be that the celebrations of these Sabbats, by the early pagan population, went on for anywhere from three days and nights to seven days and nights, culminating on the dates mentioned above. Today, most Witches just celebrate on the one day.

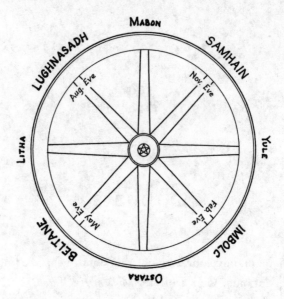

The Wheel of the Witches' Year

To early humankind the year was first divided into two parts: summer and winter. Although it was possible to grow food in the summer, it was necessary to hunt for animals for food in the winter. The God, as a god of hunting, predominated during the winter months and the Goddess, as a goddess of fertility for the crops, predominated in the summer. The changes occurred at Samhain (November Eve) and Beltane (May Eve). Later in the development of humankind, it was learned how to store the crops from the summer to last through the winter, so success in hunting became less important and the Goddess predominated throughout the whole year, though with the God by her side.

To mark the halfway point through each of the halves of the year, Imbolc (February Eve) and Lughnasadh (August Eve) came into being. The word Imbolc means "in milk" and is associated with the lactating of sheep and other domestic animals at that time. The word Lughnasadh means "married to Lugh (the sun god)." Like most of the festival names, these are of Celtic origin. The equinox and solstice celebrations tie in with the progress of the sun through the year, but the four major (and oldest) festivals are more agricultural in their associations, tying in to the land, crops, and animals.

As a Solitary Witch, feel free to celebrate the Sabbats in any way that appeals to you. You can feast, sing, dance, act out a solitary play (very traditional for all of the Sabbats), compose a special poem or song, plant a tree, or whatever. Many Witches tie in their celebration with the theme of the time of year, looking to the old myths and folk-lore for inspiration; for example, at Yule the Goddess gives birth to a son, who is the God and the sun. At Imbolc the Goddess is recovering while the young God is growing and learning of his power. At Ostara the God grows to maturity while the Goddess awakes from her sleep. Beltane marks the God's full emergence into manhood and his desire for the Goddess, who becomes pregnant by him. At mid-summer (Litha), the fertility of the Goddess is at its peak. Lugh-nasadh sees the God losing his power and starting toward death, while the Goddess feels the child within her, who will become the new God. At Mabon the God prepares to depart for the darkness of death and what lies beyond, while the Goddess acknowledges the weakening of the sun. Samhain shows the Goddess preparing for the birth she will give at Yule and the God says his farewell. For full, detailed explanations, stories, and myths associated with each of the Sabbats, I highly recommend *Eight Sabbats for Witches* by Janet and Stewart Farrar (Hale, London 1981).

The Sabbat was a time for celebration, therefore magic was not usually done at these times (unless there was some emergency—for example, healing was needed), so save this for the Esbats. However, divination was often a part of the rites; these turning points seeming to be an appropriate time to look and see what the future might hold. Below I give suggested rituals for each of the Sabbats. Work with them as they are or use them as inspiration for your own versions. You do not have to do the same thing year after year either; it is fine to compose new rituals each year or whenever you feel the need or desire. I'll say again, the Sabbats were a time for celebration, so use them to celebrate not only the turning of the wheel of the year, but also life itself and what it means to you.

In *Natural Home* magazine (May/June 2003), Carol Venolia wrote an article on celebrating the seasons. In it she told how ritualist L. Bachu celebrated Samhain by setting a table with candles and pictures of loved ones, even going to the trouble of laying out a meal of apples, chocolate, whole-grain bread, and wine for them. David Rousseau, a Canadian architect, said that he would sit with friends around a fire at the winter solstice, tossing into the fire pieces of paper on which had been written anything they considered "bad news." Each would first read their "bad news" then everyone would chant "Bad news!" as it was thrown into the fire. This is very similar to the ritual we give here (see below). Another architect, Marcia Mikesh, marked each equinox and solstice by eating only foods she had grown on her own land. There are many such simple rituals that can be made up and performed to draw us closer to nature and to an awareness of life. Make up some of your own and work them into the following rituals.

Samhain

Samhain is the turning point of the year; it is the Celtic New Year's Eve, sometimes referred to as the Feast of the Dead, Feast of Apples, or Ancestor Night. When the new religion, Christianity, adopted this festival—as was done with so many of the old pagan celebrations—they aligned it with their own festival known as All Saints, All Souls, or All Hallows. The eve of it, which is when pagans and Witches would actually do their celebrating, was All Hallow's Evening. This became shortened to Hallow's Eve or Hallowe'en. Witches call it Ancestor Night because this is the time—between the end of the old year and the start of the new—when it is felt that the veil between this world and the next is very thin and therefore it's much easier to contact the spirits of your dead loved ones. Indeed, this was how the jack-o'-lantern originated. When traveling to the Sabbat site, Witches would believe that the spirits of their dead traveled with them. To light their way, the Witches would carry lanterns, often made out of hollowed-out turnips or pumpkins with a candle inside. It was then only a short step to carving a face on such a lantern so that it could better represent the departed spirit traveling along.

The focus of Samhain is honoring the dead, along with winter preparations and divination. It is a time for getting rid of the things you don't want to have to take with you through the winter. In the old days, even the herds and flocks would be thinned, so there would be meat on hand through the winter and so there wouldn't be unnecessarily large numbers of animals to have to feed in the hard months to come. So keep this culling of unnecessary things in your mind when you compose your own ritual. Take a piece of paper and write on it all the things you would like to clear out of your life. You can list habits you would like to break, projects you want to finish, and medical condition(s) you want to alleviate. This is also a time for divination—for peering through the crack in time—thanks to the agencies of the crone aspect of the Goddess.

The circle and the altar are decorated with things appropriate to the season: small pumpkins, branches, flowers (possibly marigolds and/or chrysanthemums), nuts, apples or other fruit, and so on. Candles, both on the altar and around the circle, can be white or orange. In addition to the usual altar tools, have a small dish (a miniature cauldron would be ideal) and the piece of paper listing those things you want to get rid of. Also on the altar have photos of any ancestors, now dead, who are special to you. If you wish, you may have tarot cards or a crystal ball (depending upon your own favorite form of divination) sitting on the ground beside the altar.

The Opening the Circle ritual is done. If it is at, or close to, the full moon or the new moon then the appropriate rite is performed. After that, you return to the altar and ring the bell seven times. Raise your wand high and say:

> **"Hail to the Mighty Ones; the Lord and the Lady; Herne and Epona! I stand today at the Crack of Time; at the division between the old year and the new. Through this crack may pass those I have known and loved in the past,**

who have gone on to the Summerland. I greet their return and share my love with them as they share with me. I know that this Samhain time is special for such meeting, though it is not unique. At this time, I also give thanks to the crone aspect of the Lady and her gifts of future sight. To the Lord I pledge my love and support as he embarks upon his journey through the dark half of the year."

Lower your wand and take up the photos of your deceased loved ones. Spend some time thinking of them. You can speak to them as though they are present (which they are and you may even actually see them). Give them your love and let them know they are not forgotten. Ring the bell three times.

Now turn to your wish to rid yourself of unnecessary "baggage." Take up the list you have made and study it. As you read each item, think about it and realize how much happier you are going to be without it. *Know* that, with the act you are about to perform, you will free yourself of these problems. Now take the paper, light it from the altar candle, and hold it over the dish. Let it burn, its ashes falling into the dish. As it burns, picture the items listed on the paper falling away from you, leaving you and your body. Feel the weight of these things lifting from your shoulders. As the last of the paper burns, say **"Thank You"** to the gods. Ring the bell three times.

Now is a good time to do some divination, if you wish. Whatever is your particular favorite should be indulged in. Look to the future and see what you can reveal; see what the coming year has in store for you in the way of opportunities. Remember that nothing is set in stone (see chapter 15, *Divination*), and that what you may see is only an indication of how things may go, depending upon many different factors.

When you have finished, ring the bell three times. Now, if you wish, you may sing and/or dance about the circle. Enjoy the feeling of change. End by sitting (or kneeling or standing) and, in your own words, thank the gods for all they have given you in the past year. Feel free to ask for what you would like in the coming year.

Do the Cakes and Wine rite and end with Closing the Circle.

Winter/Yule

Yule (from the Norse *Iul*, meaning "wheel") has the shortest day and longest night of the year. It is the turning point in the dark half of the year, going from the waxing to the waning year. Yule is a time to celebrate the return of the sun and the rebirth of the God. It is a time to think about your hopes for the coming year, and your plans and aspirations.

The circle and the altar are decorated with things appropriate to the season: ivy, mistletoe, holly, pine boughs, bay, and rosemary. Candles, both on the altar and around the circle, can be green, red, or purple. In addition to the usual altar tools, have an extra (unlit) red candle (*see note below*).

The Opening the Circle ritual is done. If it is at, or close to, the full moon or the new moon then the appropriate rite is performed. After that, return to the altar and ring the bell seven times. Raise your wand high and say:

> **"Hail to the Mighty Ones; the Lord and the Lady; Herne and Epona! The Sun Lord dies yet also he lives! At this time, when the Sun is at its lowest point, I send forth my energies to the Lord to bring him life and to send him on his way toward our Lady, who waits at the entrance to springtime. This is the time for the Goddess to give birth to her Son-Lover, destined to imbue her and thus return the light. Hail, Lady! Queen of the Heavens and of the Night. Bring to us the Child of Promise!"**

Light the extra red candle from the altar candle. Sit, kneel, or stand and meditate on the passage of the God through the dark half of the year. See him at this turning point, reborn and starting on the waxing passage through to the spring. Give thanks to the gods for what you have and for the hopes and promises that lie before you. When you have finished, ring the bell three times.

Now, if you wish, you may sing and/or dance about the circle. Enjoy the feeling of change. End by sitting (or kneeling or standing) and, in your own words, thank the gods for all they have given you in the past.

Do the Cakes and Wine rite and end with Closing the Circle.

[*Note: If you are lucky enough to be able to have your circle outdoors, then instead of the extra candle on the altar, have a small fire ready for lighting in the north quarter of the circle and ignite that rather than lighting the extra candle. In dancing around the circle, you can jump over the fire as you circumambulate.*]

Imbolc

Imbolc, or Oimelc, is basically an early spring festival. It is a time to prepare for the new season; it is a time of new opportunities. This was the occasion for the old Feast of Torches. At sunset people would light lamps or candles in every room of the house, honoring the sun's rebirth. In some Scandinavian countries, a maiden is chosen to wear a crown made of thirteen candles. Many Wiccan celebrations focus on the goddess Bride (pronounced "breed") for, despite falling within the "dark half" of the year, Imbolc is actually a very Goddess-oriented Sabbat. Bride is associated with poetry, so this would be a good Sabbat at which to read (or even to do the actual writing in the circle and then read) a poem.

The last sheaf of the previous year's harvested wheat traditionally is kept to be used as the seed for the new harvest. From this sheaf, a doll was often made, known variously as a corn dolly, harvest mother, or sheaf mother. In Gaelic it was the *brídeóg,* or "biddy." Quite often this doll would be dressed in women's clothing and laid in a small bed known as the Bride bed. Symbolic corn dollies were also made, weaving and braiding the cornstalks into traditional patterns, forming squares, crosses, and similar. If you feel so inclined, a good project would be to make a corn dolly.

The circle and the altar are decorated with things appropriate to the season: small evergreen branches, bay sprigs, holly, nuts, fruit, and so on. Candles, both on the altar and around the circle, can be white or yellow. In addition to the usual altar tools, have an extra white (unlit) candle on the altar (*see Note*). On the ground beside the altar have a corn dolly or (if you haven't made one) a Priapic wand (*see chapter 5, Tools*). You may also have a crystal ball or deck of tarot cards there.

The Opening the Circle ritual is done. If it is at, or close to, the full moon or the new moon then the appropriate rite is performed. After that, you return to the altar and ring the bell seven times. Raise your wand high and say:

> **"Hail to the Mighty Ones; the Lord and the Lady; Herne and Epona! Winter draws to its end and releases its hold on the land. Torches blaze and light shines forth to welcome the progress of our God. As winter goes out of one door, so spring comes in at the next. Farewell to death and bright greetings to life; farewell to the old and greetings to the new. The wheel turns and, as it does, we move ever forward."**

Ring the bell three times. Light the white candle from the altar candle, saying:

> **"And welcome anew to the young God, who grows and embraces us all."**

If you have a corn doll then place it on the altar (if not, then the phallic wand. If you have both, lay the phallic wand on top of the corn doll. If you have neither, use your regular wand) with the words:

> **"Welcome, Lady Bride; Lady of Light; Three-in-One Goddess of us all. Young Goddess of New Beginnings."**

If you have written a poem, then recite it now. (If you feel inspired, write one now and then recite it.) When you have finished, ring the bell three times.

If you wish, you may now sing and/or dance about the circle. End by sitting (or kneeling or standing) and, in your own words, thank the gods for all they have given you in the past. If you wish to do some divination, now would be a good time to do it.

Do the Cakes and Wine rite and end with Closing the Circle.

[*Note: If you are lucky enough to be able to have your circle outdoors, then instead of the extra candle on the altar, have a small fire ready for lighting in the north quarter of the circle and ignite that rather than lighting the extra candle. In dancing around the circle, you can jump over the fire as you circumambulate.*]

Spring/Ostara

Spring is a sign that winter is truly over. Light is conquering darkness, though here they are of equal length. Ostara (also spelled Œstra, Œstara, Eostre, and Eostra) was the Anglo-Saxon goddess of spring. When the Christians borrowed this part of paganism they renamed it Easter. The Easter egg and Easter rabbit come from the fact that Ostara was a fertility goddess, with eggs and rabbits (or hares) symbols of fertility. Her name was probably a variant of Astarte, Ishtar, and Aset. Another symbol of the spring goddess is the snake, the shedding of whose skin is a strong symbol of rebirth and an ancient symbol of new life coming out of old.

The circle and the altar are decorated with things appropriate to the season: evergreen branches, wild flowers, pussy willow, daffodils, primroses, celandines, and so on. Candles, both on the altar and around the circle, can be white, green, or orange. In addition to the usual altar tools, have a small bowl filled with earth and a number of seeds of some kind. The Opening the Circle ritual is done. If it is at, or close to, the full moon or the new moon then the appropriate rite is performed. After that, you return to the altar and ring the bell seven times. Raise your wand high and say:

"Hail to the Mighty Ones; the Lord and the Lady; Herne and Epona! Welcome to Herne and Epona and welcome to the spring. Now is the time to sow the seeds of my future. To know that the seed is in the ground, and will be developing and growing through the coming weeks and months, fills me with joy in the knowledge that my hopes and dreams will eventually be bursting forth in full bloom. Lord and Lady, receive this seed I offer and nurture it, bringing it to its full potential. So Mote It Be."

Sit, kneel, or stand and contemplate for a few moments those things that you would like to see come to fruition in the near future. Spend some time deciding what is most important and how that development of what you desire might affect others around you. Be sure that nothing you bring about for yourself will have a negative impact on anyone else. Then take the bowl of earth and, with the tip of your wand, make a small space in the center, pushing down to make a hole. Then take the seeds you have and hold them in your hands, cupped between the palms. Concentrate your energies into the seeds. Ask (silently or out loud, in your own words) the gods to bless them and to see that they prosper. Then drop the seeds into the hole and, with the fingers of your dominant hand, close the earth over them. Hold up the bowl over the altar and say:

"Here are the seeds I have planted in the womb of the Lady. Let them develop and grow to full maturity. May Herne and Epona join with me in watching over them and guiding them to prosper, as my own plans may prosper. So Mote It Be."

Ring the bell three times. Now, if you wish, you may sing and/or dance about the circle. End by sitting (or kneeling or standing) and, in your own words, thank the gods for all they have given you in the past.

Do the Cakes and Wine rite and end with Closing the Circle.

Beltane

Beltane (spelled variously Bealtaine, Bhealtyainn, Bealtuinn, and similar) is opposite Samhain, as one of the main turning points of the year. The Irish Gaelic pronunciation is "b'*yol*-tinnuh" but most Witches just pronounce it as written: "Bell-tain." The festival is probably named after the Celtic sun god Bel, known as "the Bright One." As the main shift of season in the Celtic calendar, it is especially at this time that the focus turns from the God to the Goddess, who will be predominant through the summer months. Traditionally, two bale fires were lit and cattle and other livestock were driven through between the fires, to consecrate them, protect them from disease, and to give them the sun god's blessing. Couples would often take hands and, together, jump over the fires for fertility and good luck.

This was the time when the maypole was erected. The themes of the festival were sexual love, fertility, birth, and creativity, the maypole being a phallic symbol. It was a time known for joy and festivity. Phillip Stubbs, the Puritan, said of it:

> Against May, Whitsunday, or other time, olde men and wives, run gadding over-night to the woods, groves, hills and mountains, where they spend all night in pleasant pastimes; and in the morning they return, bringing with them birch and branches of trees, to deck their assemblies withal. . . . But the chiefest jewel they bring from thence is their May-Pole, which they have bring home with great veneration. . . . They have twentie or fortie yoke of oxen, every oxe having a sweet nose-gay of flowers placed on the tip of his hornes, and these oxen drawe home this May-Pole (this stinking Ydol, rather), which is covered all over with floures and hearbs, bound round about with strings, from the top to the bottome, and sometime painted with variable coulours, with two or three hundred men, women and children following it with great devotion. And this being reared up . . . then fall they to daunce about it,

like as the heathen people did at the dedication of the Idols, wereof this is a perfect pattern, or rather the thing itself. I have heard it credibly reported (and that viva voce) by men of great gravitie and reputation, that of forty, threescore, or a hundred maides going to the wood over-night, there have scarcely the third of them returned home againe undefiled. (*Anatomie of Abuses*, 1583)

This is somewhat echoed by Rudyard Kipling's words (which have been adopted by many modern Wiccans as their "May Eve Chant"):

Oh, do not tell the priests of our rites
For they would call it sin;
But we will be in the woods all night
A-conjurin' summer in!

Janet and Stewart Farrar, in *Eight Sabbats for Witches*, mention that "Bealtaine for ordinary people was a festival of unashamed human sexuality and fertility. Maypole, nuts, and 'the gown of green' were frank symbols of penis, testicles, and the covering of a woman by a man. Dancing around the maypole, hunting for nuts in the woods, 'greenwood marriages,' and staying up all night to watch the May sun rise were unequivocal activities, which is why the Puritans suppressed them with such pious horror."

As a Solitary, you would probably have difficulty erecting a maypole and dancing around it to plait the ribbons in the traditional manner. But that doesn't matter; you can still celebrate Beltain. Dance and song are a big part of the celebrations so don't hesitate to indulge in both. The sexual union of the God and the Goddess, which was such an important part of this celebration, can be echoed through self-gratification (be you male or female) if you wish, integrating it as part of your ritual (an appropriate point, see below, would be where you say: "Now is the time for the seed to be spilled that fertility may spread throughout the earth"). If you can hold your ritual outdoors, then a balefire burning in the east is a great idea.

You can even jump over it as part of your dancing, after the circle has been closed and you can move outside its limits more freely. If you have to be indoors, then many Solitary (and Coven) Witches will burn a Sterno or a large candle inside a small cauldron, or similar, in the east quarter of the circle, so that it may be jumped over when dancing around inside the circle.

The circle and the altar are decorated with things appropriate to the season: seasonal flowers, nuts, apples or other fruit, and so on. Candles, both on the altar and around the circle, can be white, green, or yellow. In addition to the usual altar tools, have a small cauldron, or other suitable container, in the east quarter (inside the circle) containing a large candle. A can of Sterno also will do. This should be lit before you start to open the circle.

The Opening the Circle ritual is done. If it is at, or close to, the full moon or the new moon then the appropriate rite is performed. After that, you return to the altar and ring the bell seven times. Raise your wand high and say:

> **"Hail to the Mighty Ones; the Lord and the Lady; Herne and Epona! The end of the dark half of the year is at hand. All hail to our Lord! Welcome to our Lady! This is a time for joy and for sharing. The richness of the soil accepted the seed; now is the time for the seed to be spilled that fertility may spread throughout the earth. I celebrate the planting of abundance, the turning of the Wheel. Farewell to the darkness and greetings to the light. Lord and Lady become Lady and Lord, as the Wheel turns."**

Ring the bell three times. You may now dance around the circle, jumping over the "bale fire" in the east as you go. If you wish, you may sing the May Eve chant:

> **"Oh, do not tell the priests of our rites**
> **For they would call it sin;**
> **But we will be in the woods all night**
> **A-conjuring summer in.**

> **And I bring you good news,**
> **By word of mouth,**
> **For women, cattle, and corn;**
> **Now is the sun come up from the south**
> **With oak and ash and thorn."**

When you have finished, return to the altar and ring the bell three times. Take up the wand, hold it high, and say:

> **"Love is the spark of life. It is always there, if I will but see it. I need not seek far for love is within me; it is that inner spark of all that I do. The light of love burns without flicker; it is a steady flame. Love is the beginning and the end of all things. So Mote It Be."**

If you wish, you may again sing and/or dance around the circle. Enjoy the feeling of change. End by sitting (or kneeling or standing) and, in your own words, thank the gods for all they have given you.

Do the Cakes and Wine rite and end with Closing the Circle.

Midsummer/Litha

Midsummer has the longest day of the year. The old Roman name for this time of year was Litha. The sun is at its highest point in the sky, with the God strong and virile. The fertility of the Goddess is at its peak. She is pregnant with the young god and pregnant with the harvest. Here, then, is a balance of fire and water. Here, also, is the turning point where we are about to enter the waning of the year which, eventually, will lead to winter.

The circle and the altar are decorated with things appropriate to the season: summer flowers, heather, oak branches, fruit, and so on. Candles, both on the altar and around the circle, can be white, orange, or yellow. In addition to the usual tools on the altar there is a red (unlit) candle. Also, have a cauldron or other container filled with water standing in the south.

The Opening the Circle ritual is done. If it is at, or close to, the full moon or the new moon then the appropriate rite is performed. After that, you return to the altar and ring the bell seven times. Raise your wand high and say:

> **"Hail to the Mighty Ones; the Lord and the Lady; Herne and Epona! The Sun shines down from on high, giving its light and life to everything and everyone on earth. Its power and joy enter into the Lady, who is the earth itself, filling her with the new life that is soon to burst forth; the life that will descend into the corn and into the plants and the trees. This is a life that is blessed; that is sacred; that is of the Lady and the Lord."**

Light the red candle from the altar candle and hold it high. Keeping it aloft, walk out to the east and then walk slowly around the circle, letting the light from the candle, representing the God, illumine the circle. As you walk, say the following three times: **"Here shines the light and the love of the God, bringing strength and joy to all."** Return to the altar and set down the candle beside the altar candle. Ring the bell three times.

Go out to the circle and walk around to the south. Standing beside the cauldron of water, stand with your feet shoulder-width apart and raise both hands upward and outward. Say:

> **"Here is the bounty of the Lady; she who, by her love, sanctifies and purifies."**

Lower your arms and kneel beside the bowl of water. Dip your fingers into it and sprinkle yourself with the water saying the following three times: **"Blessings from the Great Mother."**

Return to the altar. Take up the wand and hold it high. Say:

> **"At this festival of Litha I see the sun, my Lord, move on his course. I feel him enter into the Lady and, through her, descend into the fields and the crops. I sense the new life that flows through the Goddess."**

Lower your wand and spend a moment thinking of the blessings you enjoy and of how you might share those blessings with those less fortunate. Ring the bell three times. If you wish, you may sing and/or dance around the circle. Enjoy the feeling of change. End by sitting (or kneeling or standing) and, in your own words, thank the gods for all they have given you.

Do the Cakes and Wine rite and end with Closing the Circle.

Lughnasadh

Lughnasadh is a Celtic name referring to the celebration of the sun god Lugh and actually meaning "the commemoration of Lugh" (since he undergoes death and resurrection in his sacrificial mating with the Goddess). Another name sometimes used is Lammas, from the Anglo-Saxon *hlæf mas*, meaning "loaf mass," a celebration of the bread after the corn harvest. This is the time of the first harvest. The god makes love to the already pregnant goddess for the last time, sacrificing himself and passing into the earth. It is through such death and rebirth that the harvest is brought into being.

The circle and the altar are decorated with things appropriate to the season: seasonal flowers such as poppies, fruits (perhaps the first blackberries), grain, small loaves of bread (perhaps shaped like a sun), and so on. Candles, both on the altar and around the circle, can be white, yellow, or brown. In addition to the usual tools, there is a small loaf, or roll, on the altar.

The Opening the Circle ritual is done. If it is at, or close to, the full moon or the new moon then the appropriate rite is performed. After that, you return to the altar and ring the bell seven times. Raise your wand high and say:

> **"Hail to the Mighty Ones; the Lord and the Lady; Herne and Epona! Here do I celebrate the First Harvest, giving thanks for the continuing Wheel of Life and the continuing fertility of the Earth. May the seeds of the grain be buried in the womb of the Goddess, to be reborn in the spring. As**

there must be rain with the sun, to make all things good, so must there be pain with joy, that we may know all things. Through the sacred union of the Lord with the Lady is the harvest assured."

Ring the bell three times then take up the loaf of bread and, with it, dance around the circle, deosil, three times. Returning to the altar, say:

"May the power of the gods pass down to all. May we too enjoy the gift of bounty. May the harvest grow and spread wide to all I love. May the surplus of the land fill our bodies with strength, and may the power of the Lord and the Lady reach down to young and old alike."

Break off some small pieces of the loaf, laying them on the altar. Take your wand and touch the tip to the pieces of bread, saying: "The blessings of the gods."

Eat one of the pieces and then place the rest in the libation dish, to be given to the gods later (with the offerings of Cakes and Wine). Ring the bell three times.

If you wish, you may sing and/or dance about the circle. End by sitting (or kneeling or standing) and thank the gods for all they have given you, with the words:

"Lord and Lady I thank you for all that has been raised from the soil. May it grow in strength from now until the main harvest. I thank you for this promise of fruits to come."

Do the Cakes and Wine rite and end with Closing the Circle.

Autumn/Mabon

Autumn is the other time (after the spring equinox: Ostara) of equilibrium, when the hours of daylight and night are equal. Autumn is a sign that summer is truly over; darkness is conquering light. The accent is on resting after the labors of the harvest, before the start of the winter. This is "harvest home," the end of the grain harvest. The Goddess is settling into restfulness, starting to take on her crone aspect. As Gail Duff puts it (*Seasons of the Witch*): "The God, having laid down his life for the harvest, is about to cross over into the Land of Shadows. He stands on the threshold of light and dark, life and death. Soon he will rest in the arms of the Goddess, waiting to be reborn. Like the corn, the God has been cut down, but his seed brings the promise of new life."

The circle and the altar are decorated with things appropriate to the season: acorns, pinecones, gourds, poppies, fruit, and so on. Candles, both on the altar and around the circle, can be white, brown, or red. In addition to the usual altar tools, have a dish with an apple on it. If you do not normally use an athamé then have a sharp knife beside the apple.

The Opening the Circle ritual is done. If it is at, or close to, the full moon or the new moon then the appropriate rite is performed. After that, you return to the altar and ring the bell seven times. Raise your wand high and say:

> **"Hail to the Mighty Ones; the Lord and the Lady; Herne and Epona! Now that the season of plenty draws to its close, I take time to look about me and enjoy the beauties of autumn. Here is a balance of day and night, light and darkness. The wheel turns, and turns again. Death approaches, arrives, and passes on. New life comes into being—and so the wheel turns."**

Lay down the wand and take up the apple. Hold it for a moment, acknowledging the beauty of creation. Take the athamé or knife and cut the apple crosswise. You will see the seeds arranged like a pentagram. As you look at them say:

"Here, within this fruit, is found the symbol of life. Within all life lie the seeds of future lives. My thanks to the gods for their bounty."

Cut a slice of the apple for a libation, then sit and eat the apple, enjoying it and thinking of the blessings that have come to you—the harvest you have gathered from life. When you have finished, ring the bell three times. If you wish, you may sing and/or dance round the circle. End by sitting (or kneeling or standing) and, in your own words, thank the gods for all they have brought into your life. Feel free to ask for what you would still like to accomplish.

Do the Cakes and Wine rite and end with Closing the Circle. ⚭

13

<hr />

Magic (General)

Magic is for none but those with the steady courage to go quietly on in the face of every adversity, surely and carefully constructing a Living Cosmos within themselves, which will endure for Eternity—and beyond!

—William G. Gray, *Inner Traditions of Magic*

Magic/Witch Name

ost Wiccans have a Witch name or magical name that they use within the Craft. Unlike the name you were given at birth, this will be one of your own choosing, so choose carefully. (If you'd like to stay with your given name, that's fine.) There are certain guidelines I'd recommend for this name, which I'll get to in just a moment. When I was first initiated, in 1963, the coven I joined had a list of names from which to choose. As a Solitary, you will not have access to such a list, but that means you are not limited in any way.

When you become a Witch (and I'll deal with the actual ceremony making you one later in this book) you are going to be reborn. You'll be starting life anew. Some people make up a name, some use the name of a famous Witch of the past, some use the name of one of the deities. I personally think this last is rather presumptuous, but it has become a common practice. (Of course, in doing so you are likely to find yourself one of perhaps dozens of Witches named Cerridwen or Merlin, or similar. I would think it better to have a name that is exclusively yours.) You could choose what is essentially a "witchy-sounding" name, but why not do the thing properly? Why not select a name that is right *magically*, using numerology to do it? Even if you are not good at math, it's not hard to do.

Start by finding your birth number. On a piece of paper, write down the month, day, and year of your birth; for example: 7.24.1982. (Be sure to include the "19" in the year you put down.) Now add those digits together: $7 + 2 + 4 + 1 + 9 + 8 + 2 = 33$. Bring that to a single digit: $3 + 3 = 6$. The number **6 is your birth number**. Now to find a name that matches that birth number, and thereby is the right name for you, magically, having the same vibrations.

First choose a name that you like. As an example, let's say you like the name Amanda. Write out the numbers 1 through 9 with the letters of the alphabet underneath them:

1	2	3	4	5	6	7	8	9
A	B	C	D	E	F	G	H	I
J	K	L	M	N	O	P	Q	R
S	T	U	V	W	X	Y	Z	

Now find the numbers that would equate to Amanda:
A = 1, M = 4, A = 1, N = 5, D = 4, A = 1

Add those together and you get: $1 + 4 + 1 + 5 + 4 + 1 = 16$, $1 + 6 = 7$. But that is not the same as your birth number of 6. To make it the same, you need to add a letter or number that would give a total that would equal 6. If you added an 8 to it, it would work: $7 + 8 = 15$;

1 + 5 = 6. However, the 8 letters are H, Q, and Z, which don't seem to fit very well ... or do they? How about if you just put an H on the end of the name, making it Amandah? That gives us 1 + 4 + 1 + 5 + 4 + 1 + 8 = 24, 2 + 4 = 6, the same as your birth number! Amandah, then, could be a good Witch name for you. (You could put the H anywhere. How about Amandha or Ahmanda?) Try it with your own birth date and your own choice of name. You might have to add more than one letter, or even drop one. But usually, with just a little shuffling around, you can get the name you want. In fact, often you end up with an extra special, unique name, as in the above example.

This is my recommended method of getting an exclusive Witch name. It will be a name you like. It will (if you have had to "adjust" a little) be a unique spelling of it. And most important, it will equate to your birth number and so be very powerful for you. You don't need to use the title "Witch" in front of it. Using the above example, for instance, you wouldn't call yourself "Witch Amandah" but just Amandah. For some reason, in recent years many Wiccans have taken to dubbing themselves "Lord This" or "Lady That." If you feel happier referring to yourself this way, then join the club and be "Lady Amandah," but it's not necessary (and it isn't truly traditional).

Working Magic

What does it mean to work magic? It's not waving a "magic wand" and, with a puff of smoke, turning a person into a frog! I think everyone knows that, yet still people come to the Craft expecting to learn how to "make things happen" and expecting them to happen more or less overnight. There are a number of things that need to be considered with magic. The time factor is one of them. In some instances, magic does work quickly. But in the majority of cases it takes time. Sometimes you have to work at a thing for a number of days, weeks, or even months, to bring it about. So the first requirement of the Solitary Wicca magician is *patience*.

But perhaps the more important question is, when do you do magic? Or, to put it another way, when is magic called for? The answer is that it is done only when there's a definite need for it. You do not do magic just to see if it will work. You do not do magic just to show that it can be done. *You only do magic, when there is a real need for it.* It's not an easy way out. It's not a shortcut. You don't sit around trying to think up spells to do and magic to perform, like some sort of entertainment. Apart from anything else, magic is hard work! So don't be in a hurry to do magic. If you have a problem, see if it can't be resolved by normal means first. Only when all else fails should you turn to magic.

Another thing to be considered—in fact the most important thing—is who will be affected by your magic? We have the one true law of Witchcraft: "An it harm none, do what thou wilt." To repeat what I've said before, so long as you don't harm anyone, you can do what you like. That means do whatever magic you want to do. But there is that precautionary tag: not to harm anyone. That's not always easy to figure out; for example, a lot of newcomers to the Craft want to do love spells. "What harm can there be in getting someone to fall in love with me?" they'll ask. One good way to determine whether or not someone would be harmed is to put yourself in that person's position. Supposing there is someone who likes/admires/loves you, with or without your knowledge. Perhaps you are not especially drawn to that person (may not even know he or she exists). It may also be that you have your eyes on someone else. But then supposing magic is worked and suddenly you find yourself forced—yes, "forced" would be the right word—to love that admirer. Although that admiring magic-worker feels he or she is not harming you by making you love him or her, from your perspective there *is* harm being done. So if your magic in any way affects another, look at the situation from all possible angles to determine whether you are interfering with another's free will. If you are, then DON'T DO IT! (There *are* ways to work love magic, which I'll talk about later.) Positive magic is the only magic allowed in Witchcraft. Negative magic is no part of the Craft. If you do negative magic, of any sort, you are not a true Witch.

A most important factor in working magic is the belief in its efficacy. By that I mean, don't work magic simply *hoping* that it's going to work. Do it *knowing* that it's going to work! This is one of the little-appreciated secrets of magic. To work effective magic, you need to put every possible iota of energy into it; you need to propel the wish out toward its target with everything possible in its favor. A most important ingredient is this "knowing" that the spell will be successful. If you do it merely hoping, then it loses much of its power and energy, and will probably fall short.

Along with this goes your focus. From the very start of collecting the necessary tools and ingredients that you are going to be using, your focus should be on the end result. As an example, if you are purchasing a packet of incense for use in the ritual, then by purchasing it with your mind tuned to the end result of the ritual—the success of the magic—then you will be starting to build that energy that will work the magic successfully. That energy will pass into the incense at the time it is burned in the ritual.

As it becomes known that you are a Witch (if it does become known, of course), you will occasionally be asked to do magic for other people. Although it is possible to do this, *the most powerful person to work magic is the one most directly affected*. In other words, anyone wanting magic done should do it him- or herself (we'll talk about healing magic later, since there are slightly different energies involved there). Let's take the example of someone who has been out of work for a while and is desperate to get a job. The person asks you to do magic to help him or her find employment. You certainly could do this, but no matter how much you empathize, no matter how good a friend the person is, no matter how much you wish the person could get a job, there is no way your feelings can have the same deep-rooted need (desperation even) that the person concerned has. Therefore, the magic you would do could not have quite the same power as magic done by him or her. Only that person is aware of all the little nuances of being out of work: awareness of the bills to be paid, the sleepless nights spent worrying, the fear of becoming homeless, the lack of self-esteem, and so on. You could work the magic, yes, but that person would put far more energy, far more power, into the spell because of his or her personal involvement (especially if the person has reached the desperation point) and because of his or her personal need. Certainly you can help the person. With your knowledge, you can instruct the person on how to go about it. You might even want to work with the person, but he or she should be the primary opera- tor. All of this brings us back to the beginning and underscores the fact that the most important ingredient in magic is *need*. There must be a real need, on the part of the practitioner, for something to come about so that sufficient power will be put into the act to produce the desired effect.

Scott Cunningham suggested that there are three kinds of power that are the sources for magical energy: personal power, earth power, and divine power. In fact, these are all part and parcel of the same power, or energy. The power that is within each and every one of us—and that is channeled and directed to bring about magic—is the same power that resides deep within the earth and within all parts of the earth. It is also the same energy that has its origins in the gods. In believing in, and worshiping, the Lord and the Lady we are acknowledging that all energy comes from them. It may come directly into our bodies or it may come by way of the earth on which we stand. (You'll find, in many magical workings, that "grounding" to the earth is an important aspect of that work.) In Wicca magic, the

---

Magic plays a special role in Wicca. It allows us to improve our lives and return energy to our ravaged planet. Wiccans also develop special relationships with the Goddess and God through magic.

—Scott Cunningham, *Wicca*

Lord and the Lady are invoked when working magic, making them a viable part of the process.

Preparations and Precautions

No Witch jumps in and does magic without first carefully preparing for it. There are preparations specific to the particular magic to be done and there are also precautions to be taken no matter what magic is done. Let's look at the preparations first.

Preparations

When you are going to do magic in the circle, it is usually done after the Cakes and Wine rite and before the Closing of the Circle. It's a good idea (see "Precautions" section) to reinforce the circle by again walking around with a wand or athamé, salted water, and a censer, just before starting on the magical work, making it truly a cone of power. Having thus prepared the circle, you should also prepare yourself by doing some simple deep breathing. This, incidentally, especially should be done if ever you are not able to be in a consecrated circle yet need to work magic. Even if you are doing candle magic, color magic, hands-on healing, or similar—and perhaps are unable to cast a regular circle—you must cleanse yourself first. However, I want to stress the importance of casting a circle, if at all possible, to work magic.

Sit comfortably for this self-cleansing and reinforcing. If necessary have a chair in the circle (I recommend one with a straight back and with arms, so you can rest your arms on the arms of the chair). If you'd prefer to sit on the floor, that's all right too. Wherever you sit, be sure your spine is straight; this is the key. Start by relaxing your body with deep breathing. Close your eyes and simply breathe deeply—breathing in to fill your lungs and breathing out to completely exhaust them. Try to keep your mind blank, which is not easy. When odd thoughts from the day—from your job or your personal life, for example—come creeping in, gently push them out again and ·

concentrate on your breathing. As you breathe in, imagine white light coming into your body. See it filling you, starting at your toes and gradually moving up to all parts of the body. As you breathe out, see the grayness of negativity being pushed out and away. Feel all the little aches and pains going away as the gentle relaxation of purity comes in. Keep this up for a few minutes. As the white light builds and fills you, see it expanding even beyond your body, to form a ball of white light all around you. This is a protective barrier for you and will keep away all negativity. See it expanding to fill the sphere of the magic circle or the area in which you are going to be working. If you are doing a healing on someone who is present, then let it include that person too. When you feel you have done this sufficiently—and the time will vary from individual to individual—let your breathing return to normal and open your eyes. Always do this before any magical or psychic work. [*Note:* An additional step that may be included when working magic is the "awakening of the serpent", the activation of the chakras. I detail this below, in the "Sex Magic" section, chapter 14.]

Have all the necessary tools ready, and at hand, for any magical work you're going to be doing. You don't want to realize suddenly that something essential, like the cord, if you're going to be doing cord magic, is sitting outside the circle! If you're going to be making a poppet, be sure you have all the ingredients with you. If you need to have a photograph of someone on which to concentrate, be sure it's there. Make sure there is sufficient incense and that the circle candles are not going to burn out. You are probably going to be dancing, to raise the power for your magic. Do you need a drum or tambourine, or recorded music, in the circle with you? You will also be chanting (see "Chants, Songs, & Dances" section). Know exactly *what* you will be chanting and why.

Some Witches suggest a mild fasting before doing major magical work. This can be a good idea, though if you fast too much your concentration is more likely to be drawn to a growling stomach than to the object of your magic! I wouldn't fast for more than twenty-four hours, and even then drink plenty of water and perhaps eat a little whole-wheat bread.

Another preparation I would suggest is of the mind. Most magic is dependent upon concentration. You need to be able to "see" things, and people, in your mind's eye and to be able to concentrate on them, often for considerable time. It can help to do some exercises to develop your ability to concentrate. Many years ago, when I was in Haiti examining Vodoun, I was shown a trick to help in this area. Using a photograph of a scene, or of a person, study the picture and try to make a mental note of every little aspect of that picture. Then lay a piece of paper over half of the picture. By concentrating, fill in the missing section and see it whole. See the other half of the picture as though it were still there. If it is a picture of a house, see the details of the structure, the shape of the roof, the positions of the windows and doors, any steps, and the bushes and plants around the second half. Then remove the paper and see how accurate you are. Then try it with a more complicated picture. Do it with pictures of people also. Get to the point where you can imagine every little detail of a person or object in your mind.

Precautions

The magic done in Witchcraft is essentially *safe* magic. Witches do not conjure demons, devils, spirits, or entities of any kind. In Ceremonial Magic (quite different from Witchcraft) entities are conjured, forced to appear to the magician and to do his or her bidding. Naturally these creatures are resentful of the enforced demands and look for opportunities to strike back at the conjuror. In Witchcraft there is no such conjuring and demanding, and there are no spirits wanting to attack the Witch. The only ones we call upon are the gods themselves, and even then it is not a matter of forcing them to appear to us but of *inviting* them to come and witness our rites. True, in constructing the circle you call upon "the Guardians of the Watchtowers of the East (and other directions)" asking them to guard the circle and protect it from any negative force that may try to enter. However, these

"Guardians" are not named as anything specific; they remain somewhat nebulous and could be looked upon as aspects of the gods themselves, so this is definitely not like conjuring specific entities.

There are some Coven Witches, and even some Solitaries, who ask particular entities to help guard the magic circle when it is being constructed. Sylphs of the east, salamanders of the south, undines of the west, and gnomes of the north are brought into the circle by some. I personally advise against this. If you have the gods themselves there—the Lord and the Lady watching over you—you have no need for these elementals (and I have heard of problems developing for some who conjured such beings).

The construction of the circle, which forms a globe of protection around you, should be sufficient to keep you safe from harm. Having said that, however, I would add that *when you work magic* there is an attraction to the "center of power," which you build within your circle and that could possibly catch the attention of undesirable spirits, much as moths are attracted to flames. It is for this reason that you should refrain from breaking the circle any time you are doing magic or even preparing to do magic. Before you start your magical work, walk around and reinforce the circle by once more directing energy through your wand, or athamé, and by sprinkling the salted water and swinging the incense, as you did when you first cast the circle. This, together with the personal protection you have done (the deep breathing exercise), will keep you safe.

Grounding

Some suggest that it is necessary to "ground" the power after doing magic. My feeling is that any power that has been raised is extremely positive energy, so the grounding is not necessary. If there *is* any power left—and invariably every last bit will have gone—then it can only benefit, not harm, you. However, some individuals feel happier grounding and there is certainly no harm in doing so. All that it entails is connecting with the earth. You can do this by dropping to the ground and lying flat on it, with the palms of your hands flat on the ground also. Or you may just crouch and place the palms of your hands on the ground. (Some feel they need to actually slap the ground to make the contact.) Either way, you are allowing any surplus energy to be absorbed into Mother Earth and not leaving yourself still charged up. When I say "flat on the *ground*," don't worry if you are twelve floors up in a high-rise apartment! The energies will travel down through the structure to where it is embedded in the earth and so will complete the grounding operation.

Timing

When doing magic you want everything possible to be going for you. One of the most important ingredients is timing. Trying to get something to happen when the time is against you is like trying to get somewhere by walking up a steep hill—you can do it, but it would be a whole lot easier, and more effective, if the ground was flat! For the most part, judging your timing by the phases of the moon will be sufficient, so let's start there.

Obviously, the moon goes in cycles, or phases, from full moon down to new moon and back up to full. When growing from new moon to full moon it is known as *waxing*. When decreasing from full down to new it is *waning*. Most magic is done during the waxing cycle, since it is positive and therefore akin to the moon's own increase. However, some magic has to be done during the waning cycle; for example, magic to get rid of something would be done then, since it would be akin to the decrease of the moon. Getting rid of bad habits, bad luck, ill health—these all could be done during the waning cycle. But even then you would need to examine what it is *exactly* that you are trying to achieve; for example, if dealing with ill health, are you trying to get rid of the bad health (which should be done in the waning cycle) or trying to gain good health (which should be done in the waxing cycle)? If it's luck, are you trying to rid yourself of bad luck (needs waning cycle) or bring yourself good luck (needs waxing cycle)? You can see, then, that you need to carefully examine the exact intention and focus that you have and decide on the moon's phase from that. If in doubt, and to be on the safe side, work in the waxing/positive cycle of the moon. Always try to think positive. If you are doing magic that requires you do a ritual a number of times, then try to build up to where the final rite is done as close to the full moon (just before it rather than just after it) as possible. In my book *Advanced Candle Magick* (Llewellyn, 1996), I detail some rituals that need to be done over a long period and give a breakdown on how to determine exactly when to do them.

Days of the week can play a part in deciding on the best time to do a ritual. Certain days are traditionally associated with certain things; for instance, if you're working on something to do with marriage, you should work on a Tuesday or a Thursday (note that this is marriage as opposed to love, which would be done on a Friday). Here is a list of the various associations[7]:

DAYS AND ATTRIBUTES

Monday	Ancestors; childbearing; dreams; healing; instinct; memory; merchandise; purity; theft; virginity
Tuesday	Enemies; initiation; loyalty; matrimony; prison; protection; war; wealth
Wednesday	Business; communication; debt; fear; loss; travel
Thursday	Clothing; desires; harvests; honor; marriage; oaths; riches; treaties
Friday	Beauty; family life; friendship; fruitfulness; growth; harmony; love; nature; pleasures; sexuality; strangers; waters
Saturday	Building; doctrine; freedom; gifts; life; protection; real estate; sowing; tenacity
Sunday	Agriculture; beauty; creativity; fortune; hope; money; self-expression; victory

Some people will go to the extent of working with planetary hours for their magic. I don't think Witches need be that precise. So long as you are working with the moon, and perhaps with the day of the

[7]Why are both "marriage" and "matrimony" listed? If you are dealing with an immediate marriage—the preparations, ceremony, newlyweds, and so on—then go for the heading "marriage." If you are dealing with an older, more established marriage, then go for the heading "matrimony."

week, then that should be enough. But for those who want that extra fillip, I'll give the details. First, consider the planet ruling the day of the week with which you are concerned:

Monday	Moon
Tuesday	Mars
Wednesday	Mercury
Thursday	Jupiter
Friday	Venus
Saturday	Saturn
Sunday	Sun

So in addition to the correct day, if you are working for love, for example, you would not only start the ritual on a Friday, which is governed by Venus, but would also start it in the *hour* of Venus. How do you determine the hour of Venus (or any other particular planet)? First of all, you need to know your local times of sunrise and sunset. These vary across the country and for different times of the year.

Let's say that in your locality, at the time of year you want to do this magical ritual, sunrise comes at 6:25 A.M. and sunset at 8:20 P.M. That means there are more hours of daylight than of darkness (obviously it must be summer!). You need to divide the daily hours into twelve *parts* and the same with the nighttime hours. With a total of 835 minutes of daylight (6:25 A.M. till 8:20 P.M.) and 605 minutes of darkness (8:20 P.M. till 6:25 A.M.), dividing each into twelve parts (not hours) you have twelve 69.58-minute daylight sections (835 divided by 12), and twelve 50.42-minute nighttime sections (605 divided by 12). For the purposes of working with planetary hours, these 69.58-minute sections and 50.42-minute sections will be called "hours" even though we know they are not regular 60-minute hours.

Now the first "hour" of daylight on a Friday is the planetary hour of Venus (if you had been doing this for a Wednesday, for example, the first "hour" would be the planetary hour of Mercury). They then follow through the twelve rulers in order, in this case, each daylight "hour" taking 69.58 minutes and each nighttime "hour" taking 50.42

minutes. Different days of the year will, then, vary in the lengths of their hours according to the local times for sunrise and sunset. Here is a table:

SUNRISE
Daytime Hours

Hour	Sun	Mon	Tue	Wed	Thu	Fri	Sat
1	Sun	Moon	Mars	Mercury	Jupiter	Venus	Saturn
2	Venus	Saturn	Sun	Moon	Mars	Mercury	Jupiter
3	Mercury	Jupiter	Venus	Saturn	Sun	Moon	Mars
4	Moon	Mars	Mercury	Jupiter	Venus	Saturn	Sun
5	Saturn	Sun	Moon	Mars	Mercury	Jupiter	Venus
6	Jupiter	Venus	Saturn	Sun	Moon	Mars	Mercury
7	Mars	Mercury	Jupiter	Venus	Saturn	Sun	Moon
8	Sun	Moon	Mars	Mercury	Jupiter	Venus	Saturn
9	Venus	Saturn	Sun	Moon	Mars	Mercury	Jupiter
10	Mercury	Jupiter	Venus	Saturn	Sun	Moon	Mars
11	Moon	Mars	Mercury	Jupiter	Venus	Saturn	Sun
12	Saturn	Sun	Moon	Mars	Mercury	Jupiter	Venus

SUNSET
Nighttime Hours

Hour	Sun	Mon	Tue	Wed	Thu	Fri	Sat
1	Jupiter	Venus	Saturn	Sun	Moon	Mars	Mercury
2	Mars	Mercury	Jupiter	Venus	Saturn	Sun	Moon
3	Sun	Moon	Mars	Mercury	Jupiter	Venus	Saturn
4	Venus	Saturn	Sun	Moon	Mars	Mercury	Jupiter
5	Mercury	Jupiter	Venus	Saturn	Sun	Moon	Mars
6	Moon	Mars	Mercury	Jupiter	Venus	Saturn	Sun

Hour	Sun	Mon	Tue	Wed	Thu	Fri	Sat
7	Saturn	Sun	Moon	Mars	Mercury	Jupiter	Venus
8	Jupiter	Venus	Saturn	Sun	Moon	Mars	Mercury
9	Mars	Mercury	Jupiter	Venus	Saturn	Sun	Moon
10	Sun	Moon	Mars	Mercury	Jupiter	Venus	Saturn
11	Venus	Saturn	Sun	Moon	Mars	Mercury	Jupiter
12	Mercury	Jupiter	Venus	Saturn	Sun	Moon	Mars

Although I've said you need everything going for you that you can get, I don't personally feel that Witches need to be as precise as this. But, if you do decide to work with the planetary hours, then I'd suggest copying them into your Book of Shadows.

Raising the Power

When working magic, the climax is the "projection" of the power you have raised—sending it out to strike the target. But how do you raise that power? Everyone has "power" (for want of a better word) within their body. In parapsychology, generally, it can be used to move objects (psychokinesis), to heal, to see in a crystal ball (skrying), to work a Ouija board, and can even be observed by others as the aura (more on that in chapter 16, "Healing"). In Wicca there are certain things that can be done to increase this power. This is what we do in magic. We increase the power to the highest possible degree, and then direct it and release it to do whatever needs to be done.

The most common way of building up the power is through chant and dance. This is not exclusive to Witchcraft; it is found universally in such varied cultures as Native American, Australian Aboriginal, African, Haitian, and all forms of shamanism. One of the best known and recognized is found in Vodoun. In that religion, the initiates will raise the power in order to find ekstasis and then be "ridden by the loa," or possessed by their gods. The Vodoun drummers beat out a rhythm, which gradually rises in its intensity (conducted by the priestess, or Mambo). As this rhythm drives along, it sweeps the dancers with it, bringing them to a high state of excitement and generating tremendous power within them. The climax bursts when one of the number is taken over by a god or goddess and falls to the ground. The same general pattern is followed in all such rituals, including Witchcraft. There is a start to building the power, which then gradually works up and up until it bursts in a climax. It is easy to see a sexual parallel (this will be looked at more closely in the "Sex Magic" section, chapter 14), which is apt.

You may not have a bank of drums to propel you along to your ecstasy, but you don't need a whole bank of drums. The key ingredient here is *rhythm*. Rhythm with a sonorous beat. You can achieve this by beating a drum or tambourine, by pounding the ground, by slapping your thighs with your hands, by clapping—any one of a number of ways. If you wish, you can make use of pre-recorded music. The only problem there is that you have no control over how much it increases in volume and, more important, how much it increases in tempo. In Vodoun the priestess watches the dancers to gauge their progress. She will then signal the drummers to slow down or speed up, as necessary. If you are making your own "music," then you know how you feel and will instinctively slow or quicken the beat. But with recorded sound you are locked in to what is there.

On the other hand, when you are beating a tambourine or even clapping your hands, there is a part of you that is concentrating on that to the detriment of your going into a semi-trance, which is what you do in achieving ekstasis. I think perhaps the best method, at least to start, is for you to stamp your feet as you dance. This way, although you may be somewhat conscious of the action, it is more a part of the process and therefore less intrusive. Dance around in a circle, letting it "all hang out!" No one is there to watch you, to laugh, or criticize. Enjoy yourself. Dance, stamp, and gradually increase the speed and force of your dance. The more the blood flows through you, the more power you will be generating.

Chants, Songs, & Dances

Along with the dancing dealt with above, goes chanting or singing. As a preliminary to the actual power-raising, you can sing. In fact many Witches start by sitting and singing, then get up and start to dance while still singing. When they feel they are starting to raise the power, they switch from the song to the magical chant and then concentrate on the power-raising proper. Let's look at songs first and then the chant.

In *Wicca for Life* (Citadel, 2001) I give a selection of Sabbat songs. These could be used in this instance, if appropriate to the time of year. There is another selection—not specific to Sabbats—in my *Buckland's Complete Book of Witchcraft* (Llewellyn, 2002). Other books on the Craft also contain songs. You may want to write your own (an excellent idea) or use something that, although non-Craft, is appropriate. Of course, if you don't want to sing at all, that's fine too! But singing is a nice lead-in to the chant and a good, gradual buildup to the point where you are more consciously getting into power-building with its attendant dancing (and stamping).

Whether or not you sing, you definitely need to chant, for the chant will be your focus for the spell-casting. There are no ready-made chants here; you will need to compose your own. But the chant is, or should be, very simple. You may find some Witches who babble incoherent chants (if questioned, you'll find they have no idea what they mean!) that sound like: "Bezabi, lacha, bachababa, lamach, cahi, achababa . . . ," or "Semunis alternie advocapito . . ." You don't need these! You need a chant that means something to you, that is intelligible, and that is *specific to the spell you are working*. This is why it's best to write your own. As an example, suppose you are going to be doing a spell to help you find a new apartment. You may need to find something less expensive than where you are, or you may have to move for a variety of reasons. The essential thing here is that you find something that becomes a true home to you. So let's say the key word is "home." (Remember this key word. I'll talk more about it later.) Make up a simple rhyme with this word in it. How about: "Don't make me roam; find me a home." Hmm! Okay, but it lacks a certain "something." Let's try: "Find me a key, to a true home for me." That is better; it's short, it rhymes, and it hits the goal you have—finding a "true home."

The chant needs to be short and rhythmic, because you will be dancing and working yourself up into a state where you don't want to be trying to remember a whole lot of words. They should come almost automatically, without having to think about them. Being rhythmic means you can stamp hard on the beat: "*Find* me a *key* to a *true* home for *me*!" So the form of this chant would do, but the content still isn't quite right. When working magic, the secret is to see your spell successfully completed. In other words, don't hope that it will work, don't simply see it working, but see it *successfully finished*. In the above spell, for example, you shouldn't be thinking about getting a new apartment—you should see yourself *already in one*. You should see yourself unpacking, sleeping in the bedroom, eating in the dining room, or something similar. You should see yourself as it will be when the magic has worked (which it will!). So this chant doesn't contribute to that feeling. It asks, "Find me a key . . ." You need a chant that says you've already found it. Let's revise the chant, then, to something like: "I *have* the key to a true home for me!" You retain the same beat and emphasis, but the words are more positive. This, then, is how you decide on a chant to use. Think of the purpose of the ritual—what you want to happen—and then put together a short, simple, rhythmic phrase that you can chant while working up the power.

The steps of the dance are not important. You'll find that as you move around the circle, stamping your feet in time with the chant, that some sort of pattern emerges. But whether it does or not is not important so long as the flow of the chanting is not interrupted. You can skip, hop, jump, run—whatever feels right. As you dance and chant, see in your mind's eye the successful conclusion of the spell. See the thing done.

Musical interludes can be used directly prior to the rite to set the mood; during, as an offering to the Goddess and God or to rouse energy; and afterward in pure celebration and joy.

—Scott Cunningham, *Wicca*

Releasing the Power

I have, in the past, used the simile of an air rifle to show the process of working magic. I think it's a good one. With an air rifle, you pump it up, to build the pressure. You then sight along the top of it. When you are on target, you squeeze the trigger and fire the shot into the target. So it is with magic. The dancing and chanting to build up power is the pumping up. The more you do it—the more you work yourself up—the more power will be in the shot. Chant faster and faster, while speeding up your dancing. Chant louder and louder. You'll begin to feel as though you'll burst! You "sight" by having a clear picture in your mind of what it is you want. When you are at your peak, you squeeze the trigger and release the power into the target. This you do by actually shouting a key word, which is the trigger. In the example I used above, it would be "Home!" This word is shouted and with the shout you expend all that pent-up energy— all the force that you have been building. *Shout* the word, and see it flying to the destination of (in that example) the new apartment. You will probably feel tremendous release, both mental and physical, such that you may well collapse to the ground. That's all right. Lie there and get your breath back. Relax and know that you've done your best. When you feel able, if you so desire, you can ground out by pressing your hands to the surface of the ground, or even slapping them on the ground, and allowing any unsent energy to dissipate. As I mentioned earlier, I personally don't feel this is necessary because, if you've done the magic properly, all the energy will have been sent. Even if there are residues left, it is all positive energy that will not harm you. But some Witches like to ground, and there's certainly no harm in that.

The above has dealt with the major, most potent, way of working magic. This is the purely Witchcraft way and should always be done within a magic circle. But there are other—more gentle?—forms of magic that can be done; those will be described next. These are methods that are used by Witches but also by others who are not necessarily of the Craft. Although I urge you to do all magic inside a protective circle if you can, some of these following forms can be done without the full ritual circle and—with many of them—even without the buildup of power used for the magic described here.

Definitions of Magic

Magic is the art and science of causing change to occur in conformity with will. —Aleister Crowley

Magick is the art, science, and practice of producing "supernatural" effects, causing change to occur in conformity, and controlling events in Nature with will.
—Gerina Dunwich

Magic is the art of effecting changes in consciousness at will. —William Butler

Magic is the projection of natural energies to produce needed effects. —Scott Cunningham

We do not affect fate by our magical operations, we affect ourselves; we reinforce those aspects of our nature which are in sympathy with the powers we invoke.
—Dion Fortune

Magic is a comprehensive knowledge of all nature.

—Francis Barrett

Magic is making something happen that you want to happen. —Raymond Buckland

Magic is the act of using your will to cause change, by focusing and directing your psychic energy.

—Jennifer Hunter

Magic . . . is the art of obtaining results without resort to the ordinary mechanism of cause and effect.

—Serge Hutin

The work of magic involves transformation, and the first transformation is the shift of perception.

—Marion Weinstein

In its true sense magic is a high art and science itself, that should release the powers of the imagination for the benefit of any other part of life. —Gareth Knight

Magic is the science of the control of the secret forces of nature. —S. L. Macgregor-Mathers

[Magic is] the mastery of occult forces and their use in order to produce visible effects. —Frank Gaynor

Magick is the art and metaphysical science of manifesting personal desires through the collection and direction of energy. —Raven Grimassi

Magic is concerned with the conversion of universal energies into practical frequencies that can be utilized according to the needs of the occasion. —Murry Hope

14

Magic (Specific)

*In our modern, subjective world, it is difficult
to trust our natural instincts and reawaken
powers we possessed in the early phases of
our development. By accepting that spirit,
body and mind are linked, and harnessing
the energy of the mind, we can use magic
as a way of enhancing and taking
control of our own destinies.*
—Nicola de Pulford, *The Book of Spells*

Candle Magic

f the dozens of different classifications of magic, one of
the most common is that termed *sympathetic* or *imitative*
magic. Candle-burning is of this type. This is where an
object, such as a candle, is taken to represent a person. If
a magical act is then done to establish a link between that person
and the candle, then whatever is done to the candle will, in effect, be
done to the person. A candle can also represent a quality; for exam-

ple, attraction. By performing a ritual where the attraction candle was brought into contact with the person candle, then that person represented could be made more attractive as a result of the sympathetic magic. Based on the above, many rituals have been written and performed for a wide variety of purposes. Remember that any Witch doing such rituals *must* bear in mind the Wiccan Rede: An it harm none, do what thou wilt.

Candles . . . give a soft, natural light, and help to create the right ambience for focusing your mind. Fire is an important spiritual element.

—Nicola de Pulford, *The Book of Spells*

Whole books have been written on candle-burning magic.[8] It certainly is a popular way of working, and one which can be done with little expenditure and no risk of harm, since nothing is being conjured. It can be done almost anywhere and is especially popular when there is lack of space for a full ritual circle. The top of a bedroom chest of drawers, a coffee table, a box, or a small space on the ground can all be utilized as a candle-burning altar. I've even seen the top of the lid on a toilet water-tank used.

Let's take a look at some typical candle-burning rituals in their entirety. Ritual candles are used and recognized by their color, so first of all you need to familiarize yourself with the traditional meanings of the colors, and their association with birth signs and days of the week. You will be dealing with altar candles, astral candles, offertory candles, and day candles. I'll explain each of these.

---

[8]*Practical Candleburning Rituals* by Raymond Buckland (St. Paul: Llewellyn, 1982). *Advanced Candle Magick* by Raymond Buckland (Llewellyn, 1996).

Colors are used to specify a particular person. They are based on that person's birth date/astrological sign. There are two possible colors: a primary and a secondary. You can use the secondary color if you can't find a candle in the primary color. It is also useful if you are working with two people and they are both of the same sign; use the primary color for one and the secondary color for the other. For three people, get another candle with both colors on it. (As a last resort, if you can't find a candle in either color but need to do the ritual, then use a white candle for the person.) These, then, are the colors for the astral candles:

ASTRAL CANDLE COLORS

Astrological Sign	Birth Date	Primary Color	Secondary Color
Aquarius	Jan 20–Feb 18	blue	green
Pisces	Feb 19–Mar 20	white	green
Aries	Mar 21–Apr 19	white	pink
Taurus	Apr 20–May 20	red	yellow
Gemini	May 21–Jun 21	red	blue
Cancer	Jun 22–Jul 22	green	brown
Leo	Jul 23–Aug 22	red	green
Virgo	Aug 23–Sep 22	gold	black
Libra	Sep 23–Oct 22	black	blue
Scorpio	Oct 23–Nov 21	brown	black
Sagittarius	Nov 22–Dec 21	gold	red
Capricorn	Dec 22–Jan 19	red	brown

Next, there are the offertory candles. These are the ones used to represent qualities and states, depending upon the work being done:

OFFERTORY CANDLE
COLOR ASSOCIATIONS

red	courage; health; sexual love; strength; vigor
pink	honor; love; morality
orange	adaptability; attraction; encouragement, stimulation
yellow (gold)	attraction; charm; confidence; persuasion; protection
white	purity; sincerity; truth
green-yellow	anger; cowardice; discord; jealousy; sickness
green	fertility; finance; healing; luck
brown	hesitation; neutrality; uncertainty
blue, light	health; patience; tranquillity; understanding
blue, dark	changeability; depression; impulsiveness; sincerity
violet	healing; peace; spirituality
purple	ambition; business progress; power; tension
silver (gray)	cancellation; neutrality; stalemate; brilliance; reflection
black	confusion; discord; negativity; loss; neutrality; indecision

When I talked about the timing of magic in chapter 13, I gave a list of attributes connected with the different days of the week. I'll repeat that information here but also add the colors associated with the days of the week. The following are the day candles:

DAY-OF-THE-WEEK
CANDLE ASSOCIATIONS

Day	Color	Association
Monday	white	ancestors; childbearing; dreams; healing; instinct; memory; merchandise; purity; theft; virginity
Tuesday	red	enemies; initiation; loyalty; matrimony; prison; protection; war; wealth
Wednesday	purple	business; communication; debt; fear; loss; travel
Thursday	blue	clothing; desires; harvests; honor; marriage; oaths; riches; treaties
Friday	green	beauty; family life; friendship; fruitfulness; growth; harmony; love; nature; pleasures; sexuality; strangers; waters
Saturday	black	building; doctrine; freedom; gifts; life; protection; real estate; sowing; strength; tenacity
Sunday	yellow	agriculture; beauty; creativity; fortune; hope; money; self-expression; victory

Now to look at actual candle-burning rituals. I'll start by taking it one step at a time. It may seem a lengthy process but, once I've explained all the details, you'll see that this is actually a very simple, straightforward type of ritual that anyone could do. As a first example, let's take the case of a woman who would like to have a child but has so far been unsuccessful. Let's say her name is Mary and she was born on April 28 (the year is not important). Since you know that the best person to do magic is the one most affected by it, we'll presume that Mary is Wiccan and is doing this ritual herself. She is a Taurus so the colors for her astral candle would be red and yellow. If you can find a candle that is both red and yellow, that would be perfect. If not, then just a red one will do. Looking at the color associations for the offertory candles, you will see that green is the color of fertility. Mary will need one of those. And in order to attract that fertility to her, she will also need an orange candle (for attraction).

On her altar she should have an altar candle, which is usually white but could be a color to suit the season. (Since Mary is Wiccan, she might also like to have deity figures on her altar.) To complete the necessary "tools" she should have a small dish of anointing oil and some incense. Also there should be something with which to mark the candles (see below). A traditional instrument for this is the burin, which is a small, pointed instrument. [*Note*: Try to find small candle-holders, so that when candles are supposed to be touching one another, they are as close as possible, even though the candles themselves may not actually touch.]

First Mary needs to determine the best day to work her magic. Studying the "Days of the Week" table, Mary would see that Monday is good for magic connected with childbearing, therefore that would be the best day for working her magic. So, the day candle will need to be white, which is the color for Monday.

The basic idea behind this particular instance of sympathetic magic is that a candle representing attraction will draw a candle representing the quality of fertility forward to meet with the candle representing Mary. As these candles are manipulated—the one gradually getting closer to the other two—so they will affect who and what they represent. This is a ritual that must, obviously, be done over a period of time. A moon's span—that is, one month—is usually regarded as an appropriate length of time for magic to work. Mary will therefore set up her altar, and first light her candles, on a Monday. In the ritual, she will gradually move the green fertility candle toward her astral candle, seeing it drawn there by the attraction candle so that the three finally touch one another in the final ritual on the Monday four weeks after the start. Ideally, that final touching will occur on a Monday that is closest to (just before) the full moon. This may mean that the ritual has to be started in the waning cycle of the moon, to allow the necessary time to end at the full moon. Mary needs to study her calendar and plan her ritual accordingly. I'd suggest doing the ritual on each of the Mondays, from first to last. She can see what distance has to be covered in those four weeks and move the green candle an appropriate distance forward during each ritual.

Now to the specifics. To start with, the attraction candle is right alongside Mary's candle, on one side of the altar. The fertility candle is across the other side of the altar. Here is a suggested altar setup:

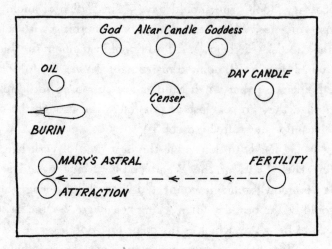

Suggested Altar Setup (I)

Having set the scene, as it were, I'll now give the ritual as Mary should do it.

For Fertility

Light the incense and the altar candle, as well as the day candle. In your own words, call upon the Lord and the Lady to witness the rite you are about to perform. You do not *have to* cast a circle about the altar, but I recommend it if possible. It doesn't have to be the full ritual circle, with quarter candles, but can be a simple, even an irregular one (if you have to walk around odd pieces of furniture!), drawn only with the wand. But if you're doing this sitting on the edge of a bed, in a cramped apartment, with the altar setup on top of a dresser in front of you, don't worry about casting the circle. *Do,* however, do the breathing preparation that I gave in chapter 13, "Magic—Preparations" section. This will serve as sufficient protection for any candle-burning magic you do.

Having invited the gods to witness the rite, state the purpose of it:

"I am here to bring fertility to myself; to make myself fertile and able to bear a child."

Anointing the Candle

Take up the astral candle and, with the burin, inscribe your name along its length. You can do this in one of the magical alphabets if you wish, though regular letters will do. Then consecrate the candle: rub it with the oil, outward from the center toward the ends, slowly turning it so that the entire candle gets oiled. Then hold it in the smoke of the incense, again turning it so that all of it gets censed.

As you do this, say words to the effect:

"Here is myself, [Your name]. It is me in every detail. All that I do to this representation, I do to me. So Mote It Be."

Stand the candle in its place. Take up the orange candle. Do the same thing, but inscribing it with the word "attraction." Consecrate it and then say:

"Here is Attraction. It has the power to draw, both directly to it and to whatever is beside it. So Mote It Be."

Stand the candle beside the astral candle. Take up the green one. Inscribe it with the word "fertility." Consecrate it and say:

"Here is Fertility. Wherever this candle moves it takes with it the power of fertility, passing that power to whomever it encounters. So Mote It Be."

Stand that candle in its place.

Now spend some time concentrating on seeing yourself pregnant, or actually with a child of your own. See, *and know*, that this is you in the future, as a result of this ritual. Light first the astral candle, then the attraction candle, and finally the fertility candle. After a few moments, move the fertility candle a short distance across the altar toward the other two. Let the three candles burn for at least thirty minutes before extinguishing them. (You should do this with a candle-snuffer or by pinching them out. Do not blow them out.) If at all possible, leave the altar setup as it is until the following Monday, when you will repeat the above ritual. If you must dismantle the altar between rituals, carefully note the respective positions of the three main candles so that you can set them back in the same spots to start the next stage of the ritual.

On the last Monday, the final move will place the fertility candle against the astral and orange offertory candle. Again, see and know that you will become pregnant. Give thanks to the Lord and the Lady, in your own words, and close the circle.

I'll give one more example of a candle-burning ritual. This is one that could be used for a variety of problems that might have developed in the home: general unhappiness, sibling rivalry, constant fighting, abuse of any sort, and so on.

For Peace in the Home

The altar is set up with six offertory candles close around your astral candle. First there are three—pink, light blue, and violet—and then three more gray (or silver) ones around those. All of these are static for the ritual; none of them will be moved. You will do this ritual on a Friday, for harmony, family life, and friendship, so the day candle will be green.

Light the altar candle, the incense, and the day candle. Sit for a few moments reviewing the situation in the home and how you

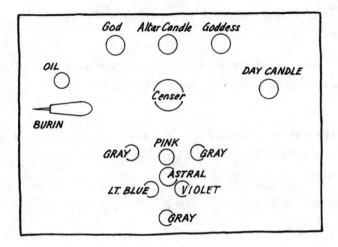

Suggested Altar Setup (II)

would like it resolved, then concentrate on it being fully resolved; everyone concerned is now happy. In your own words, call upon the Lord and the Lady to witness the rite you are about to perform. Having invited the gods to witness the rite, state the purpose of it:

**"I am here to bring peace and happiness to my home, to
make it trouble free and a place of joy and contentment."**

Take up the astral candle and, with the burin, inscribe your name along its length. You can do this in one of the magical alphabets if you wish, though regular letters will do. Then consecrate the candle: rub it with the oil, outward from the center toward the ends, slowly turning it so that the entire candle gets oiled. Then hold it in the smoke of the incense, again turning it so that all of it gets censed. As you do this, say words to the effect:

**Here is myself, [Your name]. It is me in every detail. All
that I do to this representation, I do to me. So Mote It Be."**

Stand the candle in its place in the center of the altar. Take up the pink candle. Do the same thing; consecrate it and inscribe it with the word "love." Then say:

"Here is Love. It is with me and all about me. So Mote It Be."

Place the candle alongside your astral candle. Take up the light blue one; consecrate it and inscribe it with the word "understanding." Say:

"Here is patience, tranquillity, and understanding. It is with me and all about me. So Mote It Be."

Place the candle alongside the astral candle. Take up the violet candle; consecrate it and inscribe it with the word "peace." Say:

"Here is peace and healing. It is with me and all about me. So Mote It Be."

Place that candle alongside the astral candle.

One at a time, take up the three gray candles; consecrate them and inscribe each one with the word "neutrality." Say:

"Here is neutrality. The past is gone and the future is now here. So Mote It Be."

Now spend some time concentrating on seeing your home happy and peaceful as a result of this ritual. Light first the astral candle, then the pink, light blue, and violet candles, and finally the three gray candles. Sit with them and let them burn for at least thirty minutes before you leave. Give thanks to the Lord and the Lady, in your own words, and close the circle. Leave the candles burning until they have burned themselves out.

You may repeat this ritual on a weekly or monthly basis if you wish. If so, then rather than let the candles burn out, extinguish them after an hour and relight them at the next performance of the ritual.

From these two samples, you can see that any situation can be treated by candle-burning. Simply choose the necessary candles—astral, offertory, day—place them, and, if necessary, manipulate them to indicate what you want to achieve.

Poppets

Poppet magic is another form of imitative or sympathetic magic. It has been performed for thousands of years, with examples found in ancient Egyptian times and even as far back as Paleolithic times, 25,000 years ago. In this form of magic, rather than using ready-made (or even handmade) candles, actual figures are made to represent the people to be affected. These can be of wax, clay, cloth, straw, or just about any substance. It's not necessary that they look exactly like the person they have been made to represent, though they are given a basic human shape, much like a gingerbread-man figure. Sometimes an object or objects belonging to the person, such as hair or fingernail clippings, are incorporated in the construction to provide a more direct magical connection, but that is certainly not essential.

As with candle-burning magic, colors might be used in the construction process, with colored cloth and colored clay or wax, following the traditional astral colors and color associations (see "Candle Magic" section). In addition, such things as astrological signs, or similar, may be drawn on the figure to help make the connection and exact identification. Cloth poppets are usually stuffed with appropriate herbs, whether for healing, or love, or whatever.

To make a poppet, take two pieces of cloth and, laying one on top of the other, cut out a rough gingerbread-man shape. Sew all around the figure but leave an opening at the top. (If you want to be especially neat, turn the figure inside out, so that the sewing edge is on the inside.) If you know the person's birth date, then you can use pieces of cloth of two different colors to correspond with the primary and secondary colors for the astral sign. Use the primary color on the front of the figure and the secondary color on the back. Another possibility would be to use the primary color on the front of the figure and then a color associated with the purpose of the poppet for the back; for example, if doing a healing ritual you could give it a green back (green for healing). If you don't know the birth date and astrological sign, then you can just make a white figure.

Stuff the figure with cotton, rags, or (best) any appropriate herbs (see Appendices: Magical Properties of Herbs). Think about the stuffing; it can add to the power of the figure; for example, if working to bring money why not stuff the doll with dollar bills, or cut-up Monopoly money? For love, with hopes of marriage, stuff it with confetti. There are many items such as these that could be appropriate for what you are trying to do. Come up with some of your own. When it has been stuffed, sew up the top of the figure and then mark it to show whom it represents. Embroider, paint, or use magic markers to put on a face and facial hair if there is any; add wool of an appropriate color for the hair. On the body mark the person's name, if known, and their astrological sign, if known.

As an alternative you can make the figure of wax, clay, or similar, chopping the herb(s) finely and mixing into the clay. The personal details could then be scratched onto the figure using your burin. A straw man or woman could also be constructed. In simplest form you could just cut out a flat form from cardboard and mark/paint it to represent the person. But the more work you put into it, the more powerful will be the magic.

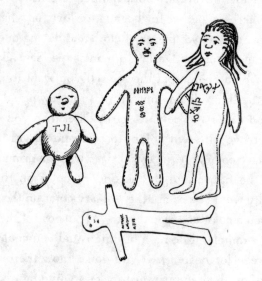

Poppets

The making of a figure, such as modeling or sewing and stuffing, puts more power into it for there is far more of your time and energy spent in making it. Once it's made, as part of the ritual you would consecrate it and name it for the person it represents. As an example of poppet magic, here's a suggested ritual for using a poppet to help someone recover from an illness (be sure to get the person's permission to do this). In this instance we'll use a cloth poppet. As in candle-burning magic, you can have a day candle on the altar. For this example it would be a white one and the ritual would be done on a Monday, for healing.

Make the poppet and write the person's name on it. If you know the person, add his or her astrological sun sign, moon sign, and rising sign. Lay the poppet on the altar.

Light the altar candle, the incense, and the day candle. Sit for a few moments reviewing the situation: what the person has suffered from and how much you want him or her to recover. In your own words, call upon the Lord and the Lady to witness the rite you are about to perform. Having invited the gods to witness the rite, state the purpose of it:

> **"I am here to bring healing and happiness to** [Name of person] **and to fill him/her with joy and contentment."**

Pick up the poppet and sprinkle it with the salted water, then hold it in the smoke of the incense, turning it so that all of it gets censed. As you do this, say words to the effect:

> **"Here is** [Name of person]. **It is him/her in every detail. All that I do to this representation, I do to** [Name of person]. **So Mote It Be."**

Now lay the poppet on the altar and, taking up your wand, touch the tip of it to the figure while you concentrate on seeing that person fully healed, and happy and joyful, as a result of this ritual. Direct your healing energies into the figure, and ask that the gods also send their healing to the person it represents. Remember, in magic you should see the thing completed, rather than simply getting better. So see the person fully recovered; see him or her laughing and moving about, fully cured. When you feel you have done this for long enough, put aside the wand and give thanks to the Lord and the Lady, in your own words. Close the circle. You may repeat this ritual on a daily, weekly, or monthly basis, if you wish. After closing the circle, carefully wrap the poppet in a piece of white linen and put it away somewhere where it will not be disturbed.

Such poppet magic is one of the best forms of creating love between two people, and we'll look at that later, in the "Love Magic" section.

Plackets

Placket magic utilizes small pockets, or "plackets," to assist in accomplishing the magic. (The word *placket* is an Old English word that means both "pocket" and "vagina"!) These are made of felt, or similar material, and in a color or colors appropriate to what is being sought. A photograph of the person, or something belonging to him or her, is placed inside the placket and kept there for a period of time. The placket is about three or four inches square, depending upon the size of the photographs that are to be inserted. In a sense, plackets are very similar to poppets but without the humanlike shape and not specific to any one particular person. If you plan to do much placket magic then make a series of these pockets to have on hand, in various colors, so that you can use an appropriate one according to the color associations and astral colors. Also make one with green on one side and red on the other, and one with green on one side and blue on the other. These will be very useful for healing magic, working with energizing (the red end of the spectrum) and soothing (blue end).

A photograph placed inside the placket is a good "connection" with the person you are trying to affect with your magic. (A letter or other writing could also be used.) It works like the nail clippings or hair that might be placed inside a poppet, in being a representation of the individual. Make certain that only the person you want to affect is in the photograph and no one else. The placket itself represents the healing, or other, force. By placing the photograph inside the placket, the individual is surrounded by the ritual energies necessary for the healing, love magic, or whatever is being worked.

Plackets

As an example of placket magic, here is the example I used for poppet magic, but this time using a placket. The aim is to help someone recover from an illness (be sure to get the person's permission to do this). For this example, it would be a white day candle on the altar and the ritual would be done on a Monday, for healing. The placket should be green, for healing, or it could be green on one side and the person's primary color on the other, if his or her birth date is known.

The placket lies on the altar, with a photograph of the person alongside it. Light the altar candle, the incense, and the day candle. Sit for a few moments reviewing the situation: what the person has suffered from and how much you want him or her to recover. In your own words, call upon the Lord and the Lady to witness the rite you are about to perform. Having invited the gods to witness the rite, state the purpose of it:

"I am here to bring healing and happiness to [Name of person] **and to fill him/her with joy and contentment."**

Take up the photograph and hold it in the smoke of the incense, turning it so that all of it gets censed. As you do this, say words to the effect:

> "**Here is** [Name of person]. **It is him/her in every detail. All that I do to this representation, I do to** [Name of person]. **So Mote It Be.**"

Pick up the placket and sprinkle it with the salted water, then hold it in the smoke of the incense, turning it so that all of it gets censed including the inside. As you do this, say words to the effect:

> "**Here is that which will cover and bring healing energies. So Mote It Be.**"

Now slide the photograph into the placket and lay it on the altar. Taking up your wand, touch the tip of it to the placket while you concentrate on seeing that person fully healed, and happy and joyful, as a result of this ritual. Direct your healing energies into the placket, and ask that the gods also send their healing to the person represented. Remember, in magic you should see the thing completed, rather than simply getting better. So see the person fully recovered; see them laughing and moving about, fully cured. When you feel you have done this for long enough, put aside the wand and give thanks to the Lord and the Lady, in your own words. Close the circle. You may repeat this ritual on a daily, weekly, or monthly basis, if you wish. Leave the photograph inside the placket for at least three days after the ritual.

Pink plackets can be used for love magic, green for finances, orange for attraction, and so on, as in the color associations.

Cord Magic

Witches have worked cord magic for centuries. There is a woodcut showing a Witch selling a knotted rope to some sailors, in Olaus Magnus's *Historia de Gentibus Septentrionalibus* (1555). This was a cord into which magic had been worked, to generate winds.

Sorcerer Selling Mariners the Winds tied up in Three Knots of a Rope
Olaus Magnus, *Historia de gentibus septentrionalibus*.

If the sailor found himself becalmed he could untie one of the knots and a wind would come up. The more knots he untied, the fiercer the wind would become. According to Magnus, "When they had their price they knit three magical knots . . . bound up with a thong, and they gave them unto the merchant sailors, observing that rule, that when they unloosed the first, they should have a good gale of wind; when the second, a stronger wind; but when they untied the third, they should have such cruel tempests that they should not be able to look out of the forecastle to avoid the rocks."

The best known Wiccan cord magic spell involves tying nine knots in your cord whilst building up the power and directing it into that cord. This power buildup can be done by dancing, chanting, or however you work best in building power. Holding the cord and concentrating the energy, the first knot is tied in the middle ————x———— with the words **"By knot of one, this spell's begun."**

The next knot is tied at one end x————x———— with the words, **"By knot of two, this spell comes true."**

The next knot is at the other end x————x————x **"By knot of three, so mote it be."**

Then a knot between the middle and one of the end ones x——x——x————x **"By knot of four, this power I store."**

The same thing at the other end x——x——x——x——x between the end one and the middle one. **"By knot of five, the spell's alive."**

Next between the first two x—x—x——x——x——x with **"By knot of six, this spell I fix."**

Then the same at the other end x—x—x——x——x—x—x with **"By knot of seven, this spell I'll leaven."**

The next knot should be next to the center x—x—x—x—x——x —x—x with **"By knot of eight, I'll cast the fate."**

Finally, the last knot x—x—x—x—x—x—x—x—x with **"By knot of nine, what's done is fine."**

All the energy is finally released into that last knot, seeing the finalizing of the work you are doing. If you are working sex magic (see "Sex Magic" section), this is where the knot is tied at the climax. All the raised power is now stored in that nine-knotted cord.

The release of that stored power is done at another, later, ritual. It can be done all at once, if necessary, or it can be done by untying one knot each day for nine days, building up to the best time. The knots should be released *in the same order in which they were tied*, not the reverse order. This way it's the final knot, which absorbed the most energy, that is again untied at the climax.

There is another simple yet effective cord magic spell. This can be used for any magic you want to do that needs to come into effect in the near future. It utilizes three cords, each twenty-one inches in length. One is red in color, one white, and one green. In ritual, sprinkle them with the salted water and then hold them in the smoke of the incense. Sit and plait the three cords together while concentrating on the magic you want to take effect (remember to see it as having been successful). As you plait them, say:

> **"I bind these cords together as I would bind my spell.**
> **I bind the cords; I bind the spell.**
> **I bind my power—work it well!"**

Carry the cords to the east and hold them up. Repeat to the south, west, and north, then return to the altar. Sit, stand, or kneel and concentrate on the aim of the spell—the intent. Build up the power and energy within yourself as you feel best. See the finished act. Then stand and, stamping out a rhythm, dance three times around the circle deosil. Tie a knot in the triple cord each time you pass the east, making three knots in all—one at each end and one in the middle— directing your power into the knots as you tie them. Tie the knot in the middle first, then the end ones. Return to the altar and lay the knotted cords on it. Touch your wand to it and say:

> **"Here is my power, deep in these cords. It is tied within so that it may not escape."**

Take the knotted cords to the east and hold them up, saying:

> **"The Air will carry this magic."**

Go to the south and say:

> **"The Fire will marry this magic."**

Go to the west and say:

> **"The Water will bear this magic."**

Go to the north and say:

> **"The Earth will wear this magic."**

Return to the altar and say:

> **"I bind these cords together as I would bind my spell.**
> **I bind the cords; I bind the spell.**
> **I bind my power—work it well!"**

Lay the knotted cords on the altar, leaving them there till you have ended the circle. Afterward, keep the cords on your person for seven days, sleeping with them under your pillow at night. Then bury them beneath an oak tree or a thorn bush. The magic with which you have imbued them will continue to emerge from the buried cords over a long period of time, supplementing any further magic you do for that particular person or purpose.

Color Magic

Color can be used in all forms of magic to reinforce it and help make it especially effective. Previously you've seen how it can be utilized in candle magic, and in poppet and placket magic. It can be worked into many other forms of magic also, such as with talismans. Basically, whatever magic you are planning, consider whether or not it could be enhanced by the use of color. Burning additional color candles, using colored paper or other material, tying colored cords or ribbons to objects, shining colored lights—all these are ways to reinforce with color. Be guided by the table of color associations, and by the colors for the days of the week and zodiacal signs that have been discussed.

Love Magic

The main thing to remember with love magic is that you must never interfere with another's free will. It is all too easy to think that by making someone else love you, you are not actually harming him or her. In a sense you are not, but the very fact that you are making the person do something that he or she would not normally do, is enough to classify that magic as negative. What, then, can be done to attract someone to you? There are two possibilities. The first is simply to work on yourself, to make yourself so attractive that others are *naturally* drawn to you. But if you've been working on that and it still seems you're not getting anywhere, then there is some magic that you can do that will not be negative. Work a love spell to bring *someone* to you, rather than a specific person.

Let's say that you are a young woman who is strongly drawn to a young man, whom we'll call Tony, but the attraction does not go both ways. In other words, Tony doesn't even seem to know you exist! Start by making a list of all the things you like about Tony: his hair color, height, eyes, physique, interests, musical taste, dress, and so on. If you know his birth date then add his sun sign to your list.

This, then, is the ideal person, in your eyes. Now, for the purposes of the magic you're about to do, forget the name Tony. Look at the list as just the "ingredients" of the person you want to fall for you. You can now work magic—candle-burning, poppet, placket, cord, or whatever—to draw to you *someone* who fits this description. Be sure to work the spell without Tony specifically in mind, just the "Tony type" you have detailed. When the magic works (as it will), if the gods feel it is right it may well turn out that it is Tony who comes running, after all. But it may also be an entirely different person you weren't even aware of before, but who fits the detailed description you put together. You may then forget all about Tony! The point is that you will have done potent love magic without directing it specifically at Tony. You will not, therefore, have been working against his, or anyone else's, free will. Below are a couple of ways of working love magic using this method.

Poppet Love Spell

Make a poppet to represent yourself, then make a second one to represent the type of person you want to attract. *Do not put a name on that second doll.* Stuff the dolls with such herbs as Adam & Eve root, elderflower, rosebuds, motherwort, yarrow, vervain, and the like (see Appendices: Magical Properties of Herbs). Concentrate on true love whilst you make the poppets. Lay them on the altar with your wand across them. Also on the altar have a twenty-one-inch length of red or pink ribbon. Light the altar candle, the incense, and the day candle. Sit for a few moments reviewing the situation: the type of person you want to bring to you (remember, no names!) and your desire for true love and happiness. In your own words, call upon the Lord and the Lady to witness the rite you are about to perform. Having invited the gods to witness the rite, state the purpose of it:

> **"I am here to bring lasting love and happiness to myself, [Your name], that I may be filled with joy and contentment."**

Take up the poppet of yourself and sprinkle it with the salted water, then hold it in the smoke of the incense, turning it so that all of it gets censed. As you do this, say words to the effect:

> **"Here am I, [Your name]. It is me in every detail. All that I do to this representation, I do to me, [Your name]. So Mote It Be."**

Return it to the altar, take up the second poppet, and sprinkle it with the salted water, then hold it in the smoke of the incense, turning it so that all of it gets censed. As you do this, say words to the effect:

> **"Here is he/she whom I would love. This represents all those qualities that I want and need; all that I desire in another. So Mote It Be."**

Now lay both poppets side by side on the altar and, holding your wand, lay it across the two figures while you concentrate on seeing yourself completely happy and fulfilled, as a result of this ritual. (It's best to concentrate solely on yourself and your love and happiness, without picturing another with you.) Remember, in magic you should see the thing completed, rather than simply working, so see yourself completely happy and filled with love.

Now take up both poppets and hold them facing one another, one in each hand, slightly apart. Say:

> **"May these two individuals be drawn together and become one. Let the love so flow between them that they are inseparable."**

Slowly move your two hands together until the poppets are against each other, face to face. Then take up the silk ribbon and bind it around the two figures, saying:

> **"May they cling to one another and stay together as one. No more shall they be separate; no more alone. Each shall be fast together with the other. So Mote It Be."**

Tie the ribbon and lay the figures back on the altar. Lay your wand across them. For the next few minutes you may either sit and direct power into the figures or dance around the circle to build the power and then direct it into them. When you feel you have done this for long enough, give thanks to the Lord and the Lady, in your own words. Close the circle. You may repeat this ritual on a daily, weekly, or monthly basis, if you wish. After closing the circle, carefully wrap the poppets in a piece of white linen and put them away somewhere where they will not be disturbed.

Love Poppets

Candle Love Spell

Set up the altar with an astral candle for yourself on one side and an orange candle (for attraction) beside it. On the other side of the altar have a white candle to represent the unknown lover, with a pink candle (for love) beside it. The day candle should be a green one and this ritual should be done on a Friday, just prior to the full moon.

Light the altar candle, the incense, and the day candle. Sit for a few moments concentrating on seeing yourself completely happy and fulfilled, as a result of this ritual. (It's best to concentrate solely on yourself and your love and happiness, without picturing another with you.) Remember, in magic you should see the thing completed, rather than simply working, so see yourself completely happy and filled with love. In your own words, call upon the Lord and the Lady to witness the rite you are about to perform. Having invited the gods to witness the rite, state the purpose of it:

> **"I am here to bring lasting love and happiness to myself, [Your name] that I may be filled with joy and contentment."**

Take up the astral candle and, with the burin, inscribe your name along its length. You can do this in one of the magical alphabets if you wish, though regular letters will do. Then consecrate the candle: rub it with the oil, outward from the center toward the ends, slowly turning it so that the entire candle gets oiled. Then hold it in the smoke of the incense, again turning it so that all of it gets censed. As you do this, say words to the effect:

> **"Here is myself, [Your name]. It is me in every detail. All that I do to this representation, I do to me. So Mote It Be."**

Stand the candle in its place on the altar. Take up the orange candle. Do the same thing; consecrate it and inscribe it with the word "attraction." Then say:

> **"Here is Attraction. It is with me and all about me. So Mote It Be."**

Place the candle alongside your astral candle. Take up the white one on the other side of the altar; consecrate it and inscribe it with the words "true love." Say:

> **"Here is the true love I seek; the other half that makes me whole. So Mote It Be."**

Take up the pink candle; consecrate it and inscribe it with the word "love." Say:

> **"Here is the love that is brought to us, filling our lives with all that we desire. So Mote It Be."**

Place that candle alongside the white candle.

Now spend some time concentrating on seeing yourself happy, joyful, and filled with love, as a result of this ritual. Light first your astral candle, then the orange one. Let them burn for a few moments then light the white candle and the pink candle. Sit with them all burning for a few more moments. Take the white and the pink candles and move them slowly across the surface of the altar, toward your astral candle and its attendant orange one. You can do this either in stages or, very slowly, in one long movement. As the candles move across, be aware of love coming into your life, of a sense of completeness. When the four candles are all together, know that you have now caught the attention of another and that the wheels of love are in motion. Give thanks to the Lord and the Lady, in your own words, and close the circle. You may leave the candles burning until they have burned themselves out, or you may repeat this ritual on a weekly or monthly basis. If on a weekly basis, extinguish the candles after an hour and relight them at the next performance of the ritual, timing things so that the candles all come together close to, and just before, the full moon. If on a monthly basis, repeat the ritual in its entirety each time, moving the white and pink candles from their starting positions across to the other two. You can keep this up repeatedly, doing the ritual every month using the same candles, until they have burned down.

Both of the above spells can also be done to deepen a love that is already there, to cement a marriage, to help a family bond. Don't be afraid of experimenting. Write your own rituals, which can be based on those I have given. So long as you keep the Wiccan Rede in mind, you will do all right.

Remembering and reliving can raise power. Raise more by drumming, chanting, clapping, pounding, breathing, singing, dancing, or any other active method you favor. Let the feelings flow free; let the power surge through you.

—Amber K, *True Magick*

Sex Magic

As you have seen, the main ingredient in working magic is the power that you raise. Without this power, no magic can be performed. In such forms as candle-burning, this power-raising may be low-key, but it's there in the concentration of inscribing the candles, for example. There are many ways to raise power: chanting, dancing, awakening the kundalini (see below), drumming, scourging, and through sex. Sex magic is the art of using the sexual experience, and especially the orgasm, for magical purposes. According to Dr. Jonn Mumford (*Sexual Occultism*), the most important psycho-physiological event in the life of a human is the orgasm. That orgasm is achieved following much the same pattern as is found in magical working and power raising—it starts slowly and very gradually builds to a climax. The literal climax of sex magic is the orgasm. Just how that is achieved is unimportant, so sex magic can be done by the Solitary just as effectively as by a couple or by a whole coven. All that matters is that the orgasm be the time of directing the power generated to the target selected.

During the excitement of sex, all of your senses become heightened, attuning you to the psychic realm much more sharply than is the case in your normal state. Just before, during, and immediately after the sexual climax, the mind is in a state of hypersensitivity, and this can be especially useful for working magic. (Many people have experienced timelessness, accompanied by subjective sensations of being "absorbed" by a sex partner during orgasm.) Successful sex magic involves interplay of all of these factors. When working sex magic, the magical process can be broken down into the following steps. First is the planning stage, when you settle upon the exact details of how to proceed. This includes the "goal" to aim at, the methods of arousal you will use, what to visualize during the act and, especially at the climax, what to set your sights on at the release of the power. Then comes the actual practice—the magical, sensual, and sexual foreplay that develops into the serious buildup of that power. Finally, there is the "explosion" of the power generated—the orgasm that sends the magical force to its target.

Perhaps with eyes closed, start by gently caressing your body, not especially trying for arousal but with gentle thoughts that will lead in that direction. At this point, the breasts and genitals are best avoided; concentrate more on the hair, face, arms, and legs instead. Thoughts can be on anyone or anything that helps with sexual direction at this time, since arousal will eventually need to come about. Gradually include breasts and genitals in your caressing, with the aim of becoming totally aroused, eventually concentrating primarily on the genital area. At some point, it will be necessary to shift the focus of your mind to the object of the magic. You should have become sufficiently aroused, by that point, that shifting this focus will not lose you the sexual stimulation.

Proceed by gently rocking back and forth, if that helps, and focusing on the person to whom the power will be directed; as always in magic, see in your mind's eye a successful result. Try to hold off the orgasm as long as possible while working on the visualization. When you can no longer hold off, at the moment of orgasm see the power shooting out from you to the target like a bolt of lightning. One Witch has described the release as a force "that pulses from my lower chakras, surging up through the others before blasting out of my crown chakra, at the top of my head."[9]

As I've said, the method of achieving orgasm is unimportant. For this reason any variety of sexual stimulation methods may be employed. This type of magic has been performed by Solitary Witches for generations; probably the majority induced the power release with their hands and fingers but some Witches certainly used such magical items as Priapic (phallic) wands. These days, such seemingly non-magical items as dildos and vibrators are also used. Sex magic is simply one method of doing magic out of many, though it's certainly not for everyone.

[9]Fiona Horne, *Witch: A Magical Journey* (New York: Thorsons, 2000).

I have mentioned the chakras (pronounced *sharkrers*) and raising the kundalini. The chakras—a Sanskrit word—are psychic centers of the body that coincide with various glands. There are seven of them, following the line of the spine from its base up to the head and then on to the top of the head. They also correspond to the seven colors of the light spectrum. Ancient wisdom teaches that these psychic centers can be opened, in order, to produce a force known as the kundalini, which surges upward. This is also known as the "serpent power." Essentially, it is power-raising within your body.

The base chakra is at the perineum, midway between the anus and the genitals. Its color is red. The next chakra comes at the fifth lumbar, at the suprarenal glands, which is equated with orange. Then there is the solar plexus at the lyden, which is yellow. The heart at the thymus is green. The throat at the thyroid is blue. The position of the third eye (between and slightly above the eyebrows) is the pineal gland and is indigo. And the "crown chakra" is at the pituitary and is violet in color. One way of raising energy is to meditate and concentrate on these seven centers. They can be activated by causing them to rotate, in order. During sexual activity, the gradual buildup toward the orgasm is automatically accompanied by (perhaps caused by) this chakra activity.

To energize the chakras, whether as an adjunct to the performing of sexual magic or for raising power for other forms of magic, sit quietly and relax. Do your light-building exercise. From the culmination of doing this white-light building, see that light become red and focus it onto the first chakra point. See, in your mind, that chakra become a vibrant red and start to spin, in a clockwise direction. (I find it helps to imagine it like one of the swirling wheels of light and sparks seen at fireworks displays.) See and feel the red light flowing into the perineum area. When you feel you have absorbed a sufficient amount of this energy, let the light move up to the next chakra area, changing color from red to orange as it does. See and feel the orange light now swirling at the position of that second chakra; at the suprarenal. Again, as you breathe deeply feel the orange light energizing that section of your body. Continue in this fashion, gradually moving the energy and changing the light color, so that it moves up to all seven chakra points. When you've done them all, let the light change back to white and again spread out to envelop the whole cone of power about you.

> *All force is vibration . . . Then we see the evolution of force in vibration brought up to the point wherein man becomes one with the Creative Energy, or the Godhead.*
>
> —Edgar Cayce, *Reading No. 900-422*

Protection

Under the "Preparations" and "Precautions" sections in chapter 13, I have given things you should do before working magic. Now let's look at some specifics of protection in various circumstances. However, first let me emphasize the necessity of doing the deep breathing and white-light building as a protective measure, to the point where you should do this at the start of *every morning*, if you feel you are in any situation where you need constant protection. The cone of power you build will not only protect you from psychic attack but also from physical harm, turning away hurtful intentions and potential evil.

A talisman can be a useful and effective tool of protection, and I will detail the making of those in the next section. Similarly, amulets, such as protective herbs and roots, can work well. Mirrors have been used for centuries as a magical means of reflecting away negative energies. They are used in the ancient Chinese art of feng shui (pronounced *fung shway*). They are also an essential ingredient in the Witch's bottle, which is detailed below. Used by themselves, flat mirrors are effective while concave mirrors will "turn enemies upside down." Convex mirrors, on the other hand, can be far-reaching. If you know the direction from which harm or animosity will be coming, then hang the mirror facing that way. If you don't know, then hang four mirrors about your home—one facing outward in each direction. A number of small mirrors hanging in a bush or tree close to the house entrance makes a good protection.

Wind chimes can also be protective, as can bells. The idea originated with the belief that the sound of the chimes would frighten away harmful spirits, but there is more to it than that. Sound is vibration and vibration has an effect on everything. Positive vibrations, from such as wind chimes, can affect negative things, thus serving to protect. Incense also can serve as a protective measure. Again, the burning of incense and its resultant smoke can cause positive vibrations and well-being.

One way to cleanse a house or apartment, ensuring protection for all who live there, is to sprinkle the corner of every room and every closet with salted water and to cense it with burning incense. I'd suggest calling on the Lord and the Lady to protect while doing this. Magical baths and washes can also be used for protection. Bathing in water into which herbs have been put to soak is a good way of protecting yourself. Look at the Magical Properties of Herbs list in the appendices and see which ones are connected with protection (such as basil, bay, dill, fennel, and rosemary). The herbs can either be thrown directly into the bath or they can be collected in a muslin bag and allowed to hang into the water.

There are numerous spells for protection. You can construct your own, based on the examples of candle-burning magic and similar, previously described. One suggestion would be to place an astral candle for yourself in the center of the altar and surround it with a number of yellow or gold candles for protection. In *Wicca For Life* (Citadel) I give some specifics, both for personal protection and for protection of the house.

The pentagram—the traditional symbol of Witchcraft—is a protective sign in itself. Wearing a pentagram serves as a talismanic protection. It represents the life force and, as such, wards against negativity. Wear a pentagram either in the form of a pendant or a ring. I have even known some Witches who have obtained a penta-gram tattoo.

All Witches should make a Witch's bottle, which has been the primary protection used by Witches for hundreds of years. The idea behind it is to not only protect the maker from any negativity directed at him or her, but to actually send back that negativity. The more the sender tries to harm you, the more he (or she) will harm himself. Take a small jar with a screw-type lid. Fill it at least half full with broken glass, broken mirror, rusty nails, pins, needles, screws, old razor blades, and so on—in effect, anything sharp. Then urinate into the jar to fill it, thus personalizing the jar and its contents. A woman can make it an especially effective bottle by including some menstrual blood. Screw on the lid and seal it with tape or wax. It should then be buried in the ground at least twelve inches deep (so that it is below any frost line). This should be done in some isolated spot where it will not be disturbed. So long as it stays there it will work for you. I recommend doing a new Witch bottle once a year, just in case the old one somehow gets cracked or broken. If you live in the city, it is worth making a special trip out to the country to bury your bottle.

Talismans and Amulets

A talisman is a human-made tool designed for magical purposes such as protection and an amulet is a natural object used for similar magical purposes; both are consecrated for use, imbuing them with magical power. Talismans and amulets are used mostly for protection but can also be used for a variety of other things, such as to bring luck, love, and money, as an aid to healing, and so on. Let's look at talismans first, since they have to be made from scratch.

Talismans can be made from virtually any material. The easiest to work with is paper (or parchment), but they can also be made of wood, metal, bone, ivory, and so on. Many occult stores and catalogs advertise ready-made, commercial talismans for various purposes. Remember, however, that the most effective (and powerful) magic is that done by the person most connected to the need. Any talisman that you make yourself, however crude it may seem, will therefore be far more powerful than one bought from a store or made for you by someone else.

At the beginning of this chapter, when talking about candle-burning magic, I gave a table of correspondences for the days of the week and associations for each day. I'll repeat that here but instead of including the colors, I will give the planets and metals associated with the days.

DAYS OF THE WEEK

Day	Planet	Metal	Association
Monday	Moon	silver	ancestors; childbearing; dreams; healing; instinct; memory; merchandise; purity; theft; virginity
Tuesday	Mars	iron	enemies; initiation; loyalty; matrimony; prison; protection; war; wealth
Wednesday	Mercury	mercury	business; communication; debt; fear; loss; travel
Thursday	Jupiter	tin	clothing; desires; harvests; honor; marriage; oaths; riches; treaties
Friday	Venus	copper	beauty; family life; friendship; fruitfulness; growth; harmony; love; nature; pleasures; sexuality; strangers; waters
Saturday	Saturn	lead	building; doctrine; freedom; gifts; life; protection; real estate; sowing; strength; tenacity
Sunday	Sun	gold	agriculture; beauty; creativity; fortune; hope; money; self-expression; victory

From this you can see which metal is best to use when making a talisman; for example, if you want a talisman to promote love, you would do best to make it on a Friday and to use copper, the metal of Venus, the goddess of love. The one obvious problem, from this table, is Wednesday and its connection to mercury, since it's not possible to make a talisman of liquid mercury (although it could be contained in a small bottle or other vessel); these days aluminum is substituted for that metal. All of the above can still be made on paper, parchment, wood, and so on, if you prefer. Actually, copper is a favorite metal, for whatever purpose, simply because it is easy to work with (also pleasant to look at and relatively easy to obtain). The above listing shows the preferred metal, but you can still deviate if you wish.

Symbols of a wide variety from almost every conceivable source are employed to provide character and to give specificity to the dynamic purpose for which the talisman has been constructed.

—Israel Regardie, *How to Make and Use Talismans*

What you put on that paper, metal, or wood to make a talisman depends upon its intended purpose. There are many old books of magic that show a wide variety of designs. But simply copying a design, however ancient, without knowing its full meaning can be hazardous. It's much better to use something that you completely understand and that is designed specifically for your personal need.

The easiest way to carry a talisman is to wear it, so discs that can be hung on chains are the most common form (and small copper discs can be purchased at craft stores). If you'd rather, you can place the talisman in a little pouch and carry it in your pocket. The choice is yours. To be effective, talismans need to be worn or carried on the person and, at night, slept with under the pillow. In this way there is a direct connection with you, a two-way exchange of energies.

On the front, or obverse, of the talisman put something that will personalize it, that will make it yours specifically. This could simply be your name and birth date, Witch name, and astrological signs, or anything like that. I would suggest using your Witch name, if you have one, since you are working with magic. I would further suggest that this be put onto the talisman in one of the so-called magical scripts. There are a number of these and I include some in the appendix, for reference. Many people who use these magic alphabets are ignorant of the original reasons for their use (to put power into the writing) and try to impress others by showing their proficiency with, for example, Theban; they write it as rapidly as they would everyday English. Doing this, however, actually shows a tremendous ignorance, since it defeats the whole purpose of using that script. If you were using ordinary, everyday writing, over-familiarity would bring about a tendency to scribble down what was to be written without really thinking about the actual writing itself—the formation of the individual letters. By using an alphabet with which you are not too familiar, on the other hand, you really have to concentrate on the actual forming of every single letter. In this way you are putting your energy, your power or *mana*, into that writing. The more power that goes into the making of a talisman, the better; because it will be more effective. With paper you will use ink to mark it; with metal you will need to engrave it. Scratching the design into the metal can be done fairly easily with any sharp engraving tool, even a sharp nail. In wood you can carve it or burn it.

On the obverse of the talisman write your Witch name in the alphabet of your choice along with your birth date or astrological signs. How you position these is up to you. Here are a couple of suggestions for someone named Heather, born March 11, 1984.

Suggested Layouts–Obverse

The other side—the reverse—is, perhaps, the more important one. Here you will put the object of the talisman: love, protection, healing, money, and so on. You could simply write the appropriate word, using a magic alphabet, or you could do something a little more intricate and therefore a little more powerful. I suggest a sigil based on a magic square. This square is made up of the nine primary numbers arranged in such a way that they add up to fifteen (known as the "constant") in every direction: across each line, up and down each line, and even diagonally across from corner to corner:

4	9	2
3	5	7
8	1	6

Now look for a moment at the key word for the talisman: love, money, protection, and so on. Let's use "strength" as an example. Numerologically, the word strength is a three number:

1	2	3	4	5	6	7	8	9
A	B	C	D	E	F	G	H	I
J	K	L	M	N	O	P	Q	R
S	T	U	V	W	X	Y	Z	

Strength: S = 1, T = 2, R = 9, E = 5, N = 5, G = 7, T = 2, H = 8, which becomes $1 + 2 + 9 + 5 + 5 + 7 + 2 + 8 = 39; 3 + 9 = 12; 1 + 2 = 3$

Going back to the magic square, a small circle will be placed on it to show the start of the word (S = 1) and a second small circle for the end of it (H = 8). A small square will be used to indicate that total number, three. With lines connecting all the letters/numbers, you will construct a pattern, or *sigil*, that represents the word "strength." Note that there are two 5s in the numerological equivalent of the word. To show this, a symbol is used that is, in effect, a "stop and go" sign: ─▷◁─

The word "strength," drawn over the magic square, will look like this:

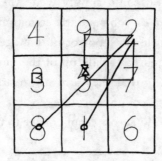

Talisman, Basic Figure

When that figure is then separated from the background square, it stands alone like this:

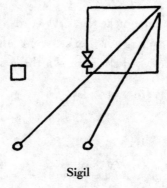

Sigil

This, then, is the sigil that is drawn on the reverse of the talisman and has all the power of the Witch focused on the word "strength." It should be made on a Saturday and, ideally, should be done on a piece of lead, though copper or paper will do.

An alternative symbol to place by itself on the reverse of the talisman would be one of the traditional magic squares. This is an arrangement of numbers (or letters) in the form of a square, similar to the one we used above but more elaborate, utilizing far more numbers. These magic squares were introduced into Europe from ancient India and China over fifteen hundred years ago. Cornelius Agrippa

(1486–1535), a famous ceremonial magician, constructed seven different magic squares that he aligned with the seven planets: Saturn, Jupiter, Mars, Sun, Venus, Mercury, and Moon. These have become standards in ritual magic and are even used in Witchcraft, tying in with the seven days of the week of the above chart. They can be used in themselves, without the need to place a sigil over them. For a strength talisman, as in our previous example, you would simply use the Saturn square, on a Saturday, again preferably on a piece of lead. The seven squares are as follows:

4	9	2
3	5	7
8	1	6

Saturn

4	14	15	1
9	7	6	12
5	11	10	8
16	2	3	13

Jupiter

11	24	7	20	3
4	12	25	8	16
17	5	13	21	9
10	18	1	14	22
23	6	19	2	15

Mars

6	32	3	34	35	1
7	11	27	28	8	30
19	14	16	15	23	24
18	20	22	21	17	13
25	29	10	9	26	12
36	5	33	4	2	31

Sun

22	47	16	41	10	35	4
5	23	43	17	42	11	29
30	6	24	49	81	36	12
13	31	7	25	43	19	37
38	14	32	1	26	44	20
21	39	8	33	2	27	45
46	15	40	9	34	3	28

Venus

8	58	59	5	4	62	63	1
49	15	14	52	53	11	10	56
41	23	22	44	48	19	18	45
32	34	38	29	25	35	39	28
40	26	27	37	36	30	31	33
17	47	46	20	21	43	42	24
9	55	54	12	13	51	50	16
64	2	3	61	60	6	7	57

Mercury

37	78	29	70	21	62	13	54	5
6	38	79	30	71	22	63	14	46
47	7	39	80	31	72	23	55	15
16	48	8	40	81	32	64	24	56
57	17	49	9	41	73	33	65	25
26	58	18	50	1	42	74	34	66
67	27	59	10	51	2	43	75	35
36	68	19	60	11	52	3	44	76
77	28	69	20	61	12	53	4	45

Moon

Squares of Saturn, Jupiter, Mars, Sun, Venus, Mercury, Moon

There are a large number of other magic squares for a wide range of purposes, the majority comprised of letters rather than numbers. These are arranged so that the words read the same from the left, right, up, and down. Many of them are illustrated in S. L. MacGregor-Mathers's translation of *The Book of Sacred Magic of Abra-Melin, the Mage* (1932). If using one of these, again I'd suggest using one of the magic alphabets for the letters. See the next page for two examples:

S	A	T	O	R
A	R	E	P	O
T	E	N	E	T
O	P	E	R	A
R	O	T	A	S

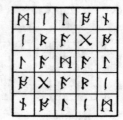

Sator Square of Protection

M	I	L	O	N
I	R	A	G	O
L	A	M	A	L
O	G	A	R	I
N	O	L	I	M

Milon Square of Divination

Great care is necessary when constructing magic squares. It should be done in a consecrated circle or at least after building the protective cone of white light. The lines should be drawn in black ink, the numbers (or letters) written in red ink. The red must not touch the black anywhere. All should be drawn with the paper or parchment set up so that your shadow doesn't fall over the work.

As mentioned earlier, an amulet is a natural object that is used in the same way as a talisman. Examples of well-known amulets are the four-leaf clover and the rabbit's foot. Both are natural objects but are carried by many people to bring luck. Another typical one, recognized and used in Witchcraft, is a stone with a natural hole through it. Known as a "Hag Stone," it represents the vagina of the goddess and is perfect to carry to promote fertility. Another example is a simple acorn, carried for strength. Similarly, in some parts of the world, a bear's claw or lion's tooth is a strength amulet. You can find potential amulets everywhere. Just decide what is right for you. If you mark or engrave it, it technically becomes a talisman but that doesn't matter; these are only labels.

Whether amulet or talisman, to complete the magical object it needs to be consecrated. The following is a suggested consecration. It may be done as part of another ritual. If so, it should be done before the Cakes and Wine rite.

In the ritual circle, sprinkle the object with salted water and hold it in the smoke of the incense. Say:

> **"Herne and Epona, here is my talisman/amulet. Bless it for its intended use, that it may serve me well, as I carry it. Let it be the focus of your love and let it keep me from all harm. So Mote It Be."**

Lay it on the altar, touch your wand to it, and concentrate your thoughts on its purpose. See it protecting you, strengthening you, bringing you love (or whatever the design of it may be). Then take it up and wear it, or carry it on your person in some way.

Herb Magic

Herbs are used a lot in magic, both as an ingredient and as magical tools in themselves. In magic, it doesn't matter whether you use fresh or dried herbs. In fact, dried herbs are probably more popular since they are more convenient. They can be used burned, like incense, or stuffed into poppets. They can also be carried, for their own magical properties. (For a full listing of the magical properties of herbs, see Appendices.)

Herbs and plants are often chosen by the planetary signs that govern them:

❋ The Sun rules such plants as angelica, bay, carnation, celandine, chamomile, chrysanthemum, eyebright, goldenseal, heliotrope, lovage, marigold, peony, rosemary, rowan, rue, St. John's wort, sesame, sunflower, and witch hazel.

❀ The Moon rules adder's tongue, bladderwrack, cabbage, calamus, chickweed, club moss, cucumber, gardenia, grape, Irish moss, jasmine, lettuce, lily, moonwort, poppy, potato, turnip, willow, wintergreen.

❀ Mercury rules agaric, bean, bittersweet, bracken, caraway, celery, clover, dill, fennel, fenugreek, fern, flax, goat's rue, horehound, lavender, lemongrass, lemon verbena, lily of the valley, mandrake, marjoram, may apple, mint, mulberry, parsley, peppermint, pimpernel, wax plant.

❀ Venus rules alder, alfalfa, aloes, wood, apple, aster, avocado, bachelor's buttons, barley, bedstraw, birch, blackberry, bleeding heart, blueflag, buckwheat, burdock, caper, cardamom, catnip, coltsfoot, columbine, corn, cowslip, crocus, cyclamen, daffodil, daisy, elder, feverfew, foxglove, geranium, goldenrod, groundsel, heather, hibiscus, hyacinth, iris, lady's mantle, larkspur, lilac, magnolia, maidenhair, mugwort, myrtle, oats, orchid, orris, passionflower, pea, pear, periwinkle, persimmon, plum, primrose, ragwort, raspberry, rhubarb, rose, rye, spearmint, spikenard, strawberry, sweet pea, tansy, tomato, tulip, valerian, vervain, violet, wheat, willow.

❀ Mars rules allspice, anemone, basil, bloodroot, briony, broom, cactus, carrot, chili pepper, coriander, cumin, damiana, deer's tongue, dragon's blood, garlic, gentian, ginger, gorse, hawthorne, High John the Conqueror, holly, hops, horseradish, hound's tongue, leek, mustard, nettle, onion, pennyroyal, pepper, peppermint, pine, poke root, prickly ash, radish, shallot, sloe, snapdragon, thistle, tobacco, Venus's-flytrap, woodruff, wormwood.

❀ Jupiter rules agrimony, anise, betony, borage, chestnut, cinquefoil, clove, dandelion, dock, endive, fig, honeysuckle, horse chestnut, houseleek, hyssop, linden, liverwort, maple, meadowsweet, nutmeg, sage, sarsparilla, sassafras, witch grass.

❀ Saturn rules beech, beet, belladonna, boneset, buckthorn, comfrey, datura, elm, hellebore, hemlock, hemp, henbane, horsetail, ivy, knot weed, lady's slipper, mimosa, morning glory, pansy, poplar, quince, skullcap, skunk cabbage, slippery elm, Solomon's seal, wolf's bane, yew.

From the above it can be determined, in general terms, which herbs are best used for what purposes; for example, the Sun is associated with beauty, creativity, hope, money, self-expression, and victory. Therefore, any herbal magic you intend to do for any of these purposes should make use of one or more of those herbs listed under the Sun, above. Here are the associations for the other planets:

❀ Moon: childbearing, dreams, healing, memory, theft, virginity

❀ Mercury: business, communication, debt, fear, loss, travel

❀ Venus: beauty, family life, friendship, fruitfulness, growth, harmony, love, nature, pleasures, sexuality, strangers, youth

❀ Mars: courage, enemies, exorcism, lust, matrimony, protection, sexual potency, war, wealth

❀ Jupiter: clothing, desires, legal matters, oaths and treaties, prosperity and riches

❀ Saturn: building, endings, freedom, exorcisms, gifts, longevity, real estate, sowing, tenacity, visions

As an example of herbal use, if you are doing magical work to ensure the best outcome of a lawsuit then you would look for herbs ruled by Jupiter (for legal matters). Sage is one of these, so burn sage as your incense for that ritual. When doing magic for protection, use an herb of Mars, such as garlic or High John the Conqueror. You might make a poppet of the person needing protection and stuff it with one or more of these herbs. For magic dealing with real estate you'd use an herb of Saturn, and so on.

You can steep herbs in oil and then use that oil for anointing candles, poppets, plackets, talismans, and so on. You can also make herbal infusions by steeping a tablespoon of an herb in about a cup of boiling water. Let it sit for several minutes, as though making tea, then strain the liquid. This can be used as a magical wash, to clean a room or even the whole house. You can even use it to wash your hair or add it to bath water.

Dried herbs can be crushed and powdered, then sprinkled in the corners of rooms and closets, under carpets, and along shelves to produce specific effects. They can, of course, be used in sachets and potpourris. Although I'm saying "herbs," you can apply much of this to dried flowers also.

> *There is more to magical success than following a set of instructions, more to it than checking the cosmic conditions . . . all the props in the world won't create magic without the concentration, focus, and pure, unbridled desire. When combined, they bring phenomenal results.*
>
> —Dorothy Morrison, *Everyday Magic*

15

Divination

*Divination is really a spiritual diagnosis
whereby we try to discover what subtle
influences are at work in our affairs. It can be
exceedingly helpful if rightly done . . . A
divination should be regarded as a weather
vane which shows which way the winds of the
invisible forces are blowing.*

—Dion Fortune, *Practical Occultism in Daily Life*

ost Witches practice some form of divination. Many
favor the cards—both regular and tarot—while others
prefer astrology, crystal-gazing, palmistry, and similar
practices. You don't *have to* practice divination; there are
many Witches who do not. But in case you want to, here are some
suggestions. There are certainly many hundreds of books written on
all of the different forms. My own, *The Fortune-Telling Book* (Visible
Ink Press, 2003), is an encyclopedia covering all possible forms,
should you need to review what is available before settling on something. For now, let's look at skrying (crystal-gazing), sortilege, cartomancy, and radiesthesia (pendulum) as typical examples.

By divination we mean the attempt to elicit from some higher power or supernatural being the answers to questions beyond the range of ordinary human understanding . . . In nearly all cultures specially gifted people, seers or mediums, are recognized as affording the necessary link with the supernatural world.

—Michael Loewe and Carmen Blacker,
Oracles and Divination

Skrying

This can be practiced using virtually any reflective surface. The first thing most people think of is a crystal ball, but a good one can be expensive and hard to find. Affordable acrylic (plastic) ones are available, but these scratch easily and the last thing you want is any blemish on the surface that will break your concentration when using it. To get the feel of the practice, before deciding whether or not this is for you, use a glass of water. Use a clear, uncolored, undecorated tumbler filled to the rim with water. Stand it on a blank surface (black velvet cloth is recommended) and position it in front of you as you sit at a table. You will be looking down onto the surface of the water. Use a single candle for illumination, and place it behind you so that you don't see it reflected in the water. The black cloth it stands on is used so there is nothing visible around it, to distract you.

Before you start, decide what it is you want to see, then clear your mind (with deep breathing and white-light building) and gaze into the water. Don't try to imagine anything there, and don't stare without blinking (your normal blinking is fine and won't interfere with the skrying). Simply stare into the water and let anything come that may.

Some people see the crystal/water get cloudy. This then thins and a picture is seen. For others, the picture seems to materialize without the clouds. What you eventually see is similar to looking at a miniature television picture, though it may be moving or still, color or black and white. Just study the picture and see what is presented. Eventually the picture will fade away, and you'll be left with the blank water again. Immediately write down everything that you saw, even if it seems not to relate to what you wanted to see. What is presented is frequently in symbolic form and has to be interpreted. This is why it's a good plan—at least when you first start—to write down what you see. That then gives you ample opportunity to study what's there and think of various possible interpretations. It can be very similar to working out what a dream might mean.

Of course, you might not see anything. Don't strain. If you've seen nothing in ten to fifteen minutes, then give up. Try again another day. Persevere and you will almost certainly see things eventually. But if you are never successful, then just turn to some other form of divination; skrying is not for everyone. However, if you are successful then practice on a regular basis—at least once a week. You will get to the point where you can decide at the start what you want to see (what is happening at a distance or what someone in particular is doing) and, after the initial mind-clearing, will go on to see it.

As I said earlier, any reflective surface will work. One tool favored by many Witches is the "magic mirror." This is a black mirror that is used instead of a ball. It's also known as a speculum. You can make one simply enough by taking a picture frame (no picture in it) and painting the back of the glass with black paint. An especially elaborate—and extremely effective—one can be made from one of the old Victorian picture frames that have the oval, convex glass. Take out the glass and reverse it, so that it is concave, and paint the back of it black. You end up with an extremely effective gazing mirror that looks very magical! Highly polished copper is another favorite for gazing. Try different things.

Sortilege

This was also known as "casting lots," and has been used for thousands of years. The word "lot" comes from the Anglo-Saxon *hlot* meaning "allotment"; *gehlot* meaning "decision." The basic form of sortilege is for objects, such as stones and bones, dice and dominoes, to be thrown down after being mixed or shaken together. Their relationship on landing is interpreted, as may be the area where they land, which may be subdivided into pertinent sections. The face of the object, or the revealed color or symbol that lands uppermost, is also significant. Black and white beans are sometimes used, as are small bones, dice, shells, and stones. When dice are used it's called "cubomancy."

Today you can use such things as dice and dominoes to throw down and interpret. There are various books that give you the meanings of the different layouts.[10] I-Ching coins or sticks also can be used. A favorite divination method with Witches is casting runes, which you can make yourself. Once again, it's better to use something you make yourself rather than something commercially produced that you buy from a store. At Præneste (Palestrina), Italy, the oracle of Fortuna had a number of oak tablets kept in a chest. Each tablet was inscribed with signs and symbols. When the oracle was consulted, an acolyte would draw out one of the tablets, at random, from the chest. This would then be interpreted by the priest. Such drawing of lots could only be done on certain days of the year, at Præneste. These oak tablets were similar, in effect, to the runes, which you can make on small pieces of wood, bone, clay, or similar.

The runes themselves were an early form of writing found in all the Germanic countries in Western Europe. The word rune means "mystery" or "secret." It stems from the old Low German word *raunen*, "to cut," or "to carve," since runes were carved into wood and cut into stone. The earliest form of runes had twenty-four letters divided into three groups of eight. Later, new letters were added and, by the ninth century in Northumbria, there were thirty-three letters. In Scandinavia, however, letters dropped out and the total fell to sixteen.

[10]For example, my *Secrets of Gypsy Fortunetelling* (Llewellyn), my *The Fortune-Telling Book* (Visible Ink Press), *The Complete Illustrated Book of the Psychic Sciences* by Walter B. and Litzka R. Gibson (Doubleday).

Runes were not simply a form of writing. The individual runes would be studied and interpreted, for divination purposes. As Ralph Elliot said in *Runes: An Introduction*, "Communication . . . remained a secondary function of runic writing throughout its long history, much more common was the use of runes to invoke higher powers to affect and influence the lives and fortunes of men." In Teutonic times the main workers of magic and divination were women. The Teutonic, or "Germanic," nations embraced the peoples of High and Low German speech, Dutch speech, Danes, and Scandinavians.

The runes themselves can be made from a wide variety of substances. One popular method is to cut small pieces of wood and to mark the runes on each piece using a wood-burning tool. A suitably sized tree branch—about one-half to three-quarters of an inch in diameter—can be sliced into a number of discs and the runes carved or burned into them. Some Wiccans collect, or buy, flat pebbles and paint the runes on these. Runes may also be carved into clay tablets and fired in a kiln, and etched or engraved into metal and then mounted on small wooden tiles.

Freyr's Ættir								
	feh	úr	thorn	ós	rád	cán	geofu	wynn

Hagal's Ættir								
	hœgl	níed	ís	géar	éoh	peorð	eolhs	sygil

Tyr's Ættir								
	tír	beore	eoh	man	lagu	Ing	éðel	dœg

Runes

The number of runes produced depends on the method of divination to be followed. Most runes used for divination are based on the twenty-four original Teutonic runes. These were divided into three groups of eight runes, each group known as an *ætt* or *ættir* (Sandinavian meaning "number of eight"). They are comprised of Freyr's or Freya's Eight, Hagal's Eight, and Tiw's Eight. Freya was the daughter of Njord and the sister of Frey. She was the goddess of love and beauty. Hagal was a minor deity about whom very little is known, though these eight runes are always attributed to Hagal. Tiw, Tyr, Tiuz, or Ziu, was a sky god often identified with the Roman Mars.

The runes, their names (Anglo-Saxon names given), and meanings (various meanings are attributed to the runes, depending upon what book you consult), are presented in the chart that follows. They are sometimes referred to as *futhark* (or *futhorc*), named after the first six letters.

Rune	Name	Meanings
FREYR'S ÆTTIR		
1	feh	money; goods; the price to pay; success and happiness
2	úr	obstacles; strength, manhood; good fortune if no risks are taken
3	thorn	great spirit; petty annoyances; take no risks
4	ós	something important to be said; be wary
5	rád	ride; saddle, a journey; long overdue change; be prudently adventurous
6	cán	torch; fire; a protection; listen to the inner voice; grasp available opportunities
7	geofu	gift; sacrifice; take others' advice
8	wynn	joy; happiness; separateness; be grateful for what you already have

Rune	Name	Meanings
HAGAL'S ÆTTIR		
9	hœgl	natural forces that damage; someone else's battle; events are beyond your control
10	níed	need; constraint; necessity; needs may not be met; problems ahead
11	ís	ice; that which cools or impedes; no movement; no hasty actions
12	géar	year; harvest; time of natural change; patience
13	éoh	avertive powers; limitations; stay calm
14	peorð	secret or hidden thing; roots of a mystery; take no chances and you may be lucky
15	eolhs	defense; protection; inspiration; health; safety; be decisive
16	sygil	sun; life force; good luck; time for a change; relax and be calm
TIW'S ÆTTIR		
17	tír	honor; time to get things moving; take action
18	beorc	fertility; growth; formation of close relationships; take the long-term view
19	eoh	horse; transport; movement; assistance needed; prudence
20	man	human being; a man; strengths and weaknesses; avoid stress
21	lagu	water; sea; fluidity; conduction; trust feelings; things are not what they seem
22	Ing	heroism; withdrawal; fertility; marriage; flexibility
23	éðel	inheritance; property; practical issues to sort out; be patient, unselfish, and active
24	dœg	day; light; fruitfulness; prosperity; on the right path; make haste slowly

Most of the runes can have a different meaning if seen reversed (some few look the same whether upright or reversed). These are as follows:

Rune	Name	Reversed Meanings
FREYR'S ÆTTIR		
1	feh	love frustrated; absence of initiative
2	úr	a chance missed; weakness
3	thorn	regret a hasty decision; disruptive opposition
4	ós	an elderly person who will prove to be a nuisance; ignorance or lack of inspiration
5	rád	traveling that will interfere with plans; error in judgment
6	cán	loss or misplacement of something valued or of a friendship; self-imposed ignorance
7	geofu	
8	wynn	be careful in business matters for three days; conflict and disharmony
HAGAL'S ÆTTIR		
9	hœgl	
10	níed	
11	ís	
12	géar	
13	éoh	
14	peorð	too high expectation that will be disappointed; presence of negativity
15	eolhs	don't get involved with people who will use you; vulnerable and unprotected situation
16	sygil	

Rune	Name	Reversed Meanings
TIW'S ÆTTIR		
17	tír	don't trust him or her, he or she won't stay long; falsehood; double standards
18	beorc	worrying news concerning a relative; obstructions
19	eoh	journey by sea; disharmony; quarrels
20	man	an enemy—the next rune will tell how to handle it; alienation; underachievement
21	lagu	keep within your limits; insensitivity; lack of feeling
22	Ing	
23	éðel	beware mechanical devices; possible accident or damage; poverty; insecurity
24	dœg	

For divination purposes, to these twenty-four runes may be added a twenty-fifth that is blank on both sides. It can have various meanings, such as an indication that the question needs to be rephrased, that the forces at work are changing too quickly at present to give a definite answer, or that the answer is simply unknowable at the present time. It can also be used as a Significator (the rune representing the person being read), in the manner of such a tarot card, if you are throwing the runes for someone else. In this latter case it would be picked out and laid down ahead of any that were to be thrown, and the position of those thrown would be interpreted in relation to the significator.

No one knows exactly what each of the runes meant originally; those shamanistic meanings have been lost in time. For this reason, the above meanings, and any others found in the many books on runes, are the meanings attributed by various authors. If you wish to work extensively with runes, it is a good idea to take each individual runic character and spend time meditating upon it in order to find what it means to *you*, personally. Then stick with those interpretations.

The runes may be cast anywhere: on the ground, a table, or a prepared surface. Some feel that it should be a prepared surface, since the runes may be viewed as sacred and as "voices of the gods." Such a prepared surface may be no more than a piece of cloth kept especially for the purpose, or it can be a richly tooled piece of leather or a decorated wooden board. The surface is traditionally referred to as the "field" for the runes. Some rune-casters will draw three concentric circles on the field or in some other way divide it into three areas. Again, different specifications are found for these three areas. One possibility: center—the inner self; second—influences; outer—future events. Another possibility: center—being; second—thinking; outer—doing. Other rune-casters do not draw anything but simply throw down the runes on the field.

The runes are usually kept in a drawstring bag. It is possible to shake up the runes inside the bag and then to reach in and draw out any specific number for a random casting. Some of the castings that have become popular are:

* Odin's Rune: Many people do this to start the day, or when they reach a point of needing an indicator of where or how to proceed. The method is simply to reach into the rune pouch and, while concentrating on any problem, stir up the runes and then pull out just one. This is "Odin's Rune" and is an indicator of where your path lies. Another method is to spread all the runes on the field, face down, and then to pass your hands lightly over the backs of them until one in particular draws you. This one is turned over as "Odin's Rune." (A further suggestion is to again draw one rune at the end of the day and to see how it compares to the first one drawn.)

* Three-Rune Spread: Draw three runes from the bag (or turn over three from the full set laid face down) and interpret; for example: 1—past, 2—present, 3—future, or 1—present situation, 2—suggested course of action, 3—new situation evolving. Come up with your own ideas on using the runes.

Although numerous ways and means for contacting spirit forces and invisible realms exist, and probably always have, divination has consistently remained the global favorite. Its continuous popularity has insured almost as many methods for its use as people who use it.

—P.M.H. Atwater, *The Magical Language of Runes*

Cartomancy

Cartomancy is divination with cards. Tarot cards are most popular, though readings can be done with regular playing cards. There are also various specialized decks on the market. The tarot originated in India and was brought westward by the Romani (Gypsies). The deck is divided into two parts, known as the Major and Minor Arcana, or the Greater and Lesser Trumps. The Major Arcana consists of twenty-two cards, each with an individual title and depicting a particular scene. The Minor Arcana is sub-divided into four suits: Wands, Cups, Pentacles, and Swords. There are fourteen cards in each suit: Ace through Ten plus Page, Knight, Queen, and King. In some decks there is simply the appropriate number of symbols shown on each card (for example, four cups or seven swords). In other decks there are separate and distinct scenes for each card, which incorporate those symbols.

You can read the cards for yourself or read them for another. The start of the process is to choose one card from the deck to represent the person being read. The best way to choose this card is to go through the whole deck until you find one card that resonates for the Querent (the person being read). A shortcut (like many shortcuts, not the best way) is to pick one of the suit cards: a Cup or Pentacle for a fair-haired person; a Wand or Sword for a dark-haired person; Page or Knight for a younger person; Queen or King for an older person.

The balance of the deck is then shuffled by the Querent, while concentrating on any question(s) they may have. Usually the deck is then cut into three piles by that person, cutting to the left with the left hand. They are restacked by the reader, and then the cards are either chosen (face down) by the Querent or drawn off the top of the pile. The number of these cards will depend upon the particular spread that is being used for the reading. For the Celtic Cross spread, for example, ten cards would be chosen. I'll use that well-known spread as an example.

The Significator is laid out first, *face up*. Then the ten cards are laid down, *face down*, in the order in which they are chosen—first chosen in the first position, and so on. This is the order for the Celtic Cross:

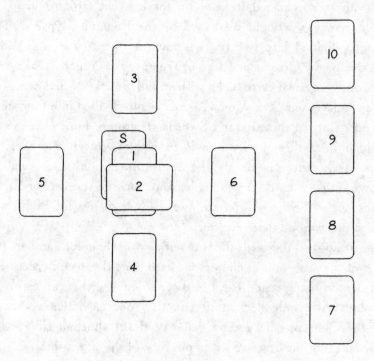

Celtic Cross Layout

First the signifactor goes in the center, then number 1 goes on top of it as "What covers him (or her)." Number 2 then goes across those two, as "What crosses him." The next four cards then go "above; below; behind; in front." The final four go up the right side as "himself; his house; his hopes and fears; the final outcome." The meanings of all these are as follows: "What covers" is the outward appearance of the person, the way he likes people to see him. It may well differ from what you, the reader, sees as the true person, the one you have picked as significator. "What crosses" represents the person(s) or situation(s) that is working against the querent at the moment. "Above" is what he aspires to. "Below," is himself deep down inside (might reveal secret hopes and/or fears). "Behind" covers the immediate past and "in front" is the immediate future . . . up to six months ahead. Number 7—"himself," is the overall person, which is a synthesis of significator and numbers 1, 3, and 4. "His house" is very close friends and close family members. "Hopes and fears" is self-explanatory. "Final outcome" is just that for this reading. You cannot see more than about a year (at most) ahead, with this or most other forms of divination. The "final outcome" is therefore only final so far as the next year is concerned.

The cards are turned over one at a time, in numerical order, and interpreted by the reader. There are standard meanings given in various books on the tarot, but try to ignore these. Every person is an individual, so is unlikely to fit the published mold. Look at what is depicted on the card and what it says to you. Say this. See how it relates to the person you are reading (even if it is yourself). Relate different cards to one another if you need to. (As I've mentioned, you'll probably see correlations between the significator, number 1, number 6, and number 7, and possibly between numbers 9 and 2 and numbers 3 and 10.) With many decks, in addition to the main characters depicted on the cards there are different images in the background of each. Sometimes it happens that a background image "speaks" to you more powerfully than does the main character. Listen to what it says.

There are many other layouts and everyone finds favorites. Try as many as you can. Some are short, featuring just three cards for past, present, and future, while others are very involved, using practically the full deck of cards. Read for yourself and read for as many people as you can, including those you know well and those you hardly know at all. This is the only way to become proficient at recognizing what the cards are trying to say. Initially you'll find yourself "reading into" what is there; in other words, adding what you happen to know about the individual rather than merely reading what is shown by the deck. It will take time but you'll learn that the cards are seldom wrong and that they have all the information you need.

Radiesthesia

This is divination using a pendulum. There are pendulums available from commercial sources but, once again, you can make your own. In fact, you can simply hang a ring on a length of ribbon or use a pendant necklace. A needle dangling from a length of thread will work. Basically any small, suspended weight will do.

Holding the chain or cord, suspend the pendulum weight so that it hangs down about seven or eight inches from your fingers. Seated at a table, let it hang down so that it is held just off the table surface.

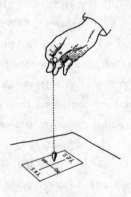

Pendulum for Radiesthesia

To allow the pendulum to hang down, I'd advise resting your elbow on the table. Some claim that the elbow should be *off* the table, but I've found that it makes for a very unsteady, tiring hold if you do that; it also doesn't make any difference to the results you obtain. Allowing the pendulum to hang down, try to keep it still so that it doesn't swing. Then ask a question. You will find that even though you try to keep it still, the pendulum will start to swing in response to the question you ask. It may swing around in a circle or, more likely, it will swing backward and forward. This could be toward you and away from you, or it could be swinging across you. Traditionally, the to and fro indicates a Yes answer to your question and the side to side, across you, indicates a No answer. If it swings around in a circle then it either cannot answer you or the question was phrased ambiguously. Try rephrasing it and see if you then get a clear answer.

You can do a lot of divination with the pendulum. You can ask questions as you think of them, though I advise trying to draw up a list ahead of time, so that you won't be asking vague or ambiguous questions. You need questions that can be answered Yes or No, but you can often get more detailed answers if you work with prepared lists, having one question lead to the next. You might want to trace a journey on a map (such as a road map or street map); perhaps following an unknown route someone else has taken. With your left finger (assuming you are right-handed) on the map, let the pendulum hang down from your right hand and to one side of the map. Trace your left finger along the route until you come to a crossroads. Then ask, "Do I go to the right?" You'll get a Yes/No answer. If No, ask "Do I go to the left?" and so on. In this way you can be led across the map by the pendulum's answers.

You can ask about the future and the past. In fact, you can cover all the usual divination questions and get responses. One of the joys of radiesthesia is its convenience. You don't have to carry any special equipment; if you wear a pendant or a ring, you're in business. In the "Color Healing" section of chapter 16, I'll talk about using the pendulum for diagnosing and prescribing.

There are many other forms of divination you should try: astrology, palmistry, numerology, and I-Ching, for example. This book is not large enough to include them all but suggested reading can be found in the bibliography. ✿

The problem with divination tools is that everyone tries to make them complicated, when, honestly, the message is the message is the message.

—Silver RavenWolf, *Solitary Witch*

16

Healing[11]

*Because discovery could mean death, witches
conducted their business in strictest secrecy.
Much of what little witches' lore survives is
found in the transcripts of the trials. These
transcripts contain testimony extracted under
torture, together with descriptions from the
witch hunters' manuals, fanciful accounts that
seem to owe more to the persecutors' lurid
imaginations than to fact. From such sources,
we gather that witches were heirs to ancient
lessons about the medicinal properties of many
substances found in nature. The witches
preserved and continued to use plant lore that
the Christian church had suppressed as
"heathen" mysteries. In patches hidden deep
in the woods, witches grew forbidden plants.*

—James Dwyer, editor, *Magic and Medicine of Plants*

[11]It's legally necessary for me to point out that the information on healing found in this book is simply an account of my experiences and of what I have gathered from folklore sources. I am not engaged in rendering medical advice; such should be sought from a competent professional. I do not advocate abandoning your health insurance coverage. First, go to a medical practitioner. When/if he or she is unable to help, then you might want to investigate the older traditional methods used by our ancestors.

ealing magic can be done with the sick person present or it can be done at a distance. It can be done in various ways, from using candles, poppets, or plackets, to direct hands-on healing. Although you might think that healing is an unselfish, positive act, you still need to get the permission of the person to be healed before proceeding with it. Many are sick for a reason . . . of which they may or may not be aware. It could be that the sickness is part of the person's life learning/experiencing process—something they have to go through. To heal them without consultation could possibly be a negative act. Therefore, do not assume that all who are ill are desperate to be healed.

As has been mentioned, we all have power within us. With some it comes out naturally; with others there is a need to exercise and practice to bring it out. That power can be used to heal others. If you are a healthy person, your power can be built up—as you do for working magic—and released into someone whose power is depleted, thus helping them become whole again.

> *The basis of herb magic—and all magic—is* the power. *This power has worn many names and forms through the centuries; at times even its existence was kept secret; at others it was common knowledge.*
>
> —Scott Cunningham,
> *Cunningham's Encyclopedia of Magical Herbs*

Hands-On Healing

As should be obvious, this is where the person is physically present with you, the healer. In Wicca, many do this healing while "skyclad," or naked. This way there is no encumbrance between healer and patient—no barrier to the passing of the power. Not all Witches work this way, but a large number do. As in all things Wiccan, no one should be forced to do anything with which they are not com-fortable, so there should be no coercion on the part of the healer (or the patient).

The patient may sit in a chair, though it may be better for him or her to stand or lie flat on the floor. When sitting, I suggest having the patient facing toward the east. If lying flat, then the person should have the head to the east and feet to the west. (I'm going to assume a female healer and male patient, for the sake of this exam-ple.) The healing starts with drawing off negativity. This is done by the Witch passing her hands down the patient's body, "drawing off" and then shaking the negativity away. The healer may stand in front of or behind the patient to do this (or kneel beside him, if the patient is on the floor), starting by doing the usual deep breathing and building of white light, in this instance building it around both her-self and the patient. Having built the cone of power, the healer places her hands at the top of the patient's head and then slowly moves them down the side of his face. The movement continues all the way down: along the face, neck, and shoulders, and down the arms and legs to the feet—moving down the outer extremities. The hands may be just touching the surface of the skin gently or may be an inch or so away from the surface. On reaching the feet the healer vigorously shakes her hands, as though physically shaking off the accumulated negativity.

She then repeats the movement and does it, down the body, a total of seven times. While doing this "drawing off," she should concen-trate her mind on her movements drawing the negativity out of the body. As she moves her hands back up to the head, she should see positive, white energy rushing in to fill the space.

After the initial seven sweeps the healer now focuses on the prob-lem area. If there is back pain, then she'll focus on the back; a knee problem, then focus on the knee, and so on. She should cup her hands around the area and focus on sending healing thoughts into it. She will gently lay her hands on the skin. The patient will invari-ably feel great heat coming from her palms and, in many instances, red handprints will be left (which will quickly fade). With hands on the patient, she will "will" healing into him. Sometimes it's good to place one hand on one side of an afflicted area and the other hand on the other side; for example, the front and back of a knee joint, or one hand on the stomach and the other on the lower back. Then the Witch concentrates on sending the healing energy pulsating back and forth between the palms of her two hands, passing and repassing through the area to be healed.

When I'm working I call upon the Lady to bring the healing and visualize the area covered in white light; I slowly turn this to the green light of healing energy. If there is inflammation, I will bring in cooling blue light. Conversely, if there is a need for heat I will bring in light from the red end of the spectrum. The healer concentrates on directing this healing energy into the area that needs it and continues to do this for as long as possible. She finishes by again making the light white and enlarging it to cover the entire body of the patient; she then removes her hands. There are many ways of doing hands-on healing and the above is just one. Some Witches use the Reiki method, some the Romani,[12] and others have their own variations.

Auric Healing

There is an electromagnetic energy that emanates from every human body. It is created by the vibration of that body. Everything is vibration: humans, animals, trees, plants, rocks, and so on. All vibrate at a rate that can be measured in what are called Angstrom units (Å), which measure a movement of one ten-millionth of a millimeter. Color (see following section) is vibration, with different colors produced by different rates of vibration. The vibration of the body, whether human, animal, or whatever, gives off a colored aura that can be seen by sensitives. This aura is sometimes referred to as the "odic force." From the fifth to the sixteenth centuries, Christian art

[12] See *Gypsy Witchcraft and Magic* by Raymond Buckland (St. Paul: Llewellyn, 1998).

often depicted this aura around the heads of especially spiritual people. In this art the aura was referred to as a *halo* or *gloria*.

In auric healing, the health of a person can be ascertained by studying their aura and then you, as healer, can concentrate on changing the colors to bring about the necessary balance that equates to good health; for example, the blue end of the spectrum soothes and calms while the red end stimulates. So for someone suffering from chills or any lack of bodily warmth, whose aura would have a lot of blue in it, you would concentrate on red surrounding him or her. Conversely, someone with a high fever, high blood pressure, or hysteria, would have a lot of red in his or her aura and would need infusions of blue.

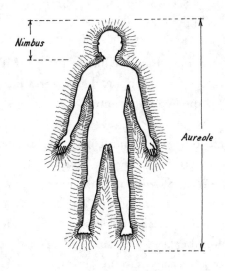

Aura

Many people can see the aura, some without really trying. Others have to practice at it. It's best seen with the person standing against either a very dark background or a very light one (different people get results from different ones). Have a friend stand facing you, against a dark wall, and look at him or her, concentrating your gaze on the position of the third eye (between and slightly above the eyebrows). You may find it helpful to squint slightly to start with. Looking at this spot, you'll become aware of the aura around the head—aware of color or colors. To start with, when you shift your gaze and try to look directly at the aura, it will disappear. Keep trying and eventually you'll be able to look more and more toward the edge of the person's face and will see the color or colors there. (If it doesn't work against a dark wall, try it against a white or light one.) It may take a number of tries, over several days, before you accomplish this, but most people are able to see the aura this way.

The aura is most obvious around the head—possibly because of brain activity—but does in fact extend around the entire body. This is more easily seen when the body is naked, though with practice, and patience, you can see it emanating through clothing. The aura around the whole body is known as the aureole, with the head section known as the nimbus. To the left of a person, the emphasis seems to be on the color orange while to the right it's blue. But the colors will change depending upon the person's health, mood, temperament, and so on (you can actually see flares of red when a person becomes angry).

The aura can also be felt. Stand close to a person and place your hands, palms in, toward his or her head, just an inch or so away from the surface of the skin. Slowly move the hands out a little then back in again. Do this a few times and you'll become aware of a warmth, a tingling sensation, or a feeling of pressure. This can be useful when doing auric healing because you can send needed color down your arms and hands and directly into the person's aura. However, you do not have to be in contact to do auric healing; it can be done even at a great distance.

For working on the nervous system, the auric colors you should project are lavender and violet for relaxing and soothing, grass green for invigorating, and orange and yellow for inspiring effects. For the blood and for most organs in the body, dark blues are soothing, greens invigorating, and bright reds stimulating. A severe headache should be treated with a lavender visualization. A stomachache should receive a light green. For bleeding, send dark blue. For a better idea of colors, see the next section on Color Healing. Auric healing is basically a branch of color healing, with the color projected by your mind and directed at changing the person's aura.

Color Healing

The principle of healing with color is to provide whatever color is lacking, or at a low level, in an ailing body. The most effective way to do this is by projection of color onto the body. Where this was done by the will in auric healing (directing color into the person's aura), in general color healing it is a physical projection of the color. This is known as chromopathy, or chromotherapy. Our bodies naturally select color from sunlight—whatever color is needed to maintain a balance. Animals and plants do the same thing. One thought is that light is absorbed into the body through the eyes, stimulating the pituitary gland and causing it to secrete certain hormones. It certainly is known that there is a reaction of the body to light and color (and this takes place even when the person is without sight). Another school of thought to which I subscribe and which seems to be endorsed by the science of radionics, says that when color rays strike the body (whether in sunlight or by artificial projection) they produce complementary vibrations within the body that signal the brain. Whether by the secretion of hormones from glands or however, there is a resultant reaction of the body.

Different colors can be projected onto the body using colored filters, such as the "gels" used for the lights in theaters, which are colored sheets of gelatine and cellulose acetate. Early researchers used colored silk attached to wooden frames. The simplest way to then project the colors is to place the sheets over a window and allow the sunlight to pass through, with the patient sitting in the colored light. For convenience, however, it's easy to make colored slides and project them with a regular photographic slide projector. (I give full details of this in my book *Color Magick: Unleash Your Inner Powers*.)

Some people forget that, like different forms of light, heat and sound, each color has its own specific frequency or wavelength, which is a measurable, provable source of energy. When this form of energy is beamed on a plant, animal, or person, something happens . . . It is true that color therapy is not always a swift method of healing, just as proper nutrition rarely brings overnight results. These natural methods do not mask symptoms as drugs do, but have been found to help rebuild and regenerate the body.

—Linda Clark, *The Ancient Art of Color Therapy*

The first step in color healing is to determine what colors are deficient. For this, and also for deciding on treatment colors and time of exposure, I utilize the pendulum (see chapter 15, "Radiesthesia" section). In this instance you would make a list of possible conditions. There are ten general disease conditions: 1. virus; 2. bacterium; 3. poison; 4. allergy; 5. toxins; 6. secretion imbalance; 7. hormone imbalance; 8. mineral imbalance; 9. vitamin imbalance; 10. psychological condition. To diagnose, you can either move your finger down the list while asking the pendulum to state Yes or No, or you can make a card with the ten conditions arranged in a semicircle and let the pendulum swing directly over them. If you are diagnosing another person, hold his or her right hand with your left hand while you allow the pendulum to swing over the card and ask about the condition. If the person cannot be present, then hold something belonging to that person, or a photograph, piece of writing, and so on. To get more specific, you can make up other cards, each offering subgroups of those ten main ones; for example, a list of viruses, a list of allergies, and so on. Similar cards can then be used to determine the color treatment (what color or colors are needed) and for treatment schedules (for how long, and how often, to project the color).

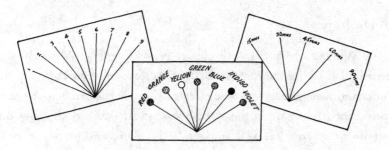

Condition and Treatment Cards

If it's not possible to treat someone personally, color can be projected onto a photograph of the person, for distant healing. There are also many other ways of using color in healing. Treating with color-charged water is one way and with colored gems laid on the body is another. Color breathing is effective, as is the auric healing, already discussed in this chapter.

Distant Healing

You can use many of the various forms of magic that have been discussed and direct them toward healing. Candle burning, poppets, plackets, and color projection all can be used. The specific forms just described—auric and color healing—can both be done at a distance. If you can possibly get something belonging to the person who needs the healing, it can be used to make the connection. The item would be known as a "witness." If nothing else, then a photograph of the person, a sample of his or her handwriting, or just the person's address written down will help. All these things allow you to focus directly on the patient. Photographs are especially useful since they help you visualize the person on whom you are working.

The basic magic of Witchcraft—the energy building and releasing—lends itself especially to distant healing. But always remember to get the permission of the person you are trying to help.

Herbology

Many Witches use herbs both magically (as I've discussed) and also medicinally. Using them medicinally calls for good knowledge of the plants and their effects and side effects. Many herbs can be poisonous if used incorrectly or in the wrong dosage. If you are able, get out into the woods and the fields and study the plants and herbs. Learn to identify them. There are numerous good books on herbs available these days; check through the books I list in the bibliography. One of the best, to my mind, is the Reader's Digest book *Magic and Medicine of Plants*, but there are certainly many other good ones. Use a section of your Book of Shadows as your personal herb notebook.

> *The realm of plants provides everything our body needs for a balanced and integrated existence. However, we are more than just a body . . . Harmony is no longer simply a matter of right diet or even right herbs, but also a matter of right feelings, right thoughts, lifestyle, actions, attunement—harmony of right relationship to our world.*
>
> —David Hoffman, *The Holistic Herbal*

Knowing the habitat, or environmental conditions, of a particular species of plant is the key to locating it. Whether or not the soil is moist, well drained, shady, sunny, acidic, or alkaline, are some of the considerations. Good herbals will not only identify a specific plant but will also describe its habitat, its growth cycle, and the time of year it is at its peak. Whether or not a plant is growing to the point of overcrowding can affect its potency, which is another considera-tion. Whether it is a native plant or an "alien" that has somehow been introduced to the area, is another.

With a number of plants growing together, select those that are most suitably situated; for example, betony prefers the shade, so if there are several betony plants with some in the shade and some in the sun choose the ones in the shade. There are also biological vari-ations that bring about differences in size, height, leaf shape, and so on, of individual plants. Collect samples of the herbs you find in your region and become expert on those few first before trying to embrace all herbs from all geographical locations.

Gathering and Drying Herbs

* *Leaves:* Choose only the greenest, fullest leaves of the herbs since they will be full of juice. Don't take any that are bruised or in any way damaged. Of herbs that seed, gather the leaves before they flower rather than after. Dry the leaves in the sun, rather than trying to do it in an oven. Then lay the leaves between sheets of brown paper, pressing them a little as you layer them. Store them in a warm, dry place, if possible near a fire.

* *Flowers:* Gather flowers when they are in their prime and when the sun has dried the dew from them. As with leaves, lay them between sheets of brown paper, one on top of another, and keep them in a warm, dry place, if possible near a fire.

* *Seeds:* Get the seeds when they are fully ripe. Let the sun dry them, then place them in brown paper bags. They don't have to be stored near a fire but should be in a dry area.

* *Roots:* Use only roots that have a good color and smell; you don't want any that have rotted. They should be neither too hard nor too soft and should be relatively dry when you gather them. The softer ones need to be thoroughly dried in

the sun, or you can hang them from a string near a fire. Leaves, flowers, and seeds are seasonal but roots are not, so don't bother storing roots that are local and plentiful, just those that are harder to find.

❀ *Barks:* Tree barks are best gathered in the spring when they come off the tree most easily. They should then be dried. The term "bark" is also applied to the outer surface of such herbs as fennel and parsley—those with pith in them. These should be split and the pith removed; the bark can then be dried. The term is also sometimes applied to the outer covering of fruit, such as oranges and lemons—what would otherwise be called rind. This should be taken when the fruit is fully ripe.

There are lots of recipes for the use of herbs, flowers, seeds, and roots, but don't be in too big a hurry to start using them. Thoroughly familiarize yourself with them and with how they should be used, and always exercise caution. ✳

17

Solitary Ethics

It's best if office is sought through office,
and honor through honor.
—Pliny the Younger, *Panegyric Oration*

or a member of a coven of Witches, there are built-in safeguards against precipitous action—action that may be regretted at a later date; for example, someone who tends to be quick tempered might well want to "get back" at someone who has done him or her wrong, using magic to do so. The rest of the coven would make that Witch see reason and moderate his or her feelings with reminders of the Wiccan Rede. But for the Solitary there is no such support. The Solitary Witch has to be on his or her guard all the time, constantly examining the possible results of actions. This is the price paid for the freedom of being solitary.

I don't believe in long lists of "rules," as are found in many Books of Shadows. However, it's worth writing down a set of "reminders" for yourself, and to review them once in a while. These should cover the following (I'm sure you will think of more):

❀ Magic should never be done for pay, for then you are obligated to produce results; magic results cannot be guaranteed.

❀ Magic should not be done just to boost your ego, or just to show someone that it can be done. In fact, in these instances magic almost certainly won't work. (The reason is that magic should only be done when there's a very real need for it. As has been shown previously, when talking about the working of magic, *need* is one of the strongest ingredients.)

❀ Don't boast of being a Witch or of having "magical powers," and never threaten others. Witchcraft is a religion of love; trying to make others fear you is not a part of it. Treat all with kindness and compassion.

❀ Do not use drugs of any sort. Drugs deplete your natural powers and harm your body and mind. Despite any stories you may hear to the contrary, real Witches don't use drugs.

❀ Magic *can* be used for your own gain and advancement, so long as none are harmed by it. Some say that you shouldn't use magic for yourself, but there's absolutely no reason you shouldn't. You are working with your own natural power to bring about the ends that you desire. Again, just make sure you harm none in what you do.

❀ Respect the beliefs and practices of others. Within the world of Wicca covens, there has grown a tremendous amount of unnecessary and un-Witchlike behavior. Petty wars flare up and some groups even forget (or choose to ignore) the Wiccan Rede and work magic against one another! Here is another of the blessings of being Solitary: you don't have to be dragged into such petty struggles for power. You are your own person.

❀ Honor all living things, human and non-human. This extends to the vegetable kingdom also, for there is life in all plants and trees.

❄ If possible, and as much as possible, hold your rites out in the open: in the woods, the fields, at the seashore, on mountain-tops, beside lakes and rivers—even if it means having to travel to get to such a site.

❄ Read and learn all you can on all aspects of Witchcraft and magic.

❄ Don't hesitate to ask questions. (No question is stupid if you don't know the answer.)

❄ Remember that you are not alone. ⚹

18

❖

Prayer and Meditation

Once a week, upon waking, go before your
shrine and pray a prayer of devotion to your
deities, ask for guidance and perform a
divination to bring about balance . . .
Consulting the deities for balance and
guidance need only be performed once a week;
after all, if you are following the tenets, there
should be little that will affect you adversely.

—Monte Plaisance, *Reclaim the Power of the Witch*

rayer is speaking directly to deity, to the Lord and the
Lady. It can be to ask for something that you feel you
very much need, to give thanks for blessings received,
or just to talk over things. This last is important. Many
people who live alone have no one with whom to talk through their
thoughts, desires, problems, frustrations, and so on. For a Witch it
seems most natural to speak (with the mind or out loud) to the gods,
and it feels as comfortable as speaking with a close friend, which is
what the deity is. Such "conversation" can help clarify a situation,

can help get your thoughts in order, and can lead you to the solutions of problems. And this is not necessarily a one-sided conversation. The gods speak back to you.

Prayer and meditation go hand in hand. Basically, prayer is asking (or thanking, or similar) while meditation is listening (for answers). It is certainly possible to separate prayer and meditation, but it works well to combine the two. Pray to ask your questions and meditate to listen for the answers.

There are many varieties of meditation; some are formal/commercial such as Transcendental Meditation. However, it is actually a simple practice that doesn't necessitate formal training. To start meditation, simply sit comfortably. Initially, you may find a chair is necessary. I recommend one with a straight back and with arms. You can rest your arms on the arms of the chair. If you'd prefer to sit on the floor, that's certainly all right. You can even lay flat on your back, though that may tend to put you to sleep. Wherever you sit, be sure your spine is straight, which is the key. Start by relaxing your body with deep breathing. Close your eyes and simply breathe deeply. Breathe in to fill your lungs and breathe out to completely exhaust them. Try to keep your mind blank—not easy to do. When odd thoughts from the day—from your job or your personal life, for example—come creeping in, gently push them out again and concentrate on your breathing. Relax your body by stages. Concentrate on relaxing your feet, then your legs; your hands, then your arms; your lower body, then upper body; your neck, then head. Feel all parts of the body gradually relaxing. As with building the cone of power, imagine white light coming into your body as you breathe in. See it filling your body. As you breathe out, see the grayness of negativity flowing out and away. Feel all the little aches and pains going away as the gentle relaxation of purity fills you. Keep this up for a few minutes. As the white light builds inside your body—down through your legs to your feet and toes; down through your arms to your hands and fingers—see it expanding even beyond your body, to form a ball or egg of white light all around you, which is the protective barrier that will keep away all negativity. When you feel you have completely relaxed, simply open your mind for the gods to come in. You may well "hear" them speaking to you, loudly and clearly. Or you may just gradually become aware of the answers to what you have been pondering; then suddenly you *know* what the answer is.

> *Meditation is emptying self of all that hinders from the creative forces rising along the natural channels of the physical man to be disseminated through those centers and sources that create the activities of the physical, mental, and spiritual man; properly done (meditation) must make one stronger mentally, physically . . . we may receive that strength and power that fits each individual, each soul for greater activity in this material world.*
>
> —Edgar Cayce, *Reading No. 281–13*

Wicca prayers are not formalized, as in Christianity. There is no "Turn to page 39, prayer number seven." Such stylized prayers can never exactly fit every situation. In Wicca you speak in your own words, from the heart. It doesn't matter whether you are articulate, or whether your grammar is correct or your phrasing perfect. All that matters is that you state what you are feeling, from deep within.

> *An Affirmation of word will serve for almost anything—health, wealth, happiness—whatever you are concentrating on at the time.*
>
> —Stuart Wilde, *Affirmations*

You don't have to be anywhere special to pray. It's certainly nice to do so in a consecrated circle and to accompany it with the detailed meditation technique I've outlined above, but it is possible to pray anywhere and at any time. The gods are always there listening to you. If you have a sudden need or desire to pray, do so. And don't forget to give thanks for what you receive, as well as to ask for what you want. ⚗

A Wiccan grace, for meals:

Gracious Abundant Universe,
We give special thanks for the beautiful, nourishing
food before us,
Knowing it will fill us with glowing, radiant health.
We acknowledge this gift and offer back
Loving thoughts for the peace and prosperity of
Mother Earth.
So Be It.

—Tara Buckland

19

---◆●◆---

Development

ou have learned how to perform the rituals: Esbats and Sabbats. You have learned forms of magic, divination, healing, and the like. I would encourage you to do all of these things, practicing as much as possible until it all seems natural to you.

I have detailed how to make your tools, and how to use them. Tools are important. They are a focal point and can also be very real aids in that they can store energies and direct them, supplementing what you do with your mind. And here I must point out that your mind is the most important, and powerful, tool that you have. In fact, you can work as a Witch with nothing more than your mind. Although I don't suggest you do this all the time (it can lead to laziness which, in turn, will lead to loss of effectiveness), in emergencies you can do all of your rites and rituals without any tools, by simply using your imagination. I mentioned this briefly when I was talking about setting up an altar and temple. I said then that if your circumstances were such that you simply did not have the available space to construct a proper temple, then you could do it in your mind. And so you can.

Here is where practice at meditation and imagination comes into play. In order to do a complete ritual—one of the Sabbats, for example—solely in your mind, with no tools or physical actions, you will need to be able to imagine every single aspect of the rite. Sitting with your eyes closed, you must "see" yourself walking the circle, lighting candles, swinging incense, and doing the full Cakes and Wine rite. To have this degree of concentration and imagination takes a great deal of willpower and just plain energy. It is not an easy way out. Some people speak glibly of doing rituals "in their mind," but not many have actually put it into practice. It can be done, however I recommend it only be done in forced circumstances. A compromise of sorts is to do the physical actions of a ritual but without actual tools; you can point your index finger in place of the wand or athamé, for example, as you walk the circle.

Your personal development should encompass as much reading as possible. This should not be restricted to works specifically on Witchcraft. Study all forms of divination and magic. Examine different systems of meditation. Look into healing of all sorts. Experiment with making talismans, and working with wood and metal. In the old days the Witch was the Wise One of the area. This meant wisdom in all things and a Witch would many times apprentice him- or herself to others (such as a blacksmith) to learn how to do things properly. Try to emulate those ancient sages.

Being a Witch should mean that your life is considerably better, in a variety of ways, than the lives of those around you. You have access to real power. In actuality, as I've mentioned, everyone has this power but most just don't know how to access or use it. You do. You should be in a position to create your own reality. You can work magic which, as has been said, is making something happen that you want to happen. Therefore, as a Witch, you should have a greater sense of self-satisfaction, possibly greater material possessions, and a far happier life than the majority of people. This is the sign of a successful Witch. And the important part of this is that it is all possible without harming others.

Magical initiates of olden times were exhorted to study and work their magic with the following four axioms in mind: **Know** what to think, **dare** to think it, **will** to do something with it, and have the sense to **keep silent** about your experiences (of the mysteries of magic). To know, to dare, to will, and to keep silent: these are the four axioms of magic. Keeping silent is, perhaps, the most important. This is why it's not good to boast about your powers. Such boasting will draw attention to you, and even today there are lots of examples of prejudice and outright persecution of Witches, no matter what the law might state. So always be circumspect where your religion is concerned. And especially be protective of any other Witches you may know or encounter. ✄

20

———◆———

Final Thoughts

lthough the main aspect of Wicca is the religious ritual, magic plays a part—and for some it is a big part. Yet magic is a fickle thing—it doesn't always work! Why is that?

When your magic doesn't work you first need to look at all the obvious possibilities for failure; for example, the actual mechanics of the magic. With candle burning, did you have the right candles? Were they properly consecrated? Did you work with the phases of the moon and, if so, did you do so correctly? With poppets, were you able to incorporate witnesses—actual items from the person represented by the poppet? Did you incorporate color into the construction of the figure(s)? In regular, basic magic—building and releasing power—did you have a clear picture of the end result desired? Everything needs to be considered and, of course, all of this should have been considered before the magic was ever started. But even with everything covered, sometimes a spell just doesn't work. This is why it must always be emphasized: *there are no guarantees with magic.*

It must be acknowledged that the gods know better than we do. However much we may want something to happen, it may be that "in the great scheme of things" it just isn't meant to happen. It may be something as simple as that the timing isn't right, which is why I suggest repeating a magical ritual—doing it three times over a three-month period before giving up. In the time spent between lives, we review what we learned and experienced in our last lifetime and we also plan what we need to learn and experience in the next one. What you are now trying to bring about by magic may not fit into that plan. There is obviously a certain amount of latitude in such a planned life, but there will be limits and coming up against a magic-related brick wall may well be one of those limits. So, if your magic doesn't work, examine it, see if there might be some other quite different approach you might try and, if that doesn't work, accept defeat.

All of which brings us back to the fact that Wicca/Witchcraft is essentially a religion and that magic is secondary to that. It is the "Old Religion;" a form of paganism. As such it is a religion of which you should be proud. I have been a part of it for well over forty years (with more than a decade before that just reading and studying) and have spent many years working on the public relations side of Wicca—righting the popular misconceptions and spreading the word. The scene today is certainly vastly different from what it was back in the 1960s. Hopefully that scene will continue to improve as Wicca becomes more accepted by other religions and individuals. But the fact remains that there are still certain people and groups who may never accept us, just as they won't accept *any* group other than their own. Rather than confront such fanatics, it is usually best to avoid them. My father had an expression: You cannot argue with an idiot! Unfortunately, that applies to many Fundamentalists.

Speaking of not being accepted, I must return to the point that Solitary Witches are frequently not "accepted," or recognized, by Coven Witches. To my mind, this is sad and simply a reflection on the lack of knowledge of those Coven Witches. However, the bottom line is that it really doesn't matter in the least whether you are "accepted" by them and whether they view you as "authentic." All that matters is that you know who you are and you are happy in the practice of your religion. If someone else has a problem with it, let them get on with it. (By the same token, a Solitary could say that he or she does not "accept" the idea of covens! But there again, it wouldn't matter and shouldn't interfere with either.) The many petty jealousies and rivalries that crop up in today's world of Wicca do nothing but drag down the Old Religion. It's sad, but I have to accept it as part of human nature. There may never be an end to it, but let's do all in our power to rise to the highest standards.

I wish you well on your Solitary path, knowing that the Lord and the Lady will always be there for you. Look ahead, rather than back. Send out love. And keep the Craft alive.

In love and light,
Raymond Buckland

APPENDICES

Glossary of Wiccan and Magical Terms

This glossary contains those terms mentioned in the above text plus other words and phrases you are likely to come across in the world of Wicca and certain aspects of magic.

Affirmation: A word, short phrase, or sentence that encapsulates thoughts and ideas in a positive statement. Repeated constantly, the affirmation gets down into your unconscious mind, reinforcing and empowering.

Amulet: A magical charm for protection, power, healing, and so on, utilizing a natural object such as a stone, nut, shell, piece of wood, or similar item.

Asperge: To sprinkle sacred water for purification, as part of a ritual. This might be done with an aspergillum or with the fingers.

Aspergillum: Tool used for asperging. Can be as simple as a few twigs or a spray of evergreen, or can be an elaborate, commercially produced metal object. It is dipped into the water and then flicked at the person or object to be asperged.

Astral: A plane of existence, invisible to the naked eye, that coexists with the physical realm.

Astral Body: An etheric copy of your physical body (and that of all living things) that extends slightly beyond the physical, such that a psychic may see its outline as an aura.

Astral Projection: To separate your astral or etheric body from your physical body and travel about the astral plane. It is said that many dreams are actually memories of astral travels.

Athamé: Ritual knife used as a tool in Witchcraft and ceremonial magic. Styles, handle colors, and markings on the knife vary with Wicca traditions.

Aura: Light emanating from living beings and vibrating at frequencies beyond the normal range of vision. It indicates the position of the etheric body. The color of the aura may vary, dependent upon a person's health, mood, emotions, and so on.

Balefire: Traditional fire lit for religious celebratory purposes during Sabbats. In medieval times there were balefires lit on hilltops across the length and breadth of Europe.

Bane: Negative energy that harms and destroys. Often associated with evil and/or applied to poison.

Banish: To dismiss spirits from a ritual circle.

Bell: A ritual tool used in Witchcraft and various forms of magic to alter the vibrations of the sacred area. It may or may not be engraved with sigils and is consecrated for ritual use.

Beltane: One of the Greater Sabbats of Witchcraft that falls on May Eve. Also known as Roodmas, Walpurgisnacht, and Cethsamhain. It marks the shift in emphasis from God to Goddess.

Besom: A broom, sometimes used in Witchcraft rituals. Some Handfasting ceremonies include having the wedded couple jump over the besom, for luck and to promote fertility. It is used by some Witches as an equivalent of the staff.

Boleen: Also spelled boline, or bolline, this is a knife with a curved blade used strictly for cutting herbs.

Book of Shadows: The book that contains all the rituals, spells, recipes, and other pertinent information of a Solitary Witch or of a coven. It is named for the time (during the persecutions) when Witches had to meet "in the shadows" and were first starting to record what had previously been a purely oral tradition. It is always handwritten by the Witch who owns it.

Broom: Equivalent of the staff, for some Witches. Generally referred to as a besom.

Burin: An awl-like tool used for marking the various signs and symbols on objects for the purposes of magic (for example, writing names on candles).

Cakes and Wine: Also known as Cakes and Ale, this is the rite in which the gods are thanked for the necessities of life. It involves the blessing of wine/ale and cakes, and consuming them, and usually takes place about halfway through a Wiccan ritual, although it can be performed as a ritual in itself.

Calling the Quarters: A part of the ritual construction of a magical circle, when the four elements of air, fire, water, and earth are called upon to be a part of the sacred space.

Casting the Circle: The consecration of an area in which a Witch or a coven of Witches will be holding a ritual.

Cauldron: Associated with the British Celtic goddess of the underworld, Keridwen, or Cerridwen, the cauldron was one of wisdom and enlightenment. It also symbolizes rebirth and transmutation and represents the womb of the Goddess. It is often used in Wiccan rituals, sometimes containing water and sometimes holding fire.

Censer: Also known as a thurible, this is the instrument in which incense is burned during rituals. It can vary from a simple container for a bed of sand, on which a hot coal can be placed, to an elaborate swinging device suspended on chains.

Centering: Done by some Witches prior to meditating or to doing magic, centering is the process of focusing on your spiritual center, allowing all mundane issues to fall away leaving calm and serenity.

Ceremonial Magic: A form of magic that involves complex ritual, centering on the conjuring and commanding of spirits, or entities, in order to accomplish various ends. The tools, dress, and procedures of ceremonial magic are laid down in various ancient books known as grimoires and are rigid and extremely complex. Conjurations are often in Latin, Greek, Hebrew, or other languages. Because of the dangers of trying to control the actions of the entities conjured, intricate circles of protection are created and employed as are talismans, sigils, and words of power.

Chakra: An area of power within the body. There are seven such centers. By focusing the mind on these areas, in a predetermined order, and energizing them, kundalini power is raised, which is a useful tool when working magic.

Chalice: The name given by some Witches to the goblet used in rituals such as Cakes and Wine. It is regarded as one of the four elemental tools, representing the element of water. In effect a miniature cauldron, it is also viewed as representative of the womb of the Goddess.

Chant: A combination of words in a rhythmic pattern, used to generate power when building toward the working of magic. Chanting can bring about an altered state of consciousness.

Charcoal: Powdered incense is burned on a charcoal briquette. Do not use the briquette sold for use in barbecues, however, for they give off noxious gases. Charcoal briquettes made specifically for the burning of incense are obtainable from religious supply houses.

Charge, The: Short for "The Charge of the Goddess." This is a popular discourse given by a Priestess to her coven, in rites when she specifically represents the Goddess. It originated in Charles Godfrey Leland's book *Aradia, the Gospel of the Witches of Italy* (1899) and was the address given by the goddess Aradia to her followers, instructing them on how and when to worship her. For Gerald Gardner's (Gardnerian) Book of Shadows, Doreen Valiente wrote a variation on this, which is the version most often used by today's Wiccans.

Charge, To: To charge an object is to pass power into it so that it will serve for ritual and/or magical purposes.

Charm: A talisman or amulet charged for magical purposes. Its focus may be for love, protection, to ward off evil, to promote fertility, or for any one of a number of purposes. Also, a spoken spell or incantation.

Cingulum: Name for the ritual cord used in magic. In some traditions it has to be nine feet in length and red. Other traditions have different specifics. Some use different colors to denote different degrees of advancement. It is often worn around the waist and is sometimes called a girdle. It can be used in different ways, such as to store magical energy by knotting that energy into the cord to be released at a later time and place. It can also be used more mundanely to measure and help describe the circle area.

Circle: The sacred, consecrated space in which rituals are held. "Without beginning and without end," it is the base of the cone of power that is raised with magical energy. Size can vary. Many traditions state that the circle must be nine feet in diameter; others are not specific. In ceremonial magic, there are frequently three concentric circles, which are nine, ten, and eleven feet in diameter. For Solitary Witches it is whatever size the individual prefers.

Cone of Power: A containment of magical energy based on the described circle drawn by a Witch in ritual. It is, in effect, both above and below the ground and is possibly more in the shape of a globe than two connected cones. There is the main cone of power, which is the circle itself in ritual, and there is a cone of power that can be generated and directed to an individual or specific place for purposes of healing, cleansing, and so on.

Consecrate: To purify and make holy. This is usually done by sprinkling (asperging) with salted water and censing in the smoke of incense, along with saying suitable words of intent. It can be done to people, places, and things. All tools to be used for magical purposes should be consecrated. Consecration can also be done with a specific consecration oil that serves the same purpose.

Cord: *see* Cingulum.

Coven: A group of Witches, usually led by a female and/or male (High Priestess/High Priest). Although "traditionally" a coven is said to consist of thirteen Witches, it can be any number. The coven meets at least once a month, to coincide with the full moon, though it can meet more regularly if desired. Most covens operate within a specific "tradition," with their own particular rules, though many are independent and describe themselves as "eclectic."

Cowan: A non-Witch. Someone who has not been initiated into the Old Religion.

Craft: Short for "Witchcraft," the Old Religion is frequently referred to, in modern times, as "the Craft." Witchcraft comes from *wiccacraeft*, meaning "the craft of the wise."

Deity: A supreme being; a God or Goddess; a form that is worshiped. Most Witches see their deities as being in anthropomorphic (human) form. Other peoples and civilizations have included deities in animal form or a combination of animal and human (for example, Egyptian deities).

Deosil: Clockwise. It is usual for Witches to move about the circle in deosil fashion, which symbolizes the movement of the sun. Many traditions do not countenance anyone moving counter-clockwise, or widdershins, which would be considered against nature. However, there are traditions that work deosil in the waxing moon and widdershins in the waning moon. Some open the circle deosil and close it widdershins.

Deva: A spirit; usually associated with plants, flowers, herbs, and trees.

Divination: The art of looking into the past, present, or future and discovering those things that are normally hidden. There are innumerable methods of doing divination, some of the most popular being through the use of tarot cards, crystal-gazing (skrying), palmistry, astrology, I-Ching, and tea-leaf reading, among others. Not every Witch is proficient at all methods but usually there is at least one system or technique that can work well for you.

Drawing Down the Moon: A Wicca ritual, usually performed at the full moon, where the Goddess is invoked and asked to descend into the body of the High Priestess and to speak to the coven through her. A similar ritual, known as Drawing Down the Sun, brings the God into the High Priest.

Eclectic: Made up of what seems best from a variety of sources. Eclectic Wicca covens will pick and decide what tools, rites, and practices they want to use, choosing from various traditions and teachings.

Element: Earth, air, fire, and water are the four traditional elements of Western magic. In Wicca, spirit is often added as a fifth element. These each represent a class of energy that together makes up reality as we know it.

Elemental: A spirit or entity, usually associated with one of the four elements. Those associated with earth are known as gnomes, those with air as sylphs, with fire as salamanders, and with water as undines.

Energy: The basis of magic. It is a "power" that can be raised by various means and can be channeled and directed to make changes occur. Every living thing has inert energy. The secret of Witch magic is to be able to amass that energy and use it.

Esbat: A Witch meeting—be it Coven or Solitary—at any time other than the Sabbat celebrations. Esbats are usually held at least once a month, at the full of the moon, but can be held more frequently if desired or necessary. It is at the Esbats that the "work" (healing, magic, divination) is performed, since the Sabbats are for celebration of the turning wheel of the year.

Evocation: A ritual summoning of any spirit or entity. It differs from an invocation in that it is an external working; for example, in ceremonial magic an entity is evoked to appear in a specific area outside the magician's main circle of protection, while in Drawing Down the Moon the deity is invoked (invited) to descend and enter into the body of the priestess.

Familiar: During the persecutions, one of the charges leveled against accused Witches was that they had "familiars." These were said to be servants of the Witch, given to them by the Devil. The familiars appeared in the form of animals: cats, rats, toads, rabbits, and so on. Since most people—elderly ones and those living alone especially—had a cat or other pet, the charge was a useful tool for the inquisitors.

Grimoire: From the Old French word for "grammar," it was the book in which a ceremonial magician kept record of his experiments with magic. By extension, it has become applied to any book of spells, charms, recipes, and magical techniques.

Grounding: The reinforcing of your connection to the earth after doing magic. Some feel it is necessary in order to disperse any residue of spent energy.

Handfasting: The Wicca marriage ceremony. There are many versions of this. A few are for a limited period of time but most are for "so long as love shall last."

Handparting: The official ending of a Wicca marriage, allowing those previously wed to go their separate ways.

Herbcraft: The study and practice of herbology; using herbs for magic and for health and healing. Traditionally Witches have a great knowledge of herbcraft but in fact not all are drawn to it.

High Priest/ess: The leader of a coven of Witches. All Witches are regarded as being priests and priestesses (hence the fact that they can practice as Solitaries), so the leader of a group is known as a *High* Priest or Priestess.

Imbolc: One of the Greater Sabbats, falling on February Eve and marking the first stirrings of spring.

Incense: An aromatic herb, spice, gum, or blend of such that can be in powdered form, or formed into cones or sticks, to be burned at rituals. Ancient belief was that the smoke of the incense carried prayers up to the gods. Additionally, it adds to the ambience of ritual and can help stimulate and condition the mind.

Initiation: A ritual experience that is a spiritual rebirth. The Witchcraft initiation signifies entry into the Old Religion and unity with its deities. A Solitary can do a self-dedication that is, in effect, an initiation. In Wicca, it is as valid as any coven initiation.

Invocation: A ritual invitation to spirits, entities, and deities to descend and enter into the invocator or some other person or object.

Law of Three: The belief in a three-fold return for all actions. Whatever (magical) energy is sent out will return at three times its strength. There is, then, no inducement to send out negative energy.

Libation: Liquid offering to the gods. Whenever wine or other ritual drink is poured, it is traditional to spill a little of it for the gods. In ritual, this is often poured into a libation cup or dish to be later poured out on the ground. Additionally, many Witches will spill a little just before they take a first sip of their drink. A small segment of food, such as from the cakes of Cakes and Wine, is also given to the deities.

Litha: The summer solstice, also known as Midsummer. One of the Lesser Sabbats of Wicca.

Lughnasadh: August Eve, also known as Lammas, is one of the four Greater Sabbats of the Witch year. Associated with the Celtic god Lugh, it is the first of the harvest festivals of the Old Religion.

Lunar Cycle: One full month; it is the twenty-eight-day period from full moon to the next full moon, or new moon to new moon.

Mabon: The autumnal equinox; one of the Lesser Sabbats of the Wicca year.

Magic: As Aleister Crowley put it: "Causing change to occur in conformity with will." Making something happen that you want to happen. There are probably hundreds of ways of working magic. The primary teaching of Wicca: whichever method you use, you do not use the magic to harm anyone.

Magic Mirror: An instrument for skrying. It is usually a black or dark reflective surface, which lends itself to the divinatory practice. It is also known as a speculum.

Mana: A Melanesian (and Polynesian) term, also known as *prana* (a Sanskrit word), it is the "power" that is the universal life force. The Chinese call it *Chi*, or *Qi*; the Japanese *Ki*.

Meditation: A discipline of mind and body that enables you to reach higher states of consciousness. It can be a great aid to a Witch, being especially useful in divination and in magical practices. It can also be extremely beneficial as a practice in itself, as a tool for spiritual growth.

Occult: A word meaning "secret" or "hidden." Although distorted by Judeo-Christian teachings to imply ominous practices, its meaning is benign. Today it is associated with those esoteric truths that are available only through initiation.

Ostara or Œstre: The Lesser Sabbat of the spring equinox, named for the Teutonic sun goddess and the Anglo-Saxon fertility goddess. The word "Easter" is taken from this.

Pagan: From the Latin *pagani*, meaning dwellers in the country, it has come to be applied to almost anyone who is not of Christianity, Judaism, or Islam. Witches come under the general heading of pagans (so all Witches are pagans, yet not all pagans are Witches).

Pentacle: Sometimes spelled *pantacle*, this is one of the working tools of Witchcraft. It is a disc of wood, copper, or other metal, and is usually engraved with certain signs and sigils (depending upon the tradition). When the metal is polished, the pentacle can be used like a skrying mirror for divination. Some covens use the tool simply like a tray, for holding such things as the cakes for Cakes and Wine. In ceremonial magic, a pentacle is often a protective talisman incorporating the design of a pentagram.

Pentagram: The five-pointed, starlike figure that, with its single point upward, has become a symbol for Witchcraft. It is also known as the Seal of Solomon, Druid's foot, and pentalpha. In old books of magic the pentagram was drawn superimposed over a human figure, indicating that it is the symbol for the life force. In Wicca, the shape is used in consecrations, for sealing the circle after it has been opened and/or closed, and as a sigil on talismans.

Placket: A cloth "pocket" into which personal items may be placed when working ritual magic. The color of the placket may be significant for the purpose of the work being done.

Poppet: A figure made to represent a person, for the sake of working sympathetic magic. It can be made of wax, clay, paper, cloth, and so on. When made of cloth it is usually stuffed with suitable material (for example, herbs) for the purposes of the ritual. In Witchcraft, such a figure would be used only for positive magic.

Power: The energy that is raised in ritual and directed to bring about magical results. It may be raised by any one of a number of methods including dancing, chanting, and sex.

Prana: *see* Mana.

Prayer: Verbal petitions to the gods, made either out loud or in the mind. The most powerful prayers are those that come from the heart and are in your own words.

Quarters: The four elemental powers and the directions associated with them (east, south, west, and north).

Rede: The Wiccan Rede is the one law of Witchcraft. It states: "An it harm none, do what thou wilt," which means that as long as you harm no one (including yourself) you may do as you wish.

Reincarnation: Rebirth of the spirit, or soul, into a new physical body. Witches believe that we go through a series of lives, learning and experiencing new things in each life until we have learned all. There are intervals between each life when the spirit reviews what has been learned in the life completed and plans what must be covered in the life to come.

Retribution: The karmic return for actions taken. In the Witch belief, karma takes place within the current lifetime. There are no rewards and punishments that are "put off" until after death; the returns come in the same lifetime that the events took place. In the Witch belief, it is a three-fold return. (*see* Law of Three)

Rite: A short ritual for a specific purpose that is usually part of a larger, general ritual; for example, the Cakes and Wine rite is part of every Esbat and Sabbat ritual.

Ritual: A set of rites that are performed for religious or magical purposes. They are performed within the confines of a magic circle.

Rune: Meaning "mystery" or "secret," a rune is a written character found in all Germanic countries. The runes were never a strictly utilitarian form of writing but were originally employed to incise wood and stone for purposes of casting for divination. Today they are often used by Witches as a magical form of writing. There are many variations on the runes.

Sabbat: A major celebration ritual of Witchcraft. There are eight Sabbats spread more or less evenly throughout the year: Samhain, Yule, Imbolc, Ostara, Beltane, Litha, Lughnasadh, and Mabon.

Sacred space: That space that is contained within the confines of the magic circle, cast and consecrated for Wiccan ritual.

Samhain: One of the Greater Sabbats of the Wicca year, falling on November Eve. It is regarded as the most important of the Sabbats, and was the original turning point of the year, with emphasis changing from Goddess to God.

Skrying: Divination by means of gazing at or into a reflective surface. Crystal-gazing is the prime example, but it can be done with everything from polished copper to ink blots.

Sigil: A symbol or sign for a specific energy or spirit, used for magical purposes. Sigils are used a lot on talismans and may also be found on most of the implements of ceremonial magic. In Witchcraft, there are certain sigils usually engraved on the handle of the athamé. Sigils may be constructed from magical squares containing numbers or letters. Sigils differ from symbols in that they are constructed to contain the very essence of their purpose, where symbols are simply representations.

Solitary: In Witchcraft, a Witch who works alone, without a coven. The original Witches were almost certainly Solitaries.

Speculum: A magic gazing mirror, usually with a dark or black surface, used for divination.

Spell: An act of magic designed to bring about change. It usually consists of both words and actions and is not necessarily religious. It is also a term given to a written recipe for magic.

Staff: A tool symbolizing power, which might also be powerful in itself, much like a large wand. In PectiWita (Scottish Witchcraft) it is one of the "working tools," being used for casting a circle and directing energy. In ancient times it was a symbol of authority.

Sword: A "coven tool," used by some groups for casting the circle, as one of the tools of initiation, and other purposes.

Sympathetic Magic: Also known as imitative magic, since ritual actions imitate real actions and objects imitate or represent people and things. There are probably more forms of sympathetic magic than any other type. Sir James Frazer (*The Golden Bough*, 1951) said that all magic is based on the Law of Sympathy: all things are connected by invisible bonds.

Talisman: From the Greek root *teleo*, meaning "to consecrate," a talisman is a human-made object endowed with magical properties for a specific purpose (for example, protection, power, healing). Made of metal, paper, parchment, wood, bone, and so on, a talisman is often marked with a sigil and with words of power. It must be consecrated before it can become effective.

Tarot: A deck of seventy-eight cards used for divination. It is probably the oldest known set of cards, although its exact origin is unknown. The deck is in two parts, the major and minor arcanas, also known as the greater and lesser trumps. There are twenty-two individual cards in the major arcana and fifty-six cards — arranged in four suits of fourteen cards — in the minor arcana.

Temple: The place of worship; the room, building, or open space that houses the ritual circle. Sometimes the term temple is applied to the consecrated circle itself.

Tetragrammaton: Greek for "four-letter unit," tetragrammaton is supposedly the most powerful of the "names and words of power" used in ceremonial magic. It is the ineffable name of god; a Kabbalistic term for the Hebrew name for God consisting of the four Hebrew letters *Yod*, *He*, *Vov*, and *He*.

Thaumaturgy: "Low magic"; the art of causing change to events, people, and places in everyday life.

Theurgy: "High magic"; to connect with deity and bring about spiritual growth.

Thurible: A censer; incense burner.

Tool: One of the necessary implements for ritual and magic working. The Witch's personal tool is the athamé or the wand. Other tools include censer, goblet, white-handled knife, burin, boleen, sword, besom, bell, and staff.

Tradition: A particular sect or denomination of Wicca, such as Gardnerian, Celtic, Druidic, Saxon, Færie, Scottish, Alexandrian, or Welsh.

Vibrations: The resonating atmosphere that can be felt within a charged and consecrated circle. All manifestation is comprised of vibrations at various wavelengths or frequencies. Magic tends to alter those wavelengths, and such things as sound (from the bell) and odors (from the incense) can bring about change.

Visualization: Being able to see clearly and distinctly "in the mind's eye." To be able to form a mental image of a person or thing, in all its detail. This is important for "seeing" the goal when working magic.

Wand: One of the working tools of a Witch. For many Witches, this is a preferred alternate to the athamé as the personal tool.

Waning Moon: The half of the moon's cycle when it is passing from full to new; gradually diminishing.

Ward: To protect through the use of magic. Also, to guard against possible magic.

Waxing Moon: The half of the moon's cycle when it is passing from new to full; gradually increasing.

White-handled Knife: A ritual knife used, much like the burin, for marking signs and sigils on other magical tools and objects.

Wiccan Rede: *see* Rede.

Widdershins: To move counter-clockwise about a ritual circle.

Wicca: The modern form of Witchcraft introduced to the general public in the 1950s by the late Dr. Gerald Brousseau Gardner. Most other forms of Wicca, whether claiming lengthier history or not, are based on the work of Gardner and Doreen Valiente, who put together the Gardnerian Book of Shadows. Wicca has become one of the fastest growing religions in the world today. It was introduced to the United States by Raymond Buckland in the early 1960s. Today there is a wide selection of traditions available and the religion has become federally recognized and acknowledged. Wicca is a pagan religion of nature, with belief in both male and female deities. It is a positive religion with strict laws against harming others.

Witch: A follower of Witchcraft/Wicca. The word comes from the Anglo-Saxon word wicca (f. *wicce*), meaning a wise one.

Witchcraft: Although Christianity (and especially its missionaries) has labeled anything non-Christian as being "witchcraft," in fact *wiccacræft* (Anglo-Saxon) is the "craft of the wise." It is an early pagan form of religion and magic-working that is not anti-Christian (or anti-anything) but merely non-Christian. Its emphasis is on healing and on acknowledgment of nature and the gods of nature.

Wizard: A male worker of magic.

Yule: One of the Lesser Sabbats of Wicca, falling on the winter solstice.

Magical Properties
of Herbs

Adam and Eve roots (*Aplectrum hemale*): For love and happiness. Ruled by Venus.

Adder's tongue (*Erythronium americanum*) — also known as lamb's tongue, serpent's tongue: Great healing properties. Ruled by the Moon.

African Violet (*Saintpaulia ionantha*): For protection and spirituality. Ruled by Venus.

Agrimony (*Agrimonia eupatoria*) — also known as cocklebur, stickle-wort, church steeples: For sleep and protection. Ruled by Jupiter.

Alfalfa (*Medicago sativa*) — also known as buffalo herb, purple medic: For prosperity and money. Ruled by Venus.

Allspice (*Pimenta officinalis*): For healing, luck, and for money. Ruled by Mars.

Aloe (*Aloe vera*) — also known as burn plant: For luck and protection. Ruled by the Moon.

Anemone (*Anemone pulsatilla*) — also known as wind flower: For health, healing, and protection. Ruled by Mars.

Angelica (*Angelica atropurpurea*) — also known as master wort, archangel: For healing, protection, and exorcism, and to bring visions. Ruled by Venus.

Anise (*Pimpinella anisum*) — also known as aniseed: For protection and purification and to bring or maintain youth. Ruled by Jupiter.

Apple (*Pyrus malus*) — also known as fruit of the gods, the silver bough, tree of love: For healing and love. Supposed to bring immortality. Ruled by Venus.

Asafoetida (*Ferula fœtida*)—also known as devil's dung: For protection, exorcism, and purification. Ruled by Mars.

Aster (*Callistephus chinensis*)—also known as Michaelmas daisy, starwort: For love. Ruled by Venus.

Bachelor's Buttons (*Centaurea cyanus*)—also known as devil's flower: For love. Ruled by Venus.

Barley (*Hordeum* sp.): For love, money, protection, and healing. Ruled by the Earth.

Basil (*Ocimum basilicum*)—also known as American dittany, St. Joseph's wort, witches' herb: Good for love, protection, and exorcism; wealth. Supposed to give the power to fly. Ruled by Mars.

Bay (*Laurus nobilis*)—also known as laurel, lorbeer, sweet bay, bay laurel, daphne, and grecian laurel: Good for healing, psychic powers, strength, and protection. Ruled by the Sun.

Bedstraw (*Galium triflorum*)—also known as cleavers, madder's cousin: Good for love. Ruled by Venus.

Beet (*Beta vulgaris*): Good for love and for making wishes come true. Ruled by Saturn.

Belladonna (*Atropa belladonna*)—also known as banewort, deadly nightshade, death's herb, great morel, devil's cherries, witch's berry: Good for producing visions. Ruled by Saturn.

Be-still (*Thevetia nereifolia*)—also known as trumpet flower, yellow oleander: Good for luck. Ruled by Venus.

Bistort (*Polygonum bistorta*)—also known as dragon weed, Easter giant, red legs, snakeweed, patience dock: Good for fertility and for developing psychic powers. Ruled by Saturn.

Bittersweet (*Celastrus scandens*)—also known as climbing staff tree, fever twig, waxwork, yellow root: Good for healing and protection. Ruled by Mercury.

Blackberry (*Rubus villosus*)—also known as cloud berry root, dewberry, bramble-kite, goutberry, thimbleberry: Good for healing, money, and protection. Ruled by Venus.

Black cohosh (*Cimicifuga racemosa*)—also known as black snake root, squaw root, rattle root, bugbane: Good for courage and protection, love and potency. Ruled by Jupiter.

Bladderwrack (*Fucus visiculosus*) —also known as cutweed, sea spirit, seawrack: Good for money, protection, psychic powers, and weather working (sea and wind spells especially). Ruled by the Moon.

Bleeding heart (*Dicentra spectabilis*): Good for love. Ruled by Venus.

Bloodroot (*Sanguinaria canadensis*) —also known as Indian plant, king root, red puccoon: Good for purification, love, and protection. Ruled by Mars.

Bluebell (*Campanula rotundifolia*) —also known as harebell: Good for luck and to find the truth. Ruled by Mercury.

Blue flag (*Iris versicolor*) —also known as fleur-de-lys, iris, poison lily, poison flag, snake lily, water flag: Good for money. Ruled by Venus.

Boneset (*Eupatorium perfoliatum*) —also known as ague weed, cross-wort, feverwort, sweating plant, thoroughstem, Indian sage, vegetable antimony: Good for protection and exorcism. Ruled by Saturn.

Borage (*Borago officinalis*) —also known as bugloss, herb of gladness, burage: Good for courage and to develop psychic powers. Ruled by Jupiter.

Briony (*Bryony alba*) —also known as gout root, mad root, ladies' seal, snake grape, tetter berry, wild hops, wood vine: Good for money, protection, and image magic. Ruled by Mars.

Broom (*Cytisus scoparius*) —also known as Irish broom, basam, besom, bizzon, genista green broom, scotch broom: Good for purification, protection, divination, and wind spells. Ruled by Mars.

Buckthorn (*Rhamnus catharticus*) —also known as purging berries, waythorn, purging buckthorn: Good for exorcisms and protection. Ruled by Saturn.

Burdock (*Arctium lappa*) —also known as burr seed, bardana, bardane, clotbur, hardock, hareburr, hurr-burr, happy major, personata: Good for healing and protection. Ruled by Venus.

Calamus (*Acorus calamus*) —also known as myrtle flag, myrtle sedge, sweet cane, sweet root, sweet grass: Good for healing, luck, money and protection. Ruled by the Moon.

Camellia (*Camellia japonica*): Good for amassing riches. Ruled by the Moon.

Caper (*Capparis spinosa*): Good for love, lust, and potency. Ruled by Venus.

Caraway (*Carum carui*): Good for health, protection, and developing mental faculties. Ruled by Mercury.

Cardamom (*Elettaria cardamomum*): Good for love and lust. Ruled by Venus.

Catnip (*Nepeta cataria*)—also known as catmint, cat's wort, field balm, nip: Good for beauty, love, and happiness. Ruled by Venus.

Celandine (*Chelidonium majus*)—also known as chelidoninum, tetterwort, kenning wort, devil's milk, swallow herb: Good for protection, legal matters, and to bring happiness. Ruled by the Sun.

Celery (*Apium graveolens*): Good for developing psychic powers and for lust. Ruled by Mercury.

Chamomile (*Anthemis nobilis*)—also known as Roman chamomile, ground apple, maythen, whig plant: Good for purification, love, money. Ruled by the Sun.

Cherry (*Prunus virginiana*)—also known as black cherry, sweet cherry: Good for divination and love. Ruled by Venus.

Chickweed (*Stellaria media*)—also known as adder's mouth, stitchwort, satin flower, tongue grass, passerina, star chickweed, winterweed: Good for love and fidelity. Ruled by the Moon.

Chicory (*Cichorium intybus*)—also known as succory, wild cherry: Good for removing obstacles, invisibility, obtaining favors, and frugality. Ruled by the Sun.

Cinnamon (*Cinnamomum zeylanicum*)—also known as sweet wood: Good for healing, protection, love and lust, spirituality, and protection. Ruled by the Sun.

Cinquefoil (*Potentilla canadensis*)—also known as crampweed, five finger grass, goosegrass, goose tansy, moor grass, silverweed, sunkfield: Good for sleep and prophetic dreams, protection, and money. Ruled by Jupiter.

Cloth-of-Gold (*Crocus angustifolia*): Good for understanding the speech of animals. Ruled by the Sun.

Clover (*Trifolium pratense, Trifolium repens*) — also known as cleaver grass, three-leaf grass, trefoil, honeystalks: Good for love and fidelity, protection, money, and success; exorcism. Ruled by Mercury.

Coltsfoot (*Tussilago Farfara*) — also known as bullsfoot, British tobacco, butter burr, foles foot, horse hoof, ass's foot, coughwort: Good for love; visions. Ruled by Venus.

Columbine (*Aquilegia canadensis*) — also known as lion's herb: Good for love and courage. Ruled by Venus.

Comfrey (*Symphytum officinale*) — also known as gum plant, healing herb, knitback, boneset, bruisewort, knit bone, miracle herb, slippery root, wallwort, yalluc: Good for money and travel safety. Ruled by Saturn.

Coriander (*Coriandrum sativum*) — also known as cilantro, Chinese parsley: Good for love and healing. Ruled by Mars.

Cowslip (*Primula veris*) — also known as arthritica, buckles, drelip, fairy cup, key of heaven, lady's key, password, plumrocks: Good for healing, retaining one's youth, and success in treasure seeking. Ruled by Venus.

Cumin (*Cuminum cyminum*) — also known as cumino, black or sweet cumin seed: Good for protection and exorcism, and fidelity. Ruled by Mars.

Cyclamen (*Cyclamen* sp.) — also known as groundbread, sow bread, swine bread: Good for protection, happiness, lust, and fertility. Ruled by Venus.

Daisy (*Leucanthemum vulgar*) — also known as bruise daisy, ox-eyes, moon daisy: Good for love and lust. Ruled by Venus.

Damiana (*Turnera aphrodisiaca*) — also known as Mexican damiana: Good for love and lust. Ruled by Mars.

Dandelion (*Taraxacum dens-leonis*) — also known as lion's tooth, priest's crown, cankerwort, puffball, swine snout, wild endive: Good for divination and contacting spirits. Ruled by Jupiter.

Datura (*Datura* sp.) — also known as ghost flower, devil's apple, jimsonweed, mad apple, thorn apple, madherb, love-will, stinkweed, sorcerer's herb, witch's thimble: Good for protection and curse breaking. Ruled by Saturn.

Deer tongue (*Liatris odoratissima*) — also known as vanilla leaf: Good for developing psychic powers; also for lust. Ruled by Mars.

Devil's shoestring (*Viburnum alnifolium*): Good for gambling luck, power, protection, employment. Ruled by Mars.

Dill (*Anethum graveolens*) — also known as filly, dill weed, aneton: Good for protection, money, love, lust. Ruled by Mercury.

Dittany (*Cunila mariana*) — also known as mountain dittany, stone mint, sweet horse mint, wild basil: Good for astral projection. Ruled by Venus.

Dock (*Rumex crispus*) — also known as curled dock, narrow dock, yellow dock: Good for healing, money, fertility. Ruled by Jupiter.

Dogsbane (*Apocynum androsæmifolium*) — also known as bitterroot, catch fly, flytrap, honey bloom, wandering milkweed, western wallflower: Good for love. Ruled by Venus.

Dogwood (*Cornus florida*) — also known as boxwood, budwood, green osier, Virginia dogwood: Good for protection and granting wishes. Ruled by Mercury.

Dragon's blood (*Daemonorops draco*) — also known as blume, calamus draconis: Good for protection and exorcism; love and potency. Ruled by Mars.

Elder (*Sambucus canadensis*) — also known as alhuren, battree, eldrum, lady ellhorn, old lady, pipe tree, tree of doom: The Romani call it *Yakori bengeskro* — "Devil's Eye." Good for exorcism and protection, healing and prosperity. Ruled by Venus.

Endive (*Cichorium endivia*): Good for love and lust. Ruled by Jupiter.

Eyebright (*Euphrasia officinalis*) — also known as euphrosyne: Good for psychic development. Ruled by the Sun.

Fennel (*Fœniculum vulgare*): Good for healing, protection and purification. Ruled by Mercury.

Fenugreek (*Trigonella fœnum græcum*) — also known as bird's foot, Greek hayseed: Good for drawing money. Ruled by Mercury.

Fern (*Aspidium filix mas*) — also known as male fern, bear's paw root, knotty brake, male shield fern, sweet brake, shield root: Good for protection, exorcism, luck, riches, and for health and eternal youth. Ruled by Mercury.

Feverfew (*Pyrethrum parthenium*)—also known as featherfew, febrifuge plant: Good for protection. Ruled by Venus.

Figwort (*Scrophularia nodosa*)—also known as knotty-rooted figwort: Good for health and protection. Ruled by Venus.

Flaxseed (*Linum usitatissimum*)—also known as linseed: Good for healing, beauty, psychic powers, protection, money. Ruled by Mercury.

Fleabane (*Erigeron canadense*)—also known as butter weed, blood staunch, colt's tail, horse weed, pride weed, scabious: Good for exorcism and protection; chastity. Ruled by Venus.

Foxglove (*Digitalis purpurea*)—also known as dead men's bells, cowflop, floptop, fox bells, witches' bells, dog's finger, fairy petticoats, fairy thimbles, digitalis, fairy gloves, folks' glove, ladies' glove, purple foxglove: Good for protection. Ruled by Venus.

Garlic (*Allium sativum*)—also known as clove garlic, poor man's treacle, stinkweed: Good for healing, protection, and exorcism. Ruled by Mars.

Gentian (*Gentiana lutea*)—also known as bitterroot, yellow gentian, felwort: Good for love and power. Ruled by Mars.

Geranium (*Pelargonium* sp.): Good for love and fertility, health, and protection. Ruled by Venus.

Ginseng (*Panax quinquefolius*)—also known as wonder of the world root, sang, dwarf ground nut, fivefingers root, garantogen, ninsin, red berry: Good for beauty, love, lust, healing, protection, wishes. Ruled by the Sun.

Goat's rue (*Galega officinalis*): Good for health and healing. Ruled by Mercury.

Goldenrod (*Solidago odora*)—also known as sweet-scented goldenrod, aaron's rod, blue mountain tea, solidago, goldruthe, wound weed, woundwort: Good for divination and bringing money. Ruled by Venus.

Golden seal (*Hydrastic canadensis*)—also known as eye root, eye balm, ground raspberry, Indian plant, jaundice root, orange root, Ohio curcuma, yellow puccoon, yellow paint root, yellow eye, turmeric root: Good for healing and for bringing money. Ruled by the Sun.

Ground Ivy (*Nepeta glechoma*)—also known as cat's foot, alehoof, haymaids, hedgemaids, gill-go-over-the-ground, lizzy-run-up-the-hedge: Good for divination. Ruled by Mercury.

Groundsel (*Senecio* sp.)—also known as groundswallower, ground glutton, grundy swallow, simson: Good for health and healing. Ruled by Venus.

Gum Arabic (*Acacia vera*): For purification. Ruled by the Sun.

Hawthorn (*Cratægus oxacantha*)—also known as bread-and-cheese tree, hagthorn, ladies' meat, mayblossom, may bush, quick thorn, tree of chastity, gaxels, haw: Good for fertility, chastity, happiness, and successful fishing. Ruled by Mars.

Heather (*Calluna* sp.)—also known as heath, ling, Scottish or common heather: Good for luck and protection, also for rain-making. Ruled by Venus.

Hellebore (*Helleborus niger*)—also known as Christmas rose: Good for exorcism, astral projection, and invisibility. Ruled by Saturn.

Hemlock (*Conium maculatum*)—also known as herb bennet, keckies, kex, musquah root, poison parsley, spotted corobane, water parsley: Good for astral projection and purification. Ruled by Saturn.

Hemp (*Cannibis sativa*)—also known as gallowgrass, marijuana, neck-weede: Good for love and healing, meditation, and visions. Ruled by Saturn.

Henbane (*Hyosciamus niger*)—also known as fetid nightshade, black nightshade, hog bean, symphonica, poison tobacco, stinking night-shade, Jupiter's bean, cassilago: Good for love. Ruled by Saturn.

Henna (*Lawsonia inermis*): Good for headaches and for love. Ruled by Mercury.

Hickory (*Carya* sp.): Good as protection from the law. Ruled by Saturn.

High John the Conqueror (*Ipomæa purga*): Good for love, happiness, success, and money. Ruled by Mars.

Holly (*Ilex aquifolium*)—also known as bat's wings, holy tree, holm chaste, hulver bush, tinne: Good for protection, especially from lightning, as well as luck and dream magic. Ruled by Mars.

Honesty (*Lunaria* sp.)—also known as money plant, silver dollar, lunary: Good for bringing money and repelling monsters. Ruled by the Moon.

Honeysuckle (*Diervilla canandensis*)—also known as goat's leaf, woodbine: Good for development of psychic powers, protection, and money. Ruled by Jupiter.

Hops (*Humulus lupulus*)—also known as beer flower: Good for inducing sleep and for healing. Ruled by Mars.

Horsetail (*Equisetum arvense*)—also known as bottle brush, Dutch rushes, horsetail rush, paddock pipes, shavegrass, pewterwort: Good for fertility. Ruled by Saturn.

Houndstongue (*Cynoglossum officinale*)—also known as tory weed, Canadian bur, dog bur, dog's tongue, gypsy flower, sheep lice, woolmat: Good for protection from dogs. Ruled by Mars.

Hyacinth (*Hyacinthus orientalis*): Good for protection, love, and happiness. Ruled by Venus.

Hyssop (*Hyssopus officinalis*)—also known as isopo, ysopo: Good for protection and purification. Ruled by Jupiter.

Irish Moss (*Chondrus cripus*)—also known as pearl moss, salt rock moss, carrageen: Good for luck, protection, and money. Ruled by the Moon.

Ivy (*Nepeta glechoma*)—also known as ale hoof, cat's paw, catfoot, carrion flower, gillrun: Good for healing and protection. Ruled by Saturn.

Jasmine (*Jasminum officinale*)—also known as jessamine, woodbine, moonlight on the grove: Good for love, money, and prophetic dreams. Ruled by the Moon.

Job's tears (*Coix lachyrma*)—also known as tear grass: Good for healing, luck, and wishes. Ruled by the Moon.

Juniper (*Juniperus communis*)—also known as gin berry, gin plant, geneva: Good for anti-theft, protection, exorcism, love, and health. Ruled by the Sun.

Knotweed (*Polygonum aviculare*)—also known as cowgrass, hogweed, knotgrass, nine joints, pigrush, pigweed, armstrong, red robin, ninety knot, sparrow's tongue: Good for health and all binding. Ruled by Saturn.

Lady's mantle (*Alchemilla vulgaris*) —also known as bear's foot, lion's foot, nine hooks, stellaria: Good for love. Ruled by Venus.

Lady's slipper (*Cypripedium pubescens*) —also known as nerve root, American valerian, noah's ark: Good for protection. Ruled by Saturn.

Lavender (*Lavendula vera*) —also known as garden lavender, elf leaf, spike, nardus: Good for protection, purification, love, chastity, sleep, and peace. Ruled by Mercury.

Lemon balm (*Melissa officinalis*) —also known as bee balm, melissa, and sweet balm: Good for love, healing, and success. Ruled by the Moon.

Lemon grass (*Cymbopogon citratus*): Good for lust, psychic powers, and to repel reptiles. Ruled by Mercury.

Lemon verbena (*Lippia citriodora*) —also known as cedron, yerba louisa: Good for love and purification. Ruled by Mercury.

Lettuce (*Lactuca sativa*) —also known as sleepwort, lattouce: Good for chastity, protection, sleep, and love divination. Ruled by the Moon.

Life-everlasting (*Gnaphalium polycephalum*) —also known as balsam weed, chafe weed, cud weed, field balsam, golden motherwort, Indian posey, poverty weed, everlasting: Good for health, healing, and longevity. Ruled by Saturn.

Lilac (*Syringa vulgaris*): Good for protection and exorcism. Ruled by Venus.

Lily (*Nymphæa odorata*) —also known as cow cabbage, pond lily, toad lily, water cabbage: Good for protection and breaking love spells. Ruled by the Moon.

Liverwort (*Hepatica triloba*) —also known as crystalwort, kidney liver leaf, liver moss, liver weed, trefoil, herb trinity: Good for love. Ruled by Jupiter.

Lobelia (*Lobelia inflata*) —also known as asthma weed, bladder podded lobelia, emetic weed, eyebright, gag root, puke weed, vomitwort, Indian tobacco: Good for love and stopping storms. Ruled by Saturn.

Loosestrife (*Lythrum salicaria*)—also known as blooming sally, lythrum, purple willow herb, rainbow weed, sage willow: Good for peace and protection. Ruled by the Moon.

Lovage (*Ligusticum levisticum*)—also known as lavose, love rod, lubestico, smellage, sea parsley: Good for love. Ruled by the Sun.

Mace (*Myristica fragans*): Good for psychic and spiritual powers. Ruled by Mercury.

Maidenhair (*Adiantum pedatum*)—also known as rock fern: Good for love and beauty. Ruled by Venus.

Mallow (*Malva rotundifolia*)—also known as blue mallows, cheeses, dwarf mallow: Good for protection and exorcism, and also love. Ruled by the Moon.

Mandrake (*Mandragora officinale*)—also known as anthropomorphon, brain thief, gallows, herb of circe, ladykins, mandagor, mannikin, racoon berry, wild lemon, semihomo: Good for protection, fertility, health, love, and money. Ruled by Mercury.

Marjoram (*Origanum marjorana*)—also known as joy of the mountain, sweet marjoram, pot marjoram, mountain mint, knotted marjoram, wintersweet: Good for health, protection, love, happiness, and money. Ruled by Mercury.

May apple (*Podophyllum peltaltum*)—also known as American mandrake, duck's foot, hog apple, racoon berry, wild lemon: Good for drawing money. Ruled by Mercury.

Meadow rue (*Thalictrum* sp.)—also known as flute plant: Good for protection. Ruled by the Moon.

Meadowsweet (*Spirea filpendula*)—also known as bride of the meadow, dollor, bridewort, gravel root, little queen, meadowwort, steeplebush, trumpet weed: Good for divination, love, peace, and happiness. Ruled by Jupiter.

Mint (*Mentha* sp.)—also known as garden mint: Good for travel, money, lust, healing, protection, and exorcism. Ruled by Mercury.

Mistletoe (*Viscum verticillatum*)—also known as golden bough, all heal, birdlime, devil's fuge, holy wood, witches' broom, wood of the cross: Good for protection, exorcism, love, health, and hunting. Ruled by the Sun.

Moonwort (*Botrychium* sp.)—also known as unshoe horse: Good for love and money. Ruled by the Moon.

Morning glory (*Ipomœa* sp.)—also known as bindweed: Good for peace and happiness. Ruled by Saturn.

Moss (*Bryum argenteum*)—also known as silver moss: Good for luck and money. Ruled by Mercury.

Mugwort (*Artemisia vulgaris*)—also known as artemis herb, felon herb, muggons, naughty man, old man, sailor's tobacco, St. John's plant: Good for strength and protection, healing, astral projection, psychic powers, and prophetic dreams. Ruled by Venus.

Mullein (*Verbascum thapsus*)—also known as bullock's lungwort, candlewick plant, flannel flower, graveyard dust, hare's beard, hig taper, jupiter's staff, shepherd's club, velvet plant: Good for protection, exorcism, courage, health, and love divination. Ruled by Saturn.

Mustard (*Sinapis nigra*): Good for fertility, protection, and psychic powers. Ruled by Mars.

Myrtle (*Myrtus communis*): Good for love and fertility, peace, youth, and money. Ruled by Venus.

Nettle (*Utica dioica*)—also known as stinging nettle: Good for healing, protection, and exorcism. Ruled by Mars.

Nutmeg (*Myristica fragrans*)—also known as mace: Good for health, fidelity, money, and luck. Ruled by Jupiter.

Oleander (*Nerium oleander*): Good for love. Ruled by Saturn.

Onion (*Allium cepa*)—also known as onyoun, oingnum: Good for protection, exorcism, healing, prophetic dreams, and lust. Ruled by Mars.

Orange bergamot (*Mentha citrata*)—also known as orange mint: Good for bringing money. Ruled by Mercury.

Orchid (*Orchis* sp.)—also known as satyrion: Good for love. Ruled by Venus.

Orris (*Iris florentina*)—also known as Queen Elizabeth root, florentine iris: Good for divination, love, and protection. Ruled by Venus.

Pansy (*Viola tricolor*)—also known as banewort, bird's eye, heart's ease, johnny jump-ups, kiss-me-at-the-garden-gate, love-in-idleness, love lies bleeding, meet-me-in-the-entry: Good for love and love divination, and rain magic. Ruled by Saturn.

Parsley (*Petroselinum sativum*) — also known as persil, devil's oatmeal, rock parsley: Good for protection and purification; lust. Ruled by Mercury.

Passionflower (*Passiflora incarnata*) — also known as maypops, passion vine, grandilla: Good for sleep, peace, and friendships. Ruled by Venus.

Patchouly (*Pogostemon cablin*) — also known as pucha-pot: Good for money, fertility, and lust. Ruled by Saturn.

Pennyroyal (*Hedeoma pulegioides*) — also known as squaw mint, stinking balm, thick weed, tick weed, pudding grass, lurk-in-the-ditch: Good for peace, protection, and strength. Ruled by Mars.

Peppermint (*Mentha piperita*) — also known as brandy mint, lammint: Good for development of psychic powers, healing, sleep, purification, and love. Ruled by Mercury.

Periwinkle (*Vinca minor*) — also known as blue buttons, devil's eye, sorcerer's violet, joy on the ground: Good for love and lust, mental and spiritual powers, money, and protection. Ruled by Venus.

Pimpernel (*Pimpernella* sp.) — also known as blessed herb, herb of mary, poorman's weatherglass, shepherd's weatherglass: Good for health and protection. Ruled by Mercury.

Poke (*Phytolacca americana*) — also known as crowberry, garget, inkberry, pigeon berry, pokeberry root, poke root, Virginia poke: Good for courage and hex-breaking. Ruled by Mars.

Poppy (*Papaver sumniferum*) — also known as blindeyes, blind buff, headaches: Good for love and fertility, money, sleep, invisibility, and luck. Ruled by the Moon.

Prickly Ash (*Zanthoxylum americanum*): Good for love. Ruled by Mars.

Purslane (*Portulaca sativa*) — also known as garden purslane, pigweed: Good for protection, love and happiness, sleep, and luck. Ruled by the Moon.

Ragweed (*Ambrosia* sp.): Good for courage. Ruled by Mars.

Ragwort (*Senecio* sp.)—also known as cankerwort, fairies' horses, staggerwort, dog standard, stammerwort: Good for protection. Ruled by Venus.

Rattlesnake root (*Polygala senega*): Good for money and protection. Ruled by Saturn.

Rhubarb (*Rheum rhaponticum*): Good for protection and fidelity. Ruled by Venus.

Rose (*Rosa gallica*): Good for love, love divination, healing, to promote psychic abilities, luck and protection. Ruled by Venus.

Rosemary (*Rosmarinus officinalis*)—also known as compass weed, dew of the sea, elf leaf, polar plant, sea dew: Good for protection, love, lust, purification, healing, psychic powers. Ruled by the Sun.

Rowan (*Sorbus acuparia*)—also known as delight of the eye, mountain ash, ran tree, sorb apple, wicken tree, wild ash, witchbane, witchwood: Good for healing, protection, success, and psychic powers. Ruled by the Sun.

Rue (*Ruta graveolens*)—also known as countryman's treacle, mother of the herbs, ruta, german rue, garden rue: Good for health and healing, exorcism, love, psychic powers. Ruled by Mars.

Sage (*Salvia officinalis*)—also known as sawge: Good for protection, wisdom, long life, and immortality. Ruled by Jupiter.

St. John's wort (*Hypericum perforatum*)—also known as amber, goat weed, tipton weed, sol terrestis: Good for health, protection, strength, love divination, and happiness. Ruled by the Sun.

Sassafras (*Sassafras variifolium*): Good for money and health. Ruled by Jupiter.

Scullcap (*Scutellaria lateriflora*)—also known as blue scullcap, helmet flower, hoodwort, mad-dogweed, blue pimpernel, madweed: Good for love, peace, and fidelity. Ruled by Saturn.

Skunk cabbage (*Symplocarpus fœtidus*)—also known as meadow cabbage, polecat weed, suntull: Good for legal matters. Ruled by Saturn.

Slippery elm (*Ulmus fulva*)—also known as Indian elm, moose elm, red elm: Good for stopping gossip. Ruled by Saturn.

Snakeroot (*Aristolochia serpentaria*) — also known as serpentary rhi-zome, snagree, pelican flower, snakeweed: Good for money and luck. Ruled by Mars.

Solomon's seal (*Convallaria multiflora*) — also known as dropberry, sealwort, seal root, lady's seal: Good for protection and exorcism. Ruled by Saturn.

Spearmint (*Mentha spicata*) — also known as brown mint, green mint, garden mint, lamb mint, mackerel mint, our lady's mint, spire mint, yerba buena: Good for love, healing and psychic powers. Ruled by Venus.

Spikenard (*Aralia racemosa*) — also known as nard: Good for health and fidelity. Ruled by Venus.

Star anise (*Illicum verum*) — also known as Chinese anise: Good for luck and psychic development. Ruled by Jupiter.

Sunflower (*Helianthus annuus*) — also known as marigold of Peru, comb flower, garden sunflower, corona solis: Good for health, fer-tility, wishes, and wisdom. Ruled by the Sun.

Sweetgrass (*Hierochloe odorata*): Good for calling spirits. Ruled by Jupiter.

Sweet pea (*Lathyrus odoratus*): Good for courage, strength, friend-ship, and chastity. Ruled by Venus.

Tansy (*Tanacetum vulgare*) — also known as buttons, hindheel, double-flowered tansy: Good for health and longevity. Ruled by Venus.

Thistle (*Cirsium arvensis*) — also known as blessed thistle, cursed this-tle, holy thistle, lady's thistle: Good for strength, protection, exor-cism, healing, and curse-breaking. Ruled by Mars.

Thyme (*Thymus vulgaris*) — also known as garden thyme: Good for health and healing, psychic powers, purification, love, and courage. Ruled by Venus.

Tonka (*Coumarouna odorata*) — also known as tonqua bean: Good for money, wishes, love, and courage. Ruled by Venus.

Turmeric (*Cucurma longa*): Good for purification. Ruled by Mars.

Valerian (*Valeriana officinalis*) — also known as all-heal, setwell, vandal root, capon's trailer, cat's valerian, bloody butcher, St. George's herb, garden heliotrope: Good for protection and purification, love, and sleep. Ruled by Venus.

Vervain (*Verbea officinalis*) — also known as brittanica, enchanter's plant, herb of enchantment, simpler's joy, traveler's joy, wild hyssop, juno's tears, pigeon's grass, verbena, van-van: Good for protection and purification, love, chastity, peace, money, sleep, and healing. Ruled by Venus.

Witch grass (*Agropyron repens*) — also known as couch grass, dog grass, quick grass, witches' grass: Good for love, lust, happiness, and exorcism. Ruled by Jupiter.

Witch hazel (*Hamamelis virginica*) — also known as winterbloom, pistachio, snapping hazel, spotted alder, wood tobacco: Good for chastity and protection. Ruled by the Sun.

Wolf's bane (*Aconitum napellus*) — also known as aconite, leopard's bane, monkshood, thor's hat, storm hat, wolf's hat, cupid's car: Good for protection, invisibility. Ruled by Saturn.

Wood betony (*Betonica officinalis*) — also known as bishopwort, lousewort, purple betony: Good for protection, purification, and love. Ruled by Jupiter.

Woodruff (*Asperula odorata*) — also known as master of the woods, sweet woodruff, herb walter, wood rove: Good for money, protection, and victory. Ruled by Mars.

Wood sorrel (*Oxalis acetosella*) — also known as fairy bells, cuckowe's meat, sourgrass, stickwort, leaved grass, wood sour: Good for health and healing. Ruled by Venus.

Wormwood (*Artemisia absinthium*) — also known as absinthium, old woman, crown for a king: Good for love, protection, psychic powers, and communicating with spirits. Ruled by Mars.

Yarrow (*Achillea millefoilum*) — also known as milfoil, nosebleed, arrowroot, carpenter's weed, military herb, old man's pepper, seven year's love, tansy, thousand seal, wound wort: Good for courage, exorcism, love, and psychic powers. Ruled by Venus.

Magical Properties
of Stones

Agate (*chalcedony variety*): distinguishes truth; grounding; healing

Amazonite (*feldspar*): creativity; joy; psychic expanding

Amber (*burmite, pimetite, puccinite, ruminate*): awakens kundalini; harmonizing; soothing

Amethyst (*quartz*): dispelling illusion; healing; meditation; promotes psychic abilities, especially channeling; psychic healing

Beryl: aligning; grounding

Bloodstone (*heliotrope*): psychic healing; reduces emotional and mental stress; stimulates kundalini

Carnelian (*chalcedony*): aligning; grounding

Chryosite (*peridot, olivine*): increases psychic awareness; prevents nightmares; purifying

Coral (*calcium carbonate*): positivity; stablizing

Diamond: panacea, covering the full spectrum of psychic/spiritual matters

Emerald (*beryl*): dreams; helps contact higher self; meditating; tranquillity

Garnet: compassion; general stimulant; grounding

Jade: courage; dispels negativity; protection; wisdom

Lapis lazuli (*lazurite*): contact with higher self; promotes psychic abilities

Lapis linguis (*azurite*): meditating; promotes psychic abilities

Lapis langurius (*malachite*): protection from the "evil eye"

Moonstone (*adularia variety of orthoclase*): compassion; governs the affections; relieves stress

Opal: amplifies chakras; enhances intuition; good for use with children; "stone of love"; protecting

Pearl: meditating; soothing

Quartz crystal: amplifying; channeling; purifying; spiritual protection

Rose quartz: creativity; eases tensions; self-confidence

Ruby (*corundum*): integrity; regeneration; spiritual devotion

Sardonyx (*cryptocrystalline quartz*): soothing emotional states

Topaz (*alumino-fluoro-silicate*): banishing nightmares; calming and soothing; emotional balance; inspiration; tranquillity

Tourmaline (*black*): clairvoyance; imagination; intuition; overcoming fear; protection

Tourmaline (*pink/green*): balance and harmony; compassion; empathy; rejuvenation; regeneration

Turquoise (*copper and aluminum phosphate*): calming; communication; loyalty; peace of mind

Zircon (*hyacinth*): self-esteem; storage of psychic power; strength

Magical Alphabets

	Theban	Passing the River	Malachim	Angelic	Runic
A					
B					
C					
D					
E					
F					
G					
H					
I					
J					
K					
L					
M					
N					
O					
P					
Q					
R					
S					
T					
U					
V					
W					
X				th	
Y				ng	
Z					

Bibliography

Algar, D. *Original Gypsy Remedies*. Essex: Algar, 1986.

Anderton, Bill. *Fortune Telling*. North Dighton: J. G. Press, 1996.

Baroja, Julio Caro. *The World of Witches*. London: George Weidenfeld & Nicolson, 1964.

Barrett, Francis. *The Magus*. New York: University Books, 1967.

Besterman, Theodore. *Crystal Gazing*. London: Rider, 1924.

Beyerl, Paul. *Master Book of Herbalism*. Custer: Phoenix Publishing, 1984.

Blofeld, John. *I-Ching: The Book of Changes*. New York: E. P. Dutton, 1968.

Blum, Ralph H. *The Book of Runes*. New York: St. Martin's Press, 1982.

Bonewits, Isaac. *Real Magic*. New York: Berkley, 1971.

Bord, Janet and Colin. *Earth Rites*. London: Granada, 1982.

———. *Ancient Mysteries of Britain*. London: Guild Publishing, 1986.

Bracelin, Jack. *Gerald Gardner: Witch*. London: Octagon Press, 1960.

Branston, Brian. *The Lost Gods of England*. London: Thames & Hudson, 1957.

———. *Gods of the North*. London: Thames & Hudson, 1980.

Buckland, Raymond. *The Tree: Complete Book of Saxon Witchcraft*. York Beach: Samuel Weiser, 1974.

———. *Scottish Witchcraft*. St. Paul: Llewellyn, 1991.

———. *Practical Color Magick*. St. Paul: Llewellyn, 1983.

———. *Practical Candleburning Rituals*. St. Paul: Llewellyn, 1982.

———. *Advanced Candle Magick*. St. Paul, Llewellyn, 1996.

———. *The Witch Book*. Canton: Visible Ink Press, 2001.

———. *The Fortune-Telling Book*. Canton: Visible Ink Press, 2003.

———. *Wicca for Life*. New York: Citadel, 2001.

———. *Buckland's Complete Book of Witchcraft*. St. Paul: Llewellyn, 1986.

———. *Signs, Symbols & Omens*. St. Paul: Llewellyn, 2003.

Budapest, Zsuzsanna. *The Holy Book of Women's Mysteries*. Los Angeles: Susan B. Anthony Coven No. 1, 1979.

Burland, C. A. *The Magical Arts*. New York: Horizon, 1966.

Campanelli, Pauline. *Pagan Rites of Passage*. St. Paul: Llewellyn, 1998.

——— and Dan Campanelli. *Wheel of the Year: Living the Magical Life*. St. Paul: Llewellyn, 1989.

Chadwick, Nora K. *Celtic Britain*. New York: Praeger, 1963.

Cheasley, Clifford W. *Numerology*. Boston: Triangle, 1916.

Cheiro (Louis Hamon). *Language of the Hand*. New York: Rand McNally, 1900.

Collins, Terah Kathryn. *The Western Guide to Feng Shui*. Carlsbad: Hay House, 1996.

Cooper, J. C. *The Aquarian Dictionary of Festivals*. London: Aquarian Press, 1990.

Crowley, Vivianne. *Principles of Paganism*. London: Thorsons, 1996.

Crowther, Patricia. *One Witch's World*. London: Robert Hale, 1998.

Cunningham, Scott. *Wicca*. St. Paul: Llewellyn, 1988.

———. *Living Wicca*. St. Paul: Llewellyn, 1993.

———. *Cunningham's Encyclopedia of Magical Herbs*. St. Paul: Llewellyn, 1985.

David, Judithann. *Michael's Gemstone Dictionary*. Orinda: Michael Educational Foundation & Affinity Press, 1986.

Donovan, Frank. *Never On a Broomstick*. Harrisburg: Stackpole, 1971.

Duke, James A. *The Green Pharmacy*. Emmaus: Rodale, 1997.

Dunwich, Gerina. *Wicca A to Z*. New York: Citadel, 1998.

Eliade, Mircea. *Rites and Symbols of Initiation: Birth and Rebirth*. New York: Harper, 1958.

Elliott, Ralph W. V. *Runes: An Introduction*. Manchester: University Press, 1959.

Evens, Bramwell. *A Romany in the Fields*. London: Epworth, 1958.

Farrar, Janet & Stewart. *The Witches' Goddess*. Custer: Phoenix Publishing, 1987.

———. *The Witches' God*. Custer: Phoenix Publishing, 1989.

———. *Eight Sabbats for Witches*. London: Robert Hale, 1981.

Fortune, Dion. *Moon Magic*. London: Aquarian Press, 1956.

———. *The Sea Priestess*. London: Aquarian Press, 1957.

Franklin, Anna and Paul Mason. *Lammas*. St. Paul: Llewellyn, 2001.

———. *Midsummer*. St. Paul: Llewellyn, 2002.

Frazer, Sir James G. *The Golden Bough*. London: Macmillan, 1890.

———. *The Worship of Nature*. London: Macmillan, 1926.

Gastor, Theodore H. *The New Golden Bough*. New York: New American Library, 1964.

van Gennep, Arnold. *The Rites of Passage*. Univ. of Chicago, 1960.

Gibbons, Euell. *Stalking the Healthful Herbs*. New York: David McKay,1966.

Gibson, Walter B. and Litzka R. Gibson. *The Complete Illustrated Book of the Psychic Sciences*. New York: Doubleday, 1966.

Goldberg, P. Z. *The Sacred Fire*. New York: Horace Liveright, 1930.

González-Wippler, Migene. *The Complete Book of Amulets and Talismans*. St. Paul: Llewellyn, 1991.

Grattan, J. H. G. and Charles Singer. *Anglo-Saxon Magic and Medicine*. Oxford University Press, 1952.

Graves, Robert. *The White Goddess*. London: Faber & Faber, 1952.

Gray, Magda (ed). *Fortune Telling*. London: Marshall Cavendish, 1974.

Green, Marian. *A Witch Alone*. London: Aquarian Press, 1991.

Grimassi, Raven. *Beltane*. St. Paul: Llewellyn, 2001.

———. *Encyclopedia of Wicca and Witchcraft*. St. Paul: Llewellyn, 2000.

Hansen, Harold A. *The Witch's Garden*. Santa Cruz: Unity Press, 1978.

Harris, Eleanor and Philip Harris. *The Crafting and Use of Ritual Tools*. St. Paul: Llewellyn, 1998.

Hawken, Paul. *The Magic of Findhorn*. London: Souvenir Press, 1975.

Hoffman, David. *The Holistic Herbal*. Shaftesbury: Element Books, 1998.

Hole, Christina. *Witchcraft in England*. New York: Scribners, 1947.

———. *A Mirror of Witchcraft*. London: Chatto & Windus, 1957.

Holzer, Hans. *Born Again: The Truth About Reincarnation*. New York: Doubleday, 1970.

Horne, Fiona. *Witch: A Magical Journey*. New York: Thorsons, 2000.

Hughes, Pennethorne. *Witchcraft*. London: Longmans Green, 1952.

Hunter, Jennifer. *21st Century Wicca: A Young Witch's Guide to Living the Magical Life*. Secaucus: Citadel, 1997.

Huson, Paul. *Mastering Herbalism*. New York: Stein & Day, 1974.

Hutin, Serge. *Casting Spells*. London: Barrier & Jenkins, 1978.

Jacob, Dorothy. *A Witch's Guide to Gardening*. London: Elek Books, 1964.

Jong, Erica. *Witch*. New York: Abrams, 1981.

K, Amber. *True Magick*. St. Paul: Llewellyn, 1990.

——— and Azrael Arynn K. *Candelmas: Feast of Flames*. St. Paul: Llewellyn, 2001.

Kraig, Donald Michael. *Modern Magick*. St. Paul: Llewellyn, 1988.

———. *Modern Sex Magick*. St. Paul: Llewellyn, 1998.

Leadbeater, C. W. *The Chakras*. London: Quest, 1972.

Leland, Charles Godfrey. *Aradia: Gospel of the Witches of Italy*. London: David Nutt, 1899.

Lethbridge, Thomas C. *Witches*. London: Routledge & Kegan Paul, 1962.

———. *Gogmagog: The Buried Gods*. London: Routledge & Kegan Paul, 1957.

Linn, Denise. *Sacred Space*. New York: Ballantine Books, 1995.

Lucas, Richard. *Common and Uncommon Uses of Herbs for Healthful Living*. New York: Arc Books, 1969.

MacNeice, Louis. *Astrology*. London: Aldus Books, 1964.

Maddon, Kristin. *Mabon*. St. Paul: Llewellyn, 2002.

Mayer, Gladys. *Colour and Healing*. Sussex: New Knowledge, 1974.

McNeill, F. Marian. *The Silver Bough* (series). Glasgow: William MacLellan, 1968.

Mermet, Abbé. *Principles and Practice of Radiesthesia*. London: Watkins, 1975.

Meyer, Joseph E. *The Old Herb Doctor*. Glenwood: Meyerbooks, 1941.

McCoy, Edain. *Ostara*. St. Paul: Llewellyn, 2002.

Medici, Marina. *Good Magic*. London: Macmillan, 1988.

Morrison, Dorothy. *Yule*. St. Paul: Llewellyn, 2000.

Moura, Ann (Aoumiel). *Green Witchcraft* (series). St. Paul: Llewellyn, 1996–2000.

Mumford, Jonn. *Sexual Occultism*. St. Paul: Llewellyn, 1975.

Murray, Margaret A. *The Witch Cult in Western Europe*. Oxford University Press, 1921.

———. *The God of the Witches*. London: Sampson Low Marston, 1931.

Paterson, Jacquelin M. *Tree Wisdom: The Definitive Guidebook to the Myth, Folklore and Healing Power of Trees*. London: Thorsons, 1996.

Petulengro, Gypsy. *Romany Herbal Remedies*. Newcastle: Borgo Press, 1982.

Plaisance, Monte. *Reclaim the Power of the Witch*. York Beach: Weiser Books, 2001.

de Pulford, Nicola. *The Book of Spells*. New York: Barrons, 1998.

RavenWolf, Silver. *Solitary Witch*. St. Paul: Llewellyn, 2003.

———. *Halloween: Customs, Spells, and Recipes*. St. Paul: Llewellyn, 1999.

Reader's Digest. *Magic and Medicine of Plants*. Pleasantville: Reader's Digest, 1986.

Shurety, Sarah. *Quick Feng Shui Cures*. New York: Hearst Books, 1999.

Spence, Lewis. *The Fairy Tradition in Britain*. London: Rider, 1948.

———. *Myth and Ritual in Dance, Game, and Rhyme*. London: Watts, 1947.

Thompson, C. J. S. *Magic and Healing*. London: Rider, 1946.

Tuitéan, Paul and Estelle Daniels. *Pocket Guide to Wicca*. Freedom: Crossing Press, 1998.

Valiente, Doreen. *The Rebirth of Witchcraft*. London: Hale, 1989.

———. *Natural Magic*. Custer: Phoenix Publishing, 1975.

Ventimiglia, Mark. *The Wiccan Prayer Book*. New York: Citadel, 2000.

Von Hausen, Wanja. *Gypsy Folk Medicine*. New York: Sterling, 1992.

Watson, Nancy B. *Practical Solitary Magic*. York Beach: Samuel Weiser, 1996.

Weiner, Michael A. *Earth Medicine—Earth Foods*. London: Collier Macmillan, 1972.

Whitlock, Ralph. *In Search of Lost Gods*. London: Phaidon, 1979.

Wilde, Stuart. *Affirmations*. Taos: White Dove, 1987.

Index

Connect with Us

Visit us online at
KensingtonBooks.com
to read more from your favorite authors, see books
by series, view reading group guides, and more.

 Join us on social media

for sneak peeks, chances to win books and prize packs,
and to share your thoughts with other readers.

facebook.com/kensingtonpublishing
twitter.com/kensingtonbooks

Tell us what you think!

To share your thoughts, submit a review,
or sign up for our eNewsletters, please visit:
KensingtonBooks.com/TellUs.